D1697125

RETAIL DESIGN INTER- NATIONAL

FOCUS: WHAT'S NEXT?

JONS MESSEDAT

avedition

CONTENTS

INTRODUCTION: WHAT'S NEXT?
RETAIL DESIGN THINKING 4
Dr. Jons Messedat

NEXT RETAIL: A SECOND LIFE FOR
DOWNTOWN RETAIL PROPERTY 8
Prof. Christoph M. Achammer, ATP architekten ingenieure

NEW URBANITY IN EUROPEAN CITY PLANNING 14
Stefan Herbert & Annika Gründel, METRO PROPERTIES

POST MALL LAB: REDESIGNING SHOPPING MALLS
FOR THE POST-CORONA ERA 26
Prof. i. Vtr. Sabine Krieg, Peter Behrens School
of Arts (PBSA) of the Hochschule Düsseldorf (HSD)
with the support of Hans Höhenrieder M. A.

COMPONENTS

GOT2B COSMETIC COUNTER, GERMANY 34
ARNO GmbH, Wolfschlugen

MAMMUT WINDOW CAMPAIGN, GLOBAL 38
Designplus GmbH, Stuttgart

HARRODS SHOP WINDOW DISPLAY
FOR LG DISPLAY, LONDON, UK 42
D'art Design Gruppe, Neuss / Seoul

DRUCK-SPÄTI, STUTTGART, GERMANY 46
raumkontakt GmbH, Karlsruhe

NIVEA HAUS, BERLIN / HAMBURG, GERMANY 50
NEST ONE GmbH, Hamburg

SPACES

SARA SHOWROOM, DUBAI, UAE 56
Ansorg GmbH, Mülheim a. d. Ruhr

OCCHIO STORE MILAN, MILAN, ITALY 60
1zu33 Architectural Brand Identity, Munich

STEFFL VIENNA, VIENNA, AUSTRIA 64
blocher partners, Stuttgart

BOBO'S BIKESHOP, STUTTGART, GERMANY 68
Bartholomae Design, Stuttgart

SALLYS WELT FLAGSHIP STORE, MANNHEIM,
GERMANY 72
Brust+Partner GmbH, Bad Schönborn

TOD'S STUDIOS, MILAN, ITALY 76
Gwenael Nicolas | CURIOSITY Inc., Tokyo

BRAUKUNSTHAUS ZILLERTAL BIER,
ZELL AM ZILLER, AUSTRIA 80
Holzer Kobler Architekturen, Zurich

LONGINES POP-UP INSTALLATION, BERLIN,
GERMANY 84
DFROST Retail Identity, Stuttgart

SCHTONY OPTIK, KIEL, GERMANY 90
HEIKAUS Architektur GmbH, Stuttgart

MARKTKAUF GELSENKIRCHEN,
GELSENKIRCHEN, GERMANY 94
Kinzel Architecture, Schermbeck

MONDENERO, DUSSELDORF, GERMANY 98
Holger Weddige, Neuss

LÄCKERLI HUUS, BASLE, SWITZERLAND 102
dioma ag, Berne

VERSACE PARIS FLAGSHIP, PARIS, FRANCE 106
Gwenael Nicolas | CURIOSITY Inc., Tokyo

GLAMBOU SHOP CONCEPT, BERLIN, GERMANY 112
DFROST Retail Identity, Stuttgart

CIFI SALES CENTER WUXI, WUXI, CHINA 116
Ippolito Fleitz Group – Identity Architects, Stuttgart

BREUNINGER SACHSENHEIM CONTENT
PRODUCTION, SACHSENHEIM, GERMANY 122
Studio Alexander Fehre, Stuttgart

HUNGRY EYES, STUTTGART, GERMANY 126
Florian Siegel & Severin Küppers, Stuttgart

CONTENTS

BRIDGE, ZURICH, SWITZERLAND Interstore | Schweitzer, Naturns	130
"REINVENTING LOCAL" – ALDI CORNER STORE, SYDNEY, AUSTRALIA Landini Associates, Sydney	134
GUIJIU BRAND EXPERIENCE STORE NANJING, NANJING, CHINA Ippolito Fleitz Group – Identity Architects, Stuttgart	138
CENTRAL FOOD HALL LAT PHRAO, BANGKOK, THAILAND Interstore | Schweitzer, Naturns	142
EBIKER BINZEN, BINZEN, GERMANY Theodor Schemberg Einrichtungen GmbH, Mettingen	148

BUILDINGS

IKEA CITY CENTER, VIENNA, AUSTRIA querkraft architekten, Vienna	154
ASTON MARTIN SHOWROOM, DOHA, UAE Vizona GmbH, Weil am Rhein	160
FEUCHT / SPORTLER INNSBRUCK, INNSBRUCK, AUSTRIA blocher partners, Stuttgart	164
CUPRA FLAGSHIP STORE, HAMBURG, GERMANY Vizona GmbH, Weil am Rhein	170
KASTNER & ÖHLER KAUFHAUS TYROL, INNSBRUCK, AUSTRIA dioma ag, Berne	174
K11 MUSEA SHOPPING MALL, B2 LEVEL, HONG KONG, CHINA Stefano Tordiglione Design Ltd, Hong Kong	180
SEAT CUPRA DUSSELDORF AUTOMEILE, DUSSELDORF, GERMANY Ansorg GmbH, Mülheim a. d. Ruhr	184
THE AUTHORS	188

EXPANDED SPACES: FREE APP FOR DOWNLOAD

ayscan Um diese Ausgabe nicht nur gedruckt, sondern auch im digitalen Raum erleben zu können, geben wir Ihnen überall, wo Sie das ayscan-Zeichen sehen, die Möglichkeit, Filme zu betrachten oder in virtuelle Rundgänge einzutauchen und die gedruckten Bilder damit um die Dimension der Bewegung zu erweitern. Laden Sie sich im App Store oder im Google Play Store ganz einfach die ayscan-App kostenlos herunter, scannen Sie mit Ihrem mobilen Endgerät die ganze Buchseite ein und kommen Sie in den umfangreichen Genuss von Bild, Film und Ton. Viel Spaß!

We want you to experience this edition both in print and digitally. Wherever you see the ayscan symbol, we offer you the possibility to watch films or to immerse yourselves in virtual tours, thus adding the dimension of movement to the printed images. Simply download the ayscan app from the App Store or the Google Play Store free of charge, use your mobile end device to scan the entire page of the book and enjoy a whole package of additional photos, films and sounds. Have fun!

INTRODUCTION

WHAT'S NEXT? RETAIL DESIGN THINKING

DR. JONS MESSEDAT

Nicht nur die zunehmende Flächen- und Ressourcenknappheit wird das Leben und Einkaufen in unseren gewachsenen Innenstädten stark verändern. Auch die Suche nach alternativen Energie- und Mobilitätskonzepten wird sich bei der Entwicklung von neuen urbanen Quartieren niederschlagen. Die Überlagerung von analogen und digitalen zu hybriden Retail-Formaten hat sich seit Jahren angekündigt und ist durch die zwei zurückliegenden „Corona-Jahre" verstärkt worden. Nun ist es spannend, darüber nachzudenken, welche Chancen sich daraus ergeben und wie unser urbaner Lebensraum auch für die nächsten Generationen lebenswert gestaltet werden kann.

Das neue Bauhaus Europa

Um diese Fragestellungen auf breiter und interdisziplinärer Ebene zu diskutieren, wurde die Idee eines neuen Bauhaus für Europa geboren. Die Kreativitätsinitiative soll helfen, die Grenzen zwischen Wissenschaft und Technologie, Kunst, Kultur und sozialer Inklusion zu überwinden und mithilfe von Design Lösungen für Alltagsprobleme zu finden. „Das Projekt ‚neues Europäisches Bauhaus' ist ein Hoffnungsträger. Wir wollen dabei herausfinden, wie wir nach der Pandemie besser zusammenleben können. Es geht darum, Nachhaltigkeit und Ästhetik zu vereinen, um den europäischen Grünen Deal in den Köpfen der Bürgerinnen und Bürger und auch in ihrem Zuhause Realität werden zu lassen. Wir brauchen alle kreativen Köpfe: Designer, Kunstschaffende, Wissenschaftler, Architekten sowie Bürgerinnen und Bürger sollen zusammen das neue Europäische Bauhaus zu einem Erfolg machen", erklärte die Präsidentin der Europäischen Kommission Ursula von der Leyen zu Beginn der Gestaltungsphase am 18. Januar 2021.

Our lives and the shopping experience in our historically evolved city centres will not only be fundamentally changed by the growing shortage of space and resources. The new urban districts that look set to evolve will also be a reflection of the quest for new alternative energy and mobility concepts. The replacement of analogue and digital retail formats with hybrid solutions has been on the cards for years, a trend that has been reinforced by the last two corona years. It is now exciting to reflect on the opportunities this creates and on how our urban habitat can be designed in such a way that future generations will still want to live there.

The New Bauhaus for Europe

To be able to discuss these questions on a broad and interdisciplinary level, the idea of a new Bauhaus for Europe was conceived. The creative initiative is intended to help overcome the borders between science and technology, art, culture and social inclusion and will use design to find solutions for everyday problems. "The project 'New Bauhaus for Europe' is a new source of hope. We want to find out how we can live together better after the pandemic. It is about combining sustainability and aesthetics in order to make the European Green Deal a reality in the minds of the citizens, even in their own homes. We need all the creative heads we can muster: designers, artists, scientists, architects and citizens are to work together to make the New Bauhaus for Europe a success", explained the president of the European Commission Ursula von der Leyen at the beginning of the design phase on 18 January 2021.

INTRODUCTION

Bauwende zum positiven Fußabdruck

Besonders kritisch werden derzeit Neubauten aus Beton hinterfragt, weil bei der Herstellung sehr viel CO_2 freigesetzt wird. Vor diesem Hintergrund ist die Initiative Architects for Future aktiv geworden, die sich im Rahmen der Fridays-for-Future-Bewegung gebildet hat. Sie fordert eine generelle „Bauwende", mit mehr Aufklärung über den Wert des Gebäudebestandes und die Nutzung der Klimapotenziale von Sanierung statt Neubau. Ein Schlüssel dazu ist der sogenannte „ökologische Fußabdruck", der als ein Indikator für Nachhaltigkeit gilt und uns vor Augen führen soll, wie stark das Ökosystem und die natürlichen Ressourcen der Erde beansprucht werden. Nora Sophie Griefahn und Tim Janßen vom Netzwerk „Cradle to Cradle – Wiege zur Wiege e. V." aus Berlin gehen davon aus, dass wir in Zukunft sogar einen positiven Fußabdruck (Öko-Effektivität) erzielen können: „Im Gegensatz zur weit verbreiteten Schule des Verzichts, der Reduktion und des negativen ökologischen Fußabdrucks geht die C2C-Denkschule davon aus, dass wir unser kreatives Potenzial nutzen können, um einen positiven Fußabdruck zu hinterlassen."

Revitalisierung von „grauer" Energie

In den europäischen Innenstädten ist es unübersehbar, dass vielerorts Bauwerke abgerissen werden, die erst wenige Jahrzehnte alt sind. Besonders häufig trifft es derzeit Architekturen der 1980er- und 1990er-Jahre, deren Energiebilanz und Flächenzuschnitte nicht mehr den technischen Anforderungen und aktuellen Nutzerwünschen entsprechen. Oftmals weckt auch der Standort Begehrlichkeiten, wenn aufgrund einer größeren Auslastung des Baugrunds bei einer Neubebauung eine höhere Rendite erzielt werden könnte. Viele etablierte Geschäfts- und Kaufhäuser sowie Malls und Shoppingcenter sind nach jahrzehntelangem Dauerbetrieb in die Jahre gekommen und müssen den veränderten Standards gerecht werden. Revitalisierung bedeutet in diesem Kontext weit mehr als eine rein bautechnische Sanierung, sondern die Herausforderung, wertvolle Substanz zu erhalten und für weitere Jahrzehnte nutzbar zu machen. So kann eine große Menge an sogenannter „grauer" Primärenergie erhalten werden, die notwendig ist, um ein Gebäude zu errichten. Obgleich ehemalige Kaufhäuser und Shoppingmalls scheinbar unmaßstäbliche Akteure im Stadtraum sind, bieten sie mit üppigen Flächenzuschnitten bei maximaler Traglast ein schier unerschöpfliches Reservoir für neue Ideen und Nutzungen. Das „Weiterbauen" von Gebäuden der vergangenen Jahrzehnte ist nicht nur ein Kosten-, sondern auch ein Resilienzfaktor, der immer mehr ins Gewicht fällt.

Construction turnaround for a positive footprint

New buildings made of concrete are currently the target of criticism because huge quantities of CO_2 are released into the atmosphere during production. Against this backdrop, the initiative Architects for Future was founded under the umbrella of the Fridays-for-Future movement. It is calling for a general "construction turnaround" including a greater understanding of the value of existing buildings and making use of the climate potential that refurbishment offers over a new build. A key element of this process is the so-called "ecological footprint". An indicator of sustainability, this metric shows us the extent to which our ecosystem and the world's natural resources are impacted by a project. Nora Sophie Griefahn and Tim Janßen from the "Cradle to Cradle – Wiege zur Wiege e. V." network from Berlin project that in future we will even be able to achieve a positive footprint (eco-effectiveness): "In contrast to the widespread school of sacrifice, reduction and negative ecological footprint, the C2C think-tank assumes that we can use our creative potential to leave a positive footprint behind us."

Revitalisation of "grey" energy

In the European city centres it cannot be overlooked that buildings are being demolished left, right and centre, some of them only a few decades old. Architecture from the 1980s and 1990s is particularly often the target because the energy balance and layout no longer fulfil the technical requirements and satisfy user desires. Often it is the location itself that is the object of desire because a new development promises a higher return through the optimal exploitation of the plot. Many well-established commercial buildings and department stores as well as malls and shopping centres have become dated and run down after decades of operation and have to meet new standards. Revitalisation in this context means much more than purely constructional renovation, but rather the challenge to preserve valuable substance and to make it usable for many decades to come. In this way, we can save a large amount of the so-called "grey" primary energy that is needed to erect a building. Although former department stores and shopping malls are seemingly unfitting players in the urban space, their generous layouts with maximum load-bearing capacity offer a truly endless reservoir for new ideas and usages. The reconstruction of buildings from past decades not only saves costs but is also a resilience factor which is steadily gaining in importance.

Klimaschutz und Nachhaltigkeit im Fokus

In Deutschland hat mit Antritt der neuen Regierung am 8. Dezember 2021 erstmals ein eigenes Bundesministerium für Wohnen, Stadtentwicklung und Bauwesen die Federführung in der Bauwirtschaft übernommen. „Dieser Schritt war längst überfällig", so Christine Lemaitre, geschäftsführende Vorständin der Non-Profit-Organisation DGNB e. V., anlässlich der Vorstellung des neuen Koalitionsvertrags am 25. November 2021: „Dass das Thema Bauen in der Vergangenheit mehr Anhängsel als Fokus eines Bundesministeriums war, war schlichtweg nicht nachvollziehbar. Jetzt wird es spannend sein zu sehen, ob das neue Ministerium auch tatsächlich die notwendige Kraft bekommt und die relevanten Entscheidungsbefugnisse bei sich bündeln kann. Entscheidend wird zudem die Frage, ob eine enge, zielgerichtete Zusammenarbeit mit dem neuen Ministerium für Wirtschaft und Klima gelingt. Schließlich sind die Themen Klimaschutz und Nachhaltigkeit ja Querschnittsthemen über Sektorgrenzen hinweg."

Es bleibt zu hoffen, dass neben der Ankündigung von Bundesministerin Klara Geywitz, jährlich 400.000 neue Wohnungen zu schaffen, im gleichen Schritt auch Mittel und Flächen für die damit untrennbar verbundenen Orte des Handels bereitgestellt werden.

Retail Design Thinking

In Zukunft müssen strategische Allianzen zwischen Handel, Kultur und Stadtentwicklung geformt werden, um neue Ankerpunkte im urbanen Raum zu schaffen. Diese Vorgehensweise entspricht dem Prinzip des Design Thinking, dessen Grundgedanke es ist, möglichst unterschiedliche Erfahrungen, Meinungen und Perspektiven hinsichtlich einer Problemstellung unter einem Dach zusammenzubringen.

Ich freue mich, dass genau an diesem Punkt die Beiträge unserer Buchpartner aus den Bereichen Planung, Projektentwicklung und Forschung ansetzen. Professor Christoph Achammer prognostiziert ein „zweites Leben" für bisher monofunktionale Handelsarchitekturen, die mit taxonomiekonformen Nutzungen urbane Funktionen übernehmen können. Er fordert alle Planungsbeteiligten auf, mutige und flexible Konzepte zu entwickeln, die vom Rebranding über das Rebuilding bis hin zum Rerenting reichen. Stefan Herbert und Annika Gründel plädieren für die Entwicklung von städtischen Quartieren nach dem Ansatz der sogenannten 15-Minuten-Stadt, in der alles Notwendige in einer Viertelstunde erreichbar sein soll. Wie dieses Ziel mit einer Verdichtung des urbanen Raums umgesetzt werden kann, demonstrieren sie am eigenen Unternehmensstandort mit dem zukünftigen METRO Campus. Sabine Krieg hat mit Studierenden an der

Climate protection and sustainability in focus

Germany has had a new government since 8 December 2021 and for the first time a Ministry for Housing, Urban Development and Construction has taken the helm in the construction and real estate industry. "This step was long overdue", according to Christine Lemaitre, managing board member of the non-profit-organisation DGNB e. V., on the occasion of the presentation of the new coalition agreement on 25 November 2021: "That construction used to be an appendage rather than the focus of a government ministry just made no sense. It will now be exciting to see whether the new ministry is given the necessary authority and can pool all the relevant decision-making powers. Another decisive question is whether a close, targeted collaboration with the new Ministry for Economic Affairs and Climate Action will work out. After all, the topics climate protection and sustainability are cross-section topics across all sectors".

Let's hope that not only the announcement of minister Klara Geywitz to create 400,000 new homes a year is achieved, but that in parallel funds and space will be provided for the commercial locations that are inextricably linked with the creation of housing.

Retail Design Thinking

In future, strategic alliances will need to be formed between commerce, culture and town development in order to create new anchor points in the urban space. This puts into practice the principle of design thinking, which essentially aims to get as many people as possible with different experiences, opinions and perspectives on a problem around the same table.

I am therefore delighted that this is exactly what the contributions of our book partners from the areas of planning, project development and research are about. Professor Christoph Achammer forecasts a "second life" for the so far monofunctional commercial architecture which he envisages will take over urban functions with usages which conform with the EU Taxonomy requirements. He calls on all parties involved in the planning to develop bold and flexible concepts which extend from rebranding and rebuilding through to re-renting. Stefan Herbert and Annika Gründel present a case for the development of city districts in accordance with the 15-minute city approach in which the essentials of life are all reachable within a quarter of an hour. With the future METRO Campus at their own company location, they demonstrate just how this goal can be realised by densifying the urban space. Together with students at the Peter Behrens School of Arts (PBSA), Sabine Krieg has

Peter Behrens School of Arts (PBSA) Transformationsmodelle für den Gebäudetypus „Shoppingcenter" entwickelt, die in Zukunft öffentliche und soziale Nutzungen, wie beispielsweise Nachbarschaftszentren, aufnehmen können.

Die konkreten Projekte in den drei Kategorien Components, Spaces und Buildings geben Anregungen für die Umsetzung des nächsten (next) Retail Design: vom frechen Druck-Späti, der mit der Berliner Kiezkultur spielt, über die avantgardistische Zeitreise des Schweizer Uhrenherstellers Longines bis zum archetypischen IKEA City Center, das sich wie ein überdimensionales Billy-Regal zur Stadt Wien öffnet. Das Gebäude soll ein guter Nachbar werden, beschreiben die Architekt:innen von querkraft ihre Vision. Vielleicht liegt darin ein Schlüssel zum „Next Retail". Es gilt, urbane Lebensräume zu schaffen, die Wertschätzung ausdrücken und den Menschen in Zukunft die Wahl zwischen räumlicher Dichte und sicherer Distanz erlauben.

developed transformation models for shopping centres. The ideas for the future include public and social usages such as neighbourhood centres.

The actual projects presented in this edition in the three categories Components, Spaces and Buildings provide inspiration for the realisation of the (next) Retail Design: from the cheeky print pick-up point, which makes reference to the late-night shops in the Berlin hood culture, via an avantgarde journey back in time taken by the Swiss watchmaker Longines through to the archetypical IKEA City Center, which opens to the city of Vienna like an oversized Billy shelf unit. The querkraft architects describe their vision for the lifestyle store as becoming a good neighbour. Maybe that is one of the keys to "Next Retail". It is all about creating habitats which express appreciation and in the future will allow people the choice between spatial density and safe distance.

NEXT RETAIL:
A SECOND LIFE FOR DOWNTOWN RETAIL PROPERTY

PROF. CHRISTOPH M. ACHAMMER, ATP ARCHITEKTEN INGENIEURE

Dass kommerzielle Handelsimmobilien in Europas Innenstädten mehr und mehr zum analogen Überbleibsel verkommen, konnte im Jahr 2021 auch für Branchenfremde keine Überraschung mehr sein. Die Digitalisierung und der Boom des Online-Shoppings sind wahrlich nicht pandemisch rasant über die Welt des stationären Einzelhandels hereingebrochen – diese Entwicklung hämmert seit vielen Jahren laut an die Retail-Tür. Und dennoch verhielt sich eine ganze Branche gefühlt abwartend bis ablehnend gegenüber einem Trend, der sich durch die diversen Shutdowns des gesellschaftlichen Lebens lediglich beschleunigt hat.

Lange schon ist bestens beforscht und bekannt, dass Retailment – das Gespür für den richtigen Mix aus Shopping und Erlebnis – der einzige Weg gegen die gähnende Leere monofunktionaler Handelsimmobilien ist. Die Menschen kommen nicht (mehr), um einen ohnehin auch nicht mehr gegebenen Bedarf zu decken, sie wollen überrascht werden!

Verödung: Ein ökonomisch-städteplanerisches Problem

Gründe für die Zurückhaltung progressiver baulicher Revitalisierungs-Sprünge seitens der Betreiber:innen gibt es freilich viele. Auch nachvollziehbare – wie etwa den Denkmalschutz oder politische und bürokratische Erschwernisse. Oder aber sinkende Mieten und damit wenig Lust auf neue Investitionen. Eine Transformation dieses Ausmaßes gelingt aber nicht ohne Investitionen und muss flexibel genug ausgerichtet sein, um prognostizierte Megatrends zu überdauern. Dies ist fordernd und riskant. Doch in den funktionslos gewordenen, oft großflächigen, stadtbildprägenden Immobilien liegt ein großes Potenzial, die Urbanität von

Even for people outside the retail business, it did not go unnoticed in 2021 that commercial retail property in Europe's inner cities is increasingly degenerating into an analogue relic. Digitalisation and the online shopping boom did not, however, hit the world of bricks-and-mortar retailing with the speed of a pandemic – this development has been knocking loud and clear at the retail door for many years. And yet, the whole industry seems to have been in a wait-and-see mode or even in denial of a trend which was in fact only accelerated by the various shutdowns of public life.

It has long been a well-researched and well-known fact that retailment – the instinct for the right mix of shopping and experience – is the only way to counteract the emptiness of mono-functional retail properties. People no longer come to satisfy needs which they anyway no longer have – they want to be surprised!

Desertification: An economic problem for town planners

There are, of course, countless reasons for the hesitancy among operating companies to take the necessary leaps and bounds towards progressive constructional revitalisation. Some of the reasons, such as the protection of listed buildings or political and bureaucratic hurdles, are quite understandable. Or maybe falling rent prices have caused a reluctance to reinvest. But a transformation on this scale will not succeed without investments and must be aligned flexibly enough to survive the forecast megatrends. This is challenging and risky. Yet, although the often large-scale properties that shape the urban landscape have lost their

"The Circle" gehört zu den spektakulärsten Schweizer Hochbauten der letzten Jahrzehnte. Die ATP-Tochter Mint Architecture entwickelte den Auftritt von Jelmoli, der die architektonische Handschrift aufgreift und in ein einzigartiges Shoppingerlebnis übersetzt.
"The Circle" is one of Switzerland's most spectacular high-rise buildings of recent decades. ATP subsidiary Mint Architecture developed the Jelmoli store, picking up their signature architecture and translating it into a unique shopping experience.

morgen mitzubestimmen. Und ganze Städte interessanter, sauberer, sicherer, grüner und freundlicher zu machen.

Daher sind wir als Architekt:innen und Ingenieur:innen gefordert, Immobilienhaltern flexible, ganzheitliche Lösungen aufzuzeigen: vom Konzept bis hin zur Neuvermarktung ihrer Immobilie – Rebranding, Rebuilding, Rerenting. Denn gelingt es uns nicht, die Hauptakteure für eine langfristig Erfolg versprechende Nutzung zu begeistern, dann droht die Verödung ganzer Regionen und damit eine echte Gefahr für das Gefüge der Stadt.

Flächenrecycling: Bühne frei für neues Leben

In erster Linie braucht es ein Umdenken in Bezug auf die Nutzung der einst monumentalen – klassischen – Warenhäuser und ihrer jüngeren Geschwister, der geschlossenen Einkaufszentren. Mit der Rückkehr ins „New Normal" hat dieser Paradigmenwechsel, so behaupte ich, eher marginal zu tun. Denn es sind in Wahrheit zwei Extreme in verschiedene Richtungen, die einen Trend verdichten, der lange vor dem Virus da war: Auf der einen Seite ist da der ewige Digitalisierungsskeptiker, der nun durch die Handelsbeschränkungen auch die Defizite des monostationären Handels erkannt und sich zu einem Einkauf im Flächenparadies Internet hat hinreißen lassen. Und auf der anderen Seite der eigentlich mäßig Extrovertierte, der nach Monaten des Social Distancing nun auch eine neue Sehnsucht nach Begegnung verspürt.

function, they still have a great deal of potential to co-shape the urbanity of tomorrow and to make whole cities more interesting, cleaner, greener and friendlier in the process.

It is therefore our task as architects and engineers to present flexible, holistic solutions to the owners of these properties: from the concept through to the re-marketing of their property – rebranding, rebuilding, re-renting. Because if we fail to get the main players excited about a usage which promises long-term success, whole regions are at risk of desertification, posing a real danger for the fabric of the city.

Recycling space: Curtain up for a new life

The first challenge is to rethink the use of the once monumental, traditional department stores and their younger siblings, the closed shopping centre. I would suggest that this paradigm change has very little to do with the return to the "new normal". Because in fact there are two extremes in different directions which are consolidating a trend that was there long before the virus: On the one hand, there is the eternal digitalisation sceptic who, faced with trading restrictions, has now come to recognise the deficits of mono-purpose stationary retailing and finally started ordering in the extensive shopping paradise of the internet. And, on the other hand, the moderate extrovert who, after months of social distancing, is now longing for new encounters.

Das „Lifestyle House" ist als Concept Store konzipiert und bietet auf vier Etagen ein fein kuratiertes Sortiment nach Themen und Geschichten.
The "Lifestyle House" is conceived as a concept store and offers an exquisitely curated selection sorted by topics and stories on an area spanning four floors.

Die Auswirkungen der Pandemie mögen zu Beschleunigungs- und Lerneffekten geführt haben, aber der bestimmende Trend bleibt die Tatsache, dass sich unser bedarfsorientiertes Konsumverhalten weiter in die virtuelle Welt ausbreitet und sich damit die Fläche, die wir real fürs Einkaufen benötigen, verringert, während der Wunsch nach Begegnung immer mehr Platz einfordert.

Wer nun die Digitalisierung des Handels als das versteht, was sie ist, nämlich das pragmatische und damit emotionslose Beschaffen von Waren, der erkennt auch eine Chance, aus dem sinkenden Flächenbedarf die richtigen Schlüsse zu ziehen und durch deutlich nutzerorientierte, technische, bauliche und funktionale Veränderungen The Next Retail zu kreieren.

Die Aufgabe, vor der wir stehen, erfordert mehr als einen kreativen Entwurf

Eine langfristig erfolgreiche Revitalisierung muss sich meines Erachtens entlang drei Faktoren orientieren:

Erstens: Es braucht einen Perspektivwechsel. Die Immobilie muss den Nutzer:innen einen Erlebnismehrwert bieten. Aus ihrer Sicht ist es weiterhin entscheidend, alles sehen, hören, riechen und „begreifen" zu können. Sie sehnen sich nach realen Orten, die ihnen den Aufenthalt wieder angenehm machen. Es geht nicht mehr darum, den letzten Quadratmeter Verkaufsfläche herauszuquetschen, sondern um Gebäude, die im Quartier, in der Stadt Ambiente schaffen. Dazu gehören die Vergrößerung der öffentlichen Flächen, die qualitative Aufwertung von Gastronomie und die Schaffung von „Verweilorten" mit entsprechendem Angebot, das zum Bleiben einlädt, und das ergänzte Angebot von anderen Nutzungen zulasten von Handelsflächen besonders in Ebenen über dem ersten Obergeschoss. Für die Revitalisierung der meist in sich geschlossenen, fassadenverblendeten Shoppingcenter heißt das, die Besucher:innen durch ihre Wegeführung nicht weiter zu zwingen, möglichst lange im Inneren den Ausgang zu suchen, sondern ihre Räume nach außen aufzubrechen und in Kommunikation mit der Stadt zu treten.

Zweitens: Es wird in Zukunft gut durchdachte, gemischte Nutzungskonzepte brauchen, die alle Bereiche des Lebens abdecken – Wohnen, Arbeiten, Einkaufen, Essen und Trinken. Vom Shoppingcenter, das Urban-Farming-Konzepte integriert, über die Work-Life-Blending-Immobilie im „Meister-Eder-Prinzip" – unten wird gearbeitet, oben gewohnt – bis hin zum Cultural Hub mit kuratierten Ausstellungsflächen und innovativen Pop-up-Stores ist alles denkbar. Denn integrative Mischquartiere erfüllen das Bedürfnis nach Erlebnis und Begegnung in der Regel besser als klassische monofunktionale Warenhauskonzepte.

The pandemic may have resulted in acceleration and learning effects, but the decisive trend is undeniably that our needs-orientated consumer behaviour is continuing to spread into the virtual world and reducing the space we need for actual shopping, while the desire for personal encounters is calling for more and more space.

Those who understand the digitalisation of retailing as the pragmatic and thus unemotional procurement of goods, also recognise an opportunity to draw the right conclusions from the declining need for space and, based on this realisation, to create The Next Retail by implementing clearly user-orientated, technical, constructional and functional changes.

The task we are facing requires more than a creative design

For a revitalisation to be sustainable I believe it has to be guided by three factors:

First: A change of perspective is required. The property must offer the users added experiential value. From their perspective, being able to see, hear, smell and "grasp" everything remains decisive. They long for real places which make their stay there pleasant. It is no longer about squeezing the last square metre shop floor out of the building, but about buildings which create ambiance in a district or in the city. This includes enlarging the public spaces, upgrading the food and drink offerings and creating "dwell places" which invite visitors to linger for a while. Other usages at the expense of the retail space, particularly on the levels above the first floor, are also needed. The revitalisation of the shopping centres, most of which have a closed façade, will involve no longer forcing visitors through the navigation to stay inside the centre for as long as possible, searching for the exit, but to open up the space to the outside and to enter into communication with the city.

Second: In future, well thought through, mixed usage concepts will be needed which cover all areas of life – living, working, shopping, eating and drinking. From the shopping centre with integrated urban farming concepts, via work-life blending properties – like living above the shop – through to the cultural hub with curated exhibition spaces and innovative pop-up stores. Really anything is conceivable since as a rule integrative mixed-usage districts satisfy the need for experience and encounter better than conventional, mono-functional department store concepts.

Und drittens: Der Weg zur nachhaltigen Umnutzung erfordert ein breites Spektrum an Kompetenzen und muss zwingend integral begleitet werden. Investoren, die weitsichtig genug sind, jetzt bedeutend umzubauen, brauchen Projektentwickler, die ihnen aufgrund ihrer Erfahrung realistische Kalkulationen machen und neue Formen von Mietverträgen aufzeigen können, um die Wertentwicklung und Nutzenmaximierung der kommerziellen Flächen über den gesamten Lebenszyklus ihrer Immobilie auch richtig einordnen zu können. Sie brauchen Placemaker, die sich wissenschaftlich mit den Megatrends der Zukunft beschäftigen, um langfristig erfolgreiche nutzer- und erlebnisorientierte Konzepte verfolgen zu können. Sie brauchen Architekt:innen und Ingenieur:innen, die darin erprobt sind, als Team zusammenzuarbeiten, um sämtliche Gebäudetypologien möglichst verschwendungsfrei in realitätsnahen Gebäudemodellen planen und deren Ausführung – in quality, in time und in budget – überwachen zu können.

And third: The journey to sustainable repurposing requires a broad spectrum of competencies and needs to be supported by integrated concepts. Investors who are farsighted enough to rebuild on a significant scale need project developers who use their experience to make realistic cost estimates and present new forms of rental agreement, thus helping the investors to fully understand the value development and benefit maximisation of the commercial spaces over the whole lifecycle of their property. They need placemakers who take a scientific look at the megatrends of the future to allow them to pursue user-centric and experience-orientated concepts which are successful in the long term. They need architects and engineers who are used to working as a team in order to plan all typologies of building with as little waste as possible in true-to-life building models and who are able to monitor the execution in the requisite quality, on time and within the budget.

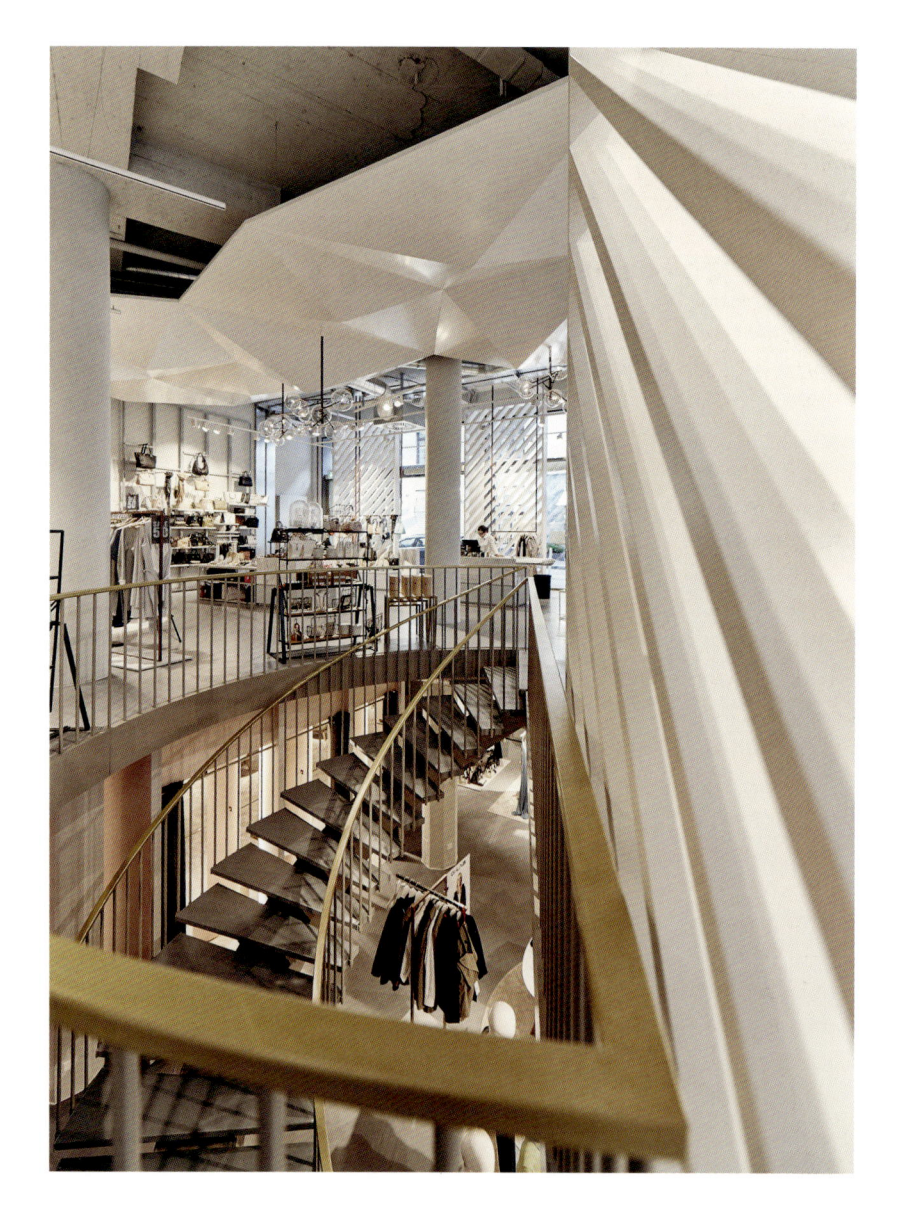

Der Multibrand Fashion Store „The Gallery" an der Zürcher Löwenstraße nutzt die Grandezza früherer Kinoarchitektur und bereitet der urbanen Shopperin eine Bühne zum Einkaufen, Verweilen und Genießen.
The multibrand fashion store "The Gallery" on the Löwenstrasse in Zurich alludes to the grandeur of early cinema architecture and thus sets the stage for the urban customer to do her shopping in a relaxing atmosphere and enjoy her stay.

Und sie brauchen multidisziplinäre Teams, die ihnen und ihren Geldgebern aufgrund ihrer Erfahrung auch den Wert der Nachhaltigkeit ihrer Immobilie ausweisen können und fähig sind, im Zuge der Renovierung die ersten Schritte auf der Road to Zero Carbon umzusetzen. Denn mit taxonomiekonformen Häusern kann den gesetzlichen Richtlinien und den Forderungen der Finanzindustrie, der Umwelt und der nachfolgenden Generationen Folge geleistet werden.

Ich behaupte mit tiefer Überzeugung: Nur wo in einer solchen Konstellation in bester Verantwortung für Mensch, Umwelt und Wirtschaft zusammengearbeitet wird, und zwar miteinander und nicht, wie in der Baubranche immer noch mehrheitlich üblich, nacheinander oder – schlimmer noch – gegeneinander, gibt es für ausgediente innerstädtische Handelsimmobilien ein zweites Leben und damit eine Chance für eine neue Urbanität der Zukunft.

What is more, they need multidisciplinary teams who have the requisite experience to recognise and convey to their investors the sustainable value of their property. In the course of the renovation, it is also important that they take the first steps on the road to net zero. Buildings that conform with the EU Taxonomy Directive not only meet the legal requirements, but also satisfy the demands of the financing industry, the environment and generations to come.

It is my firm belief that only in a constellation where responsibility is taken for people, the environment and business in the best possible way, where all the stakeholders work together (and not as is still common practice in the building trade after each other and – worse still – against each other), will obsolete city-centre retail properties be given a second life and thus present an opportunity for the new urbanity of the future.

NEW URBANITY
IN EUROPEAN CITY PLANNING

STEFAN HERBERT & ANNIKA GRÜNDEL, METRO PROPERTIES

Der Begriff Urbanität ist in der Gesellschaft und in Fachkreisen überwiegend positiv konnotiert. Klar ist, Urbanität ist das Schlagwort der Gegenwart im europäischen Städtebau. Was aber ist unter Urbanität zu verstehen und wie sieht diese im 21. Jahrhundert aus? Die Definition ist – aus unserer Sicht – unstrittig. Wir verstehen urbane Räume als städtebaulich dichte und vielseitig nutzbare Flächen. Aber handelt es sich bei Urbanität um einen rein stadtplanerischen Raum? Oder ist sie vielmehr auch ein Lebensgefühl, eine Haltung? So ist urbaner Lebensstil in aller Munde und ein vermeintlich erstrebenswerter Zustand. Wie aber entsteht das urbane Lebensgefühl in einem neuen Quartier? Wie muss zukunftsweisende Stadtplanung aussehen und welche Antworten auf den klimatischen, demografischen und digitalen Wandel muss sie geben, um den urbanen Gedanken weiterzutragen?

Im frühen 21. Jahrhundert ist unser Denken und Handeln primär von klimatischen Herausforderungen, demografischen Entwicklungen und Ressourcenknappheit geprägt. Hinzu kommen Wohnungsnot und Flächenknappheit, der Umgang mit Verkehr und alternativen Mobilitätskonzepten sowie der steigende Bedarf nach flexiblen Wohn- und Arbeitsmodellen. In europäischen Metropolen ist Bauland Mangelware; die Innenstädte stehen flächenbezogen unter erheblichem Druck. Stadtnahe Flächen mit geringer baulicher Ausnutzung bzw. gegenwärtig kommerziell oder industriell genutzte Areale geraten daher zunehmend ins Visier der Architekt:innen und Stadtplaner:innen. Es gilt, unterschiedliche Funktionen und Lebensbereiche in einer pulsierenden, modernen Quartiersentwicklung zusammenzuführen und zu integrieren. Essenziell ist dabei die Schaffung gleichermaßen flexibler wie robuster Gerüste.

The term urbanity generally has positive connotations in society and among professionals. Urbanity is certainly a buzzword in current European city planning. But what does it mean and what does it look like in the 21st century? The definition, in our opinion, is undisputed. In terms of city planning, we consider urban spaces to be densely populated areas which can be used for multiple purposes. But does urbanity refer solely to a space from a city planning perspective? Or is it rather an attitude towards life? Everyone is talking about urban lifestyle and it is considered to be something to aspire to. But how does an urban attitude to life evolve in a new district? What should forward-looking city planning look like and what responses does it have to climatic, demographic and digital change in order to perpetuate the urban idea?

In the early 21st century, our thoughts and actions are primarily shaped by climate challenges, demographic trends and a shortage of resources. Other concerns include a lack of housing, traffic management and alternative mobility concepts as well as the need for flexible living and working models. Building land in the big European cities is in short supply and city centres are starting to feel the pressure. Sparsely developed plots near cities or areas that are currently used for commercial or industrial purposes are therefore becoming an increasingly interesting option for architects and town planners. The challenge is to combine and to integrate different functions and areas of life in a pulsating, modern district development. In doing so, it is essential to create frameworks that are both flexible and robust.

NEW URBANITY IN EUROPEAN CITY PLANNING

Der urbane Raum hat in seiner Geschichte immer wieder seine Fähigkeit zum Wandel und zur Veränderung bewiesen. So hat nicht zuletzt die weltweite COVID-19-Pandemie deutlich gezeigt, was für Faktoren lebenswerte Städte ausmachen und die Bedürfnisse der Menschen befriedigen. COVID-19 forcierte die Beantwortung der Frage, wie sich städtische Räume entwickeln müssen, um krisenfester, nachhaltiger und damit attraktiver zu werden.

Die Profession der Stadtplaner:innen und Architekt:innen hat nicht nur die Aufgabe, sondern vielmehr die Verpflichtung, innovative sowie zukunftsgerichtete Ansätze zu erarbeiten und umzusetzen, die den sich ändernden gesellschaftlichen Prämissen auch Rechnung tragen.

Over time, urban spaces have again and again demonstrated their ability to transform and change. The recent worldwide COVID-19 pandemic, for instance, has once again shown what factors make cities worth living in and are capable of filling the needs of the people who live there. COVID-19 has forced those responsible to address the question of how urban spaces need to develop if they are to become more stable, more sustainable and thus more attractive.

City planning professionals and architects are tasked, or rather obligated to develop and implement innovative, future-orientated approaches which do justice to the changing societal premises.

METRO Campus: Städtebaulicher Entwurf von ACME, Stadt Land Fluss, Kieran Fraser Landscape Design.
METRO Campus: City planning design by ACME, Stadt Land Fluss, Kieran Fraser Landscape Design.

METRO Campus Platz mit Blick auf die Markthalle (rechts).
METRO Campus square with a view of the covered market (right).

Der dritte Ort – Ein Raum der Begegnung

Ist von öffentlichem Raum die Rede, so wird in der Soziologie oft der Terminus des so genannten „dritten Ortes" verwendet. Der Begriff definiert öffentlichen Raum als einen Ort der Gemeinschaft, des gesellschaftlichen Miteinanders und sozialen Austauschs. Doch wie ist öffentlicher Raum zu gestalten, um diese Funktion zu erfüllen und somit dem ihm zugedachten Zweck gerecht zu werden?

Veränderte Stadt- und Einwohnerstrukturen sowie zunehmend flexible Lebensentwürfe erfordern zukunftsweisende Gestaltungskonzepte zur Bildung attraktiver, autarker und resilienter Stadtquartiere. Die Qualität von städtischen Räumen bestimmt maßgeblich, ob wir uns wohl- und sicher fühlen, Kreativität entfalten und aufeinander zugehen. Architektur und Städtebau können diese Räume für Begegnung, Kommunikation und Austausch schaffen.

The third place – space for encounter

When talking about public space, sociologists often use the term, the "third place". The term defines public space as a place of community, of social interaction and exchange. But how should public space be designed to fulfil this function and thus do justice to its designated purpose?

Changed city and inhabitant structures as well as increasingly flexible life plans require visionary design concepts in order to develop city districts which are attractive, autonomous and resilient. The quality of urban spaces is decisive for whether we feel good and safe, whether we can give free rein to our creativity and feel comfortable about approaching others. Architecture and city planning can create these spaces for encounter, communication and exchange.

Das Comeback der Innenstädte

Innenstädte unterliegen dem kontinuierlichen Wandel. Unterschiedliche Bereiche wie Handel, Wohnen, Arbeiten, aber auch Freizeit, Kultur, Gastronomie und Tourismus charakterisieren die Innenstadt und ermöglichen (gesellschaftliche) Vielfalt. Im Idealfall. Doch wo einst Diversität herrschte, entspricht die Innenstadt heute einer Monokultur wiederkehrender Handels- und Gastronomieketten, oftmals gesichtslos und beliebig austauschbar. Diese singuläre Ausrichtung der Innenstädte auf Handel und Büroflächen bietet wenig Mehrwert für den öffentlichen Raum. Sie ist weder nachhaltig noch zukunftsträchtig.

Die Grenzen der diversen funktional getrennten Sektoren wirken oftmals anachronistisch. Im Zuge der zunehmenden Verstädterung und der Verdichtung innerstädtischer Areale wird die räumliche Trennung verschiedener Flächennutzungen, sofern möglich und sinnvoll, bereits revidiert. Die Wohn-, Arbeits- und Lebensverhältnisse wandeln sich und verschmelzen sowohl zeitlich als auch räumlich.

Es muss der Gedanke erlaubt sein, ob die Innenstädte der Zukunft zu diesem Zweck nicht von zunehmender Mischnutzung geprägt sein können oder sollten, um sie zu beleben und zu Orten der Begegnung werden zu lassen. Dazu bedarf es einer Stadtplanung mit flexiblen, vorausschauenden und nachhaltigen Flächennutzungen sowie einer leistungsfähigen Infrastruktur. Denkbare, zukunftsfähige Modelle könnten in dem Kontext Nutzmischungen wie Wohnen auf dem Supermarkt oder die Transformation von Gewerbeflächen zu Wohnraum sein.

The comeback of the city centre

City centres are subject to a constant transformation process. Different zones like retail, living, working, but also leisure, culture, restaurants and bars as well as tourism characterise the city centre and rub shoulders here, creating (social) diversity in the process. At least that is the ideal scenario. Yet, where once diversity prevailed, today's inner city is a monoculture of recurring retail and food and drink chains and is often faceless and interchangeable. Such focusing solely on retailing and offices is neither future-proof nor sustainable and provides no added value for the public space.

The boundaries of functionally segregated sectors often appear to be anachronistic. The increasing urbanisation and density of inner city areas already bring with them an urge to revise the spatial division of various usages wherever possible and appropriate. The conditions of living and working are changing, and they are merging in both time and space.

We therefore have to entertain the idea that the inner cities of the future can and should be increasingly used for mixed purposes in order to revive them and make them places of encounter. This requires town planning that makes use of building space in a flexible, forward-looking and sustainable manner based on powerful infrastructure. In this regard, living above a supermarket or the transformation of office space into commercial space could become conceivable and future-proof models.

Park Quartier: Arbeiten und Wohnen inmitten offener und belebter Grün- und Parkflächen.
Park district: Working and living amidst open and lively green spaces and park areas.

So ist die Diskussion zu Wohnhochhäusern in Deutschland aus unserer Sicht zu eindimensional geführt. Hohe Dichte wird oftmals mit ghettoähnlichen Strukturen assoziiert und ist dementsprechend vorurteilsbelastet. Dabei wird verkannt, dass nicht die städtebauliche Dichte, sondern vielmehr die Verortung im Stadtgefüge, die singuläre Ausrichtung und die meist nichtöffentlichen Ergeschosszonen zu einem Mangel an urbanem Leben führen. Ein Gebäude mag architektonisch ansprechend entworfen, klimagerecht gebaut und mit attraktiven, nachhaltigen Grün- und Außenanlagen gestaltet sein; einen Mehrwert für die Gesellschaft stiftet es nur dann, wenn die Erdgeschossflächen divers genutzt werden und öffentlich zugänglich sind.

Der oftmals sehr rigiden Haltung gegenüber gemischt genutzten Immobilien, sei es aus Sicht der Stadtplanung oder Investoren, stehen mancherorts kreative Lösungen im Städtebau entgegen. Jüngst umgesetzte Immobilienentwicklungen sind lediglich an bereits existierende Stadtquartiere angeschlossen und nutzen deren bestehende Infrastrukturen ohne die erforderliche Anpassung. Gemischt genutzte Gebäudekomplexe oder Quartiere erhöhen natürlich zunächst die Komplexität im Planungs- und Bauprozess. Allerdings erweisen sie sich auch als attraktiver und zudem krisenfest.

Wir plädieren generell für mehr Pragmatismus in dieser Debatte und einen Blick über die Landesgrenzen, insbesondere in den asiatischen Raum. Die Ergebnisse weniger restriktiver Stadtplanung sind überraschend innovative und kreative Lösungen im Umgang mit knappen urbanen Flächen. Dabei scheint der bisweilen etwas naive, aber pragmatische Planungsansatz auf den ersten Blick im europäischen oder im deutschen Städtebau nicht anwendbar. Doch gerade die Bereitschaft zur Infragestellung des Status quo ist aus unserer Sicht eine wesentliche Qualifikation aller Stadtplaner:innen und Architekt:innen.

METRO PROPERTIES hat die in Asien gesammelten Erfahrungen frühzeitig in seine internationalen Standortentwicklungen einfließen lassen. Dabei geht es weniger um festgelegte Nutzungsmodelle oder Architektur, sondern vielmehr um die generelle Fragestellung, wie Gebäude einen attraktiven Stadtraum formen oder zumindest einen Beitrag zu diesem leisten können. Im Mittelpunkt aller städtebaulichen Planungen müssen die Motivation und der Wille stehen, etwas Sinnhaftes und Einzigartiges zu schaffen. In diesem Diskurs spielt auch die optimale Ausnutzung von Flächen und Grundstücken eine entscheidende Rolle. Gebäude, die die vorgegebenen Dichteparameter absolut ausnutzen und mit unterschiedlichen Nutzungen programmiert sind, tragen zur Lebendigkeit und Attraktivität eines Areals bei.

In our opinion, the discussion surrounding high-rise residential buildings in Germany is too one-dimensional. High density is often associated with ghetto-like structures and as such is subject to prejudices. However, this stance fails to recognise that it is not density in the city that leads to a lack of urban life, but rather the location in the city framework, the singular orientation and the fact that ground floor zones are generally not publicly accessible. The design of a building may be architecturally appealing, climate friendly and include attractive, sustainable green and outdoor spaces; however, it only creates added value for the community if the ground floor zones are used in diverse ways and are publicly accessible.

In contrast to the often very rigid attitude towards mixed-use properties, be it from the perspective of the city planners or the investors, some places have benefited from more creative city planning solutions. Real estate developments of recent times are merely annexed to existing city districts and use their existing infrastructure without any adjustments. Initially, multi-use building complexes or districts do, of course, make the planning and construction process more complex. However, they also turn out to be more attractive and, on top of that, they are more stable in the face of crises.

We call for more pragmatism in this debate and would encourage a look over the borders, especially into Asia. The results of a less restrictive city planning are surprisingly innovative and creative solutions to the problems that are posed by the short supply of urban space. At first glance the slightly naïve but pragmatic planning approach appears to be incompatible with European or German city planning. However, questioning the status quo should in our opinion be a key characteristic of all town planners and architects.

METRO PROPERTIES already incorporated the experience gathered in Asia in its international location developments at an early stage. It is not so much about fixed usage models or architecture but rather about the general question of how buildings can form an attractive city space or at least make a contribution to this. At the heart of all city planning must be the will and drive to create something that makes sense and that is unique. In this discourse, the optimum use of space and land plays a decisive role. Buildings which fully exploit the density parameters and that are programmed with different usages help make an area lively and attractive.

METRO LAB – Thinktank und Innovation am METRO Campus.
METRO LAB – Think tank and innovation on the METRO Campus.

Eine weitere Herausforderung im modernen Städtebau ist die zunehmende Verdrängung gewerblicher Flächen aufgrund gestiegener Mietpreiserwartungen. Dabei sorgen gerade die inhabergeführten Betriebe und Geschäfte für Individualität und Charakter im Stadtbild. In Quartiersentwicklungen sollten daher auch Flächen für produzierendes Gewerbe, Ateliers und Handwerkerbetriebe vorgesehen werden. METRO PROPERTIES findet in Amsterdam mit dem eigens konzipierten „New Work City Concept" (siehe Retail Design International Vol. 6) eine Antwort auf diese Prämisse. Das Konzept sieht eine multiple, programmierbare dichte städtische Struktur vor, die vielen Ansprüchen gerecht wird und Vielfalt im städtischen Gefüge ermöglicht. Eine eingeschossige singuläre Nutzung auf städtischem Grund ist weder wirtschaftlich noch nachhaltig und vertretbar, da die Flächen rar sind. Demzufolge verfolgt das Redevelopment eine Verdichtungsstrategie. Im Zentrum steht dabei der Anspruch, verschiedene Funktionen optimal bzw. symbiotisch miteinander zu verknüpfen. Dies muss derart erfolgen, dass sowohl die Bewirtschaftung als auch die Interaktion bzw. Nutzung der Räume durch die einzelnen Akteure möglichst störungsfrei verlaufen. Die diversen Funktionen und Strukturen beeinflussen sich dabei gegenseitig positiv und führen zu Synergieeffekten.

An unseren METRO Standorten gilt es, vorhandenes Potenzial zu nutzen, um Räume zu schaffen, die in neu entstehende urbane Strukturen integriert werden und somit zum öffentlichen Leben beitragen.

Another challenge in modern city planning is that commercial areas are increasingly being crowded out due to higher rental price expectations. And yet, it is precisely owner-managed businesses and stores which add individuality and character to the cityscape. District developments should therefore also include space for the production industry, for ateliers and tradespeople. In Amsterdam, METRO PROPERTIES has found an answer to this premise in the "New Work City Concept" (see Retail Design International Vol. 6) that it has developed. The concept provides for a multiple, programmable dense urban structure which satisfies many aspirations and requirements and allows diversity to enter the city structures. Since space is at a premium, single-storey mono-use on city land is neither economically efficient nor sustainable and reasonable. The redevelopment therefore pursues a consolidation strategy. At the heart of this is the desire to connect various functions with one another in the best possible way or even symbiotically. This must be done in such a way that the management and interaction or use of the spaces by the individual players is as seamless as possible. The various functions and structures have a positive impact on each other and generate synergy effects.

At our METRO locations we strive to use the existing potential in order to create spaces which are integrated in new evolving urban structures and thus contribute to public life.

Grüne Quartiersgasse im Green Lane Quartier.
Green district alley crossing the Green Lane quarter.

Ein Plädoyer für städtische Quartiere

Eine inspirierende Bewegung, die im Zuge der Corona-Pandemie enorme Aufmerksamkeit erhalten hat, ist die 15-Minuten-Stadt. Ein Ansatz, der die Städte der Zukunft dezentral und in Quartieren denkt. In Deutschland klingt dies nach urbaner Utopie, in anderen Städten Europas ist es schon heute gelebte Realität. In Metropolen wie Paris oder Barcelona setzt man bereits auf das zukunftsträchtige Konzept: Das Notwendige, das Menschen brauchen, soll in einer Viertelstunde zu Fuß, mit dem Fahrrad oder den öffentlichen Verkehrsmitteln zu erreichen sein – der Arbeitsplatz, die Schule, Geschäfte, Kulturstätten und die medizinische Versorgung. Ein eigenes Auto würde überflüssig werden. Angesichts des Klimawandels und der Energiewende wird das Leitbild der autogerechten Stadt zunehmend hinterfragt, eine Neudefinition der damit verbundenen urbanen Strukturen erscheint daher dringend geboten. Solche Quartiere könnten Blaupausen für die urbane Zukunft sein. Hier kann in kleinem Rahmen ausprobiert werden, was im Großen funktionieren soll.

Der Reiz des urbanen Lebens scheint ungebrochen und ist gleichzeitig Teil des Problems. Paradoxerweise vermag die Urbanisierung jedoch auch der große Hebel im Kampf gegen den Klimawandel zu sein. So können Städte aufgrund ihrer hohen Dichte bedeutende Mengen an Ressourcen schonen und durch die Integration von verschiedenen biodiversen Grünflächen städtische Ökosysteme bilden – zum Beispiel durch den Ausbau regenerativer Energien, flächensparender und kompakter Stadtstrukturen, emissionsarmer Mobilitätskonzepte sowie energieeffizienter Gebäude.

Die aufgeführten Faktoren beeinflussen wesentlich den zukünftigen städtebaulichen Planungsprozess und damit das Erscheinungsbild unserer Städte. Schon heute sind Diversität und Inklusion wichtige Aspekte der Quartiersentwicklung – in Bezug auf soziale Mischung und auf das Zusammenspiel verschiedener Nutzungen.

A plea for city districts

An inspiring movement which has received a lot of attention during the corona pandemic is the 15-minute city. This decentralised approach thinks of the city of the future in terms of districts. While in Germany, this sounds like an urban utopia, in other European cities the idea has already been brought to life. In conurbations like Paris or Barcelona, the promising concept has already been implemented: The essentials of people's lives should be reachable in a quarter of an hour on foot, by bike or public transport – the workplace, schools, shops, cultural venues and healthcare. It would not be necessary to own a car. In light of the climate change and the new energy era, the guiding principle of a car-friendly city is increasingly being questioned; a new definition of the urban structures associated with it is therefore urgently needed. Such districts could be blueprints for the urban future. Here, it is possible to try out plans and ideas on a small scale.

Urban life has lost none of its charm, and that is in itself part of the problem. Paradoxically, however, urbanisation can also be a significant lever in the fight against climate change. Due to their high density, cities can save significant amounts of resources and form urban ecosystems by integrating various biodiverse green spaces – for example by expanding the use of renewable energies, space-saving and compact city structures, low-emission mobility concepts and energy-efficient buildings.

The aforementioned factors significantly impact on future city planning processes and thus the appearance of our cities. Diversity and inclusion are already an important aspect of district development – in terms of social mix and the interaction of different usages.

NEW URBANITY IN EUROPEAN CITY PLANNING

Neue Urbanität in Düsseldorf

METRO PROPERTIES begegnet dem rapiden weltweiten Wachstum von Städten, indem wir unsere Standorte optimal und nachhaltig in die Städte von morgen integrieren – mit Konzepten, die dem demografischen Wandel, sich verändernden Umweltbedingungen und Arbeitswelten sowie Lebensgewohnheiten mit innovativen Lösungen Rechnung tragen. In einer Welt mit zunehmend flexiblen Lebensentwürfen schaffen wir Orte der Begegnung und Lebensqualität – so auch an unserem globalen METRO Konzernsitz in Düsseldorf.

Düsseldorf ist eine attraktive Stadt. Der anhaltende Zuzug neuer Bewohner:innen in die Landeshauptstadt Nordrhein-Westfalens ist ungebrochen. Die Nachfrage nach urbanem Wohnraum und Nutzflächen übersteigt das begrenzte innerstädtische Angebot bei Weitem.

Der METRO Campus ist eine über Jahrzehnte gewachsene Institution im Düsseldorfer Stadtteil Grafenberg. Die Lage zwischen Innenstadt, Grafenberger Wald, Düsseltal und Flingern macht das Areal heute einzigartig. Beim Ankauf im Jahr 1967 lag das Areal noch in einem Industriegebiet am Rande der Stadt. Heute, Jahrzehnte später, befindet es sich in unmittelbarer Innenstadtlage. Aus städtebaulicher und immobilienwirtschaftlicher Sicht verfügt der Standort über ein enorm hohes Entwicklungspotenzial. Unser METRO Campus bietet 9,2 Hektar Fläche, die für eine alternative Nutzung grundsätzlich in Betracht kämen.

New urbanity in Dusseldorf

METRO PROPERTIES encounters the rapid worldwide growth of cities by sustainably integrating its locations into the cities of tomorrow in the best possible way – with concepts that take account of demographic change, changing environmental conditions and working worlds and life habits by implementing innovative solutions. In a world with increasingly flexible life plans, we create places of encounter and quality of life – and this also applies to our global METRO headquarters in Dusseldorf.

Dusseldorf is an attractive city. The influx of new residents to the state capital of North Rhine Westphalia continues unabated. The demand for urban living space and usable areas exceeds the limited space available downtown by far.

The METRO Campus is an institution in the Dusseldorf district of Grafenberg that has grown over decades. Today, the location between city centre, Grafenberg forest, Dusseltal and Flingern makes the areal unique. When it was purchased back in 1967, the areal was still on an industrial estate on the periphery of the city. Today, decades later, it is directly in the city centre. From a town planning and real estate perspective, the location has huge development potential. Our METRO Campus offers an area of 9.2 hectares which in principle is suitable for an alternative usage.

METRO Campus Lageplan.
METRO Campus site plan.

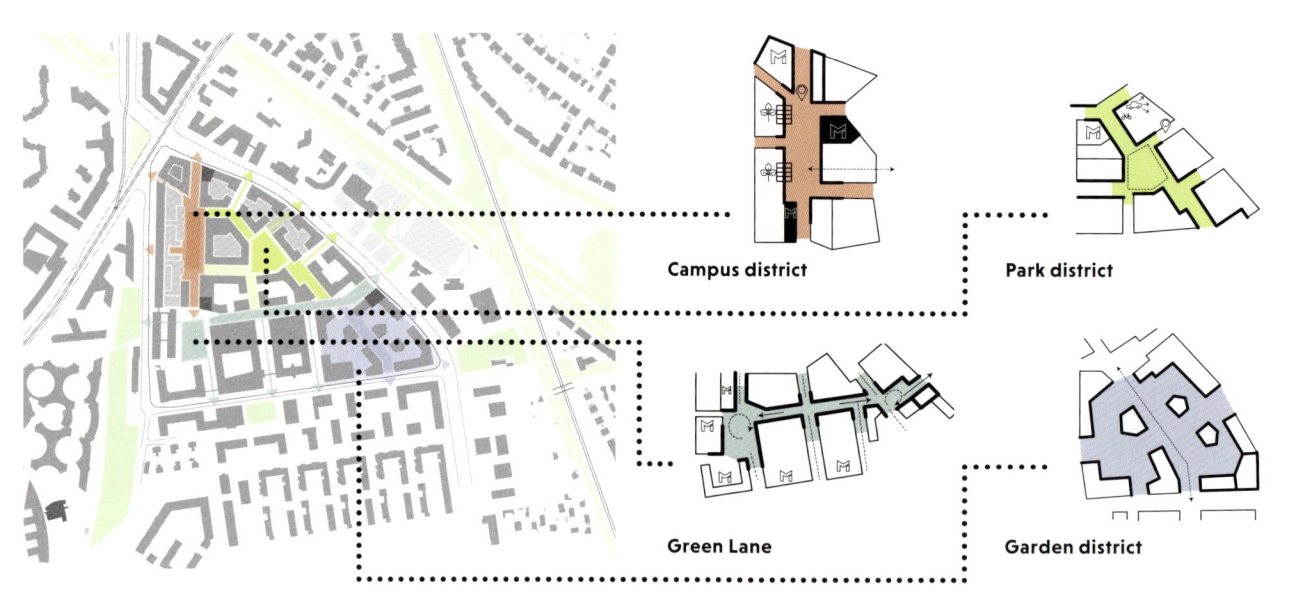

METRO Campus: Existierende und neue Gebäude formen vier Quartiere, in deren Zentren jeweils neuer öffentlicher Raum entsteht.
METRO Campus: Existing and new buildings form four quarters with new public space being created at their centres.

METRO Campus – Raum für Visionen

Aufgrund der Dimension und Relevanz des Planungsgebiets initiierte METRO PROPERTIES in Zusammenarbeit mit der Landeshauptstadt Düsseldorf einen städtebaulichen Wettbewerb. Die enge Zusammenarbeit mit der Landeshauptstadt und der Lokalpolitik hatte einen hohen Mehrwert im gesamten Verfahren. Aber auch die Stimmen weiterer Experten, der Bürger sowie der METRO Mitarbeiter:innen fanden Gehör: vom Zukunftsforscher über Mobilitäts- und Klimaexperten, vom Rat der Künste über Vertreter aller politischen Fraktionen sowie Verantwortliche aus (Landschafts-) Architektur und Städteplanung. Alle Perspektiven wurden im kollaborativen städtebaulichen Wettbewerbsprozess gehört. So war sichergestellt, dass diverse Blickwinkel und Expertisen in die städteplanerischen Entwürfe einfließen.

Von Beginn an war die kritische Auseinandersetzung mit der konzeptionellen Ebene der Stadtplanung von enormer Bedeutung. Wie können sich existierende Gebäude unter Beibehaltung ihrer Identität und Qualität in die städtische Struktur einfügen, ohne zu Fremdkörpern zu werden? Wie ist es möglich, im Rahmen der geltenden Bauvorschriften kreative, nachhaltige und flexible Entwicklungskonzepte zu fördern?

Zielsetzung der Auslobung war die Erarbeitung eines innovativen, sozioökonomisch robusten städtebaulichen Konzepts, welches das 9,2 Hektar große METRO Campus Areal in ein lebenswertes Quartier der Zukunft führen soll. Die existierenden METRO Bürobauten sollen dabei sinnvoll in das städtebauliche Gesamtgefüge des neuen Quartiers integriert und der Öffentlichkeit partiell zugänglich gemacht werden.

METRO Campus – space for visions

Due to the dimension and relevance of the planning area, METRO PROPERTIES in collaboration with the state capital Dusseldorf launched a city planning competition. The close cooperation with the state capital and local politicians added extra value to the whole procedure. But other experts, citizens and METRO staff were also heard: from future researchers via mobility and climate experts, from the arts council via representatives of all political factions and those responsible from (landscape) architecture and town planning. All perspectives were factored into the collaborative city planning competition process. This ensured that various perspectives and expertise were incorporated in the city planning design concepts.

From the outset, the critical analysis of the conceptional level of city planning was of great importance. How can existing buildings be incorporated in the city structure without losing their identity and quality and without looking out of place? How is it possible within the framework of the applicable building requirements to encourage creative, sustainable and flexible development concepts?

The aim of the competition was to develop an innovative, socio-economically robust city planning concept which will lead the 9.2 hectares of the METRO Campus areal into a liveable district of the future. The existing METRO office buildings are to be intelligently integrated in the overall city planning of the new district and be made partially accessible to the public.

Der prämierte städtebaulich-freiraumplanerische Entwurf von ACME, Stadt Land Fluss und Kieran Fraser Landscape Design interpretiert unsere Zielsetzung auf herausragende Weise. Er sieht die Entwicklung eines urbanen, gemischt genutzten Quartiers mit einer prägnanten baulich-räumlichen Struktur, einer eigenständigen Identität und einer vielschichtigen sowie diversen Stadtlandschaft vor.

Der heutige Bestand überdeckt eine 150-jährige Bebauungsgeschichte. Die Stadt Düsseldorf wuchs mit der Industrialisierung des 18. und 19. Jahrhunderts. Viele namhafte Düsseldorfer Industriefamilien, wie beispielsweise die Familie Haniel, betrieben hier ihre wichtigsten Forschungs- und Produktionsstätten. Das nördliche Quartier an der Grafenberger Allee war für 90 Jahre der Sitz von H. Schmincke & Co., dem berühmten Produzenten von Pigment- und Künstlerfarben. Südlich angesiedelt lag das Gelände eines historischen Walzwerkes.

Die Architektur des neuen Stadtquartiers soll die Innovationshistorie des Gebiets in seiner Materialität fortschreiben. Die architektonische Identität der Blöcke wird genutzt, um Quartiere zu gliedern und die unterschiedlichen Landschaftsräume genauer zu definieren. Das städtebauliche Konzept umfasst vier neu geschaffene öffentliche Quartiersteile, bestehend aus sowohl existierenden als auch neuen Gebäuden. Im Zentrum eines jeden Quartiers liegt ein neuer öffentlicher Raum mit spezifischer Identität und Qualität.

Im Campus-Quartier gruppieren sich vielfältige Nutzungen um einen aktiven Campus-Platz, als funktionales und gestalterisches Herzstück des neuen städtischen Viertels, als Schnittstelle zwischen der METRO AG Hauptverwaltung und der Neubebauung; ein lebendiger Stadtplatz und Marktplatz für die weitere Umgebung. Die westlich verlaufende Green Lane ist ein kommerzielles soziales Quartier und erschließt die südlichen METRO Gebäude, vereint mit Neubebauung. Das Park-Quartier ist ein Ort des Wohnens und Arbeitens im Kiez, zwischen dem Campus und der Walter-Eucken-Straße, erschlossen durch die Quartiersgasse und mit grünen Hofblöcken, gruppiert um einen neuen offenen grünen Quartierspark. Charakterisiert durch schützende Randbebauung und Punktbauten entsteht das Garten Quartier, welches Schulen, Kindergarten, großzügige private und gemeinschaftliche Grün- und Freiflächen sowie öffentliche grüne Dächer umfasst. Vielseitige Gemeinschaftsgärten laden zum Gärtnern, Spielen und Verweilen ein. Sie bieten den Bewohnerinnen und Bewohnern neben den gemeinschaftlichen Aktivitäten auch Ruhe und Entspannung sowie einen wohltuenden Weitblick über die Dächer der Stadt.

The award-winning design for usage in a city planning context by ACME, Stadt Land Fluss und Kieran Fraser Landscape Design interprets our goal in an outstanding way. It provides for the development of an urban, mixed-use district with a striking structure of buildings, a distinct identity and a multi-layered and diverse city landscape.

The existing buildings cover 150 years of development history. The city of Dusseldorf grew with the industrialisation of the 18th and 19th centuries. Many well-known Dusseldorf industrial families, such as the Haniel family, operated their most important research and production plants here. For 90 years, the northern district on Grafenberger Allee was home to H. Schmincke & Co., the famous producer of pigment and artist paints. To the south, are the grounds of a historical rolling mill.

The architecture of the new city district is to continue the innovation history of the area in terms of the materials used. The architectural identity of the blocks are used to divide up the districts and to define the various landscape areas more precisely. The city planning concept comprises four newly created district parts consisting of both existing and also new buildings. At the centre of each district is a new public space with a specific identity and quality.

In the Campus district, a number of uses are grouped around an active Campus square as function and design centrepiece of the new urban district, as interface between the METRO AG headquarters and the new buildings; a lively city square and marketplace for the surrounding area. Green Lane, to the west, is a commercial/social district and incorporates the METRO building, combined with new builds. The Park district is a neighbourhood for living and working, between the Campus and Walter-Eucken-Strasse. Accessed via the district lane, its green courtyard blocks are grouped around a new open green district park. Characterised by protective perimeter development and individual buildings, the Garden district consists of schools, nurseries, generous private and public green and open spaces as well as public multi-purpose community gardens that invite residents to garden, play and linger for a while. Besides these shared activities, these areas also offer space for peace and relaxation and a delightful view over the rooftops of the city.

Die abwechslungsreiche, aber dennoch klare Struktur des städtebaulichen Entwurfs ermöglicht eine multifunktionale Codierung der Gebäude und eine Aktivierung der üblicherweise abweisenden Erdgeschossflächen. Unterschiedliche Plätze mit verschiedenen Atmosphären und Angeboten bilden das Rückgrat des Zukunftsquartiers. Die vorgeschlagene heterogene Flächennutzung der Erdgeschosse und die konsistente Arrondierung von Wohnungsflächen in den Obergeschossen führt zu einer adäquaten Verdichtung des Quartiers.

In der Projektierung des METRO Campus Projekts haben wir uns die aufgeworfenen Fragen zu Herzen genommen und als Prämisse in die Auslobung des internationalen städtebaulichen Wettbewerbs einfließen lassen. Essenziell war die Entscheidung, dass neben der METRO Hauptverwaltung kein klassisches Wohngebiet entstehen soll, sondern ein urbanes Quartier, das dieses Prädikat auch zu Recht trägt. Große Teile der Erdgeschosszonen obliegen der öffentlichen Nutzung, sei es durch Handel, Gastronomie, Dienstleistungen, soziale Infrastruktur sowie Mobilitätskonzepte. Die Funktionen sind derart angeordnet, dass sie an den Hauptadern des autoarmen Quartiers liegen. Die Einbindung in den vorhandenen Kontext sowie der Anschluss an vorhandene Stadträume und Grünflächen bilden das Rückgrat einer stabilen städtebaulichen Figur.

Das Thema Nachhaltigkeit ist ein wesentlicher Aspekt in der Quartiersplanung. So wirkt die intensive Begrünung der Dachflächen und öffentlichen Plätze bis hin zum Regenwassermanagement nebst klimatischer Optimierung der Baublöcke dem Heat-Island-Effekt entgegen und sorgt für ein komfortables Mikroklima. Zudem werden in ausgewählten Bereichen artenreiche Vegetationsflächen und vielfältige Habitate für Pflanzen und Tiere geschaffen. Nicht begehbare Dachflächen sind extensiv begrünt. Wo möglich und sinnvoll, werden Dachflächen als Solargründächer angelegt. Das Konzept sieht weiterhin als effizientes Erschließungssystem ein autoarmes Quartier im Sinne des Mobilitätsszenarios „Modellquartier" vor.

Ausblick

Das Konzept des METRO Campus der Zukunft vereint Wohn- und Arbeitsraum, durchmischt mit Gastronomie, Markthalle, Einzelhandel, Handwerk und Ateliers, Naherholungs- und Freizeitangeboten, eingebettet in Parks und Gärten. Es entsteht die Vision eines städtischen Raums, der über ein klassisches Wohngebiet mit hoher Dichte hinausgeht und vielfältige Nutzungen zulässt – ein diversifiziertes, lebendiges und klimagerechtes Quartier inmitten der Rheinmetropole Düsseldorf.

The varied, but clear structure of the city planning concept allows a multifunctional coding of the buildings and the activation of the otherwise unapproachable and off-putting ground floor zones. Various squares with different atmospheres and offerings form the backbone of the future district. The proposed heterogenous use of the space on the ground floors and the consistent realignment of the residential space on the upper floors results in an adequate density in the district.

In the planning of the METRO Campus project, we took the questions that were raised to heart and incorporated them as premises in the specifications of the international city planning competition. What we are not looking for next to the METRO headquarters is a conventional residential area, but instead an urban district which deserves to be given this name. Large parts of the ground floor zones are designated for public usage, be it retail, bars and restaurants, services, social infrastructure or mobility concepts. The functions are arranged in such a way that they are located on the main arteries of the virtually car-free district. The integration in the existing context and the connection to existing city areas and green spaces form the backbone of a stable city planning character.

Sustainability is a key aspect of the district planning. The intensive planting of the roofs and public squares, rainwater management as well as the climatic optimisation of the building blocks counteract the heat island effect and ensure a pleasant micro-climate. In addition, vegetation areas with many different species and many different habitats for flora and fauna will be created in selected zones. Inaccessible roof areas are to be extensively planted, where possible, as solar green roofs. As efficient access system, the concept also provides for a virtually car-free district in line with the mobility scenario for the "model district".

Outlook

The concept of the future METRO Campus combines residential and working space, blended with bars and restaurants, a covered market, retail outlets, trades and studios, local leisure and recreational possibilities, embedded in parks and gardens. It is the realisation of a vision of an urban area which goes beyond a conventional, high-density residential area that allows multifaceted usage – a diversified, lively and climate-friendly district in the midst of the Rhine Metropolis Dusseldorf.

NEW URBANITY IN EUROPEAN CITY PLANNING

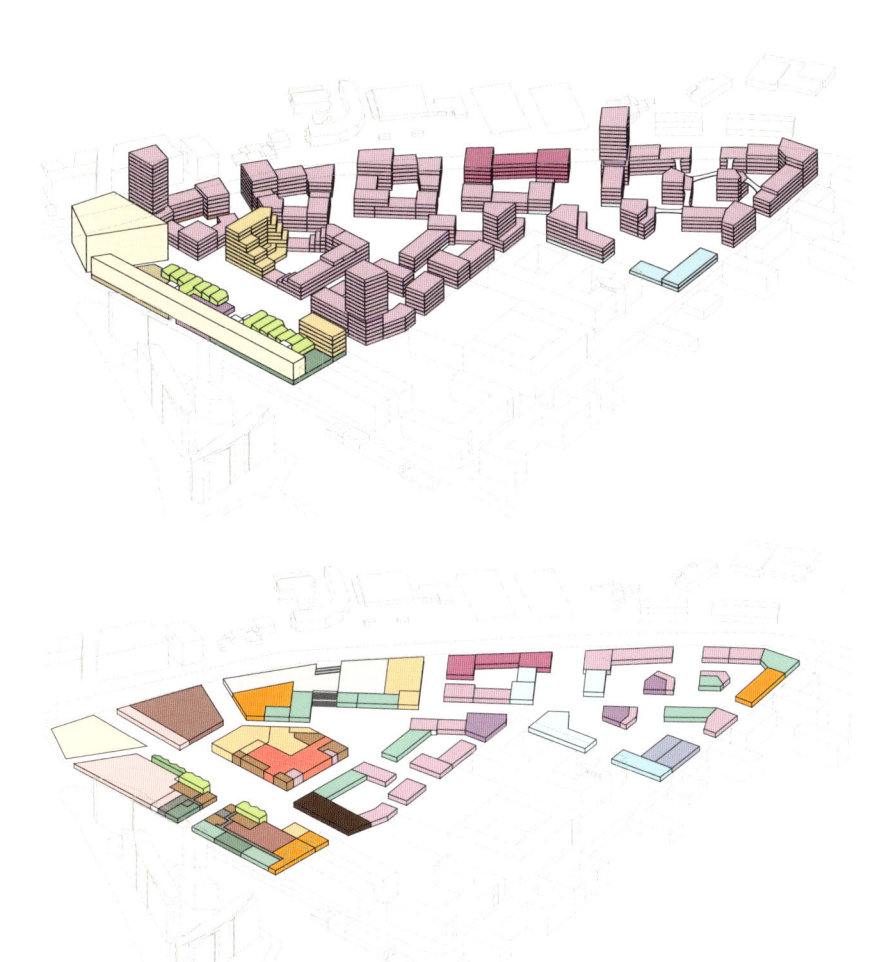

Mögliche Programmierung der Erd- (unten) und Obergeschoss-flächen (oben).
Possible usage of the ground floor (bottom) and upper floor levels (top).

Über METRO PROPERTIES

METRO PROPERTIES ist das Immobilienunternehmen der METRO AG, eines führenden internationalen Großhandels- und Lebensmittelexperten mit weltweit mehr als 95.000 Mitarbeiter:innen und Aktivitäten in 30 Ländern. Die am Markt etablierte Gesellschaft betreibt, entwickelt und vermarktet ein internationales Portfolio von rund 700 operativen Objekten. Das Tochterunternehmen von METRO unterstützt aktiv die Wachstumsstrategie des Konzerns. Das Immobilienunternehmen vereint umfassende Groß- und Einzelhandelskompetenz, hochentwickelte Immobilienkompetenz und Implementierungsfähigkeit. METRO PROPERTIES arbeitet mit lokalen Gemeinden, Geschäftspartnern und ausgewählten Investoren zusammen, um innovative und nachhaltige Konzepte für den Großhandel, den Einzelhandel und gemischte Nutzungsmodelle zu entwickeln. Sowohl national als auch international verfolgt das Unternehmen ein aktives und wertsteigerndes Immobilienmanagement. Geschäftspartner und Kunden erhalten weltweit kompetente Betreuung. Neben dem Hauptsitz in Deutschland ist METRO PROPERTIES mit Standorten in Polen und der Türkei präsent. In anderen Ländern ist es durch das regionale Management und das METRO Team vertreten.

About METRO PROPERTIES

METRO PROPERTIES is the real estate arm of METRO AG, a leading international wholesale and food expert with more than 95,000 employees worldwide and operations in 30 countries. The well-established company develops and markets an international portfolio of around 700 operating properties. The METRO subsidiary actively supports the growth strategy of the multinational organisation. The property company combines wholesale and retail competence, highly developed real estate competence and the ability to implement this know-how. METRO PROPERTIES works with local communities, business associates and selected investors to develop innovative and sustainable concepts for wholesale, retail and mixed-use models. Both nationally and internationally the company pursues active and value-enhancing property management. Business partners and customers receive competent support and service around the world. Besides the head office in Germany, METRO PROPERTIES is present in Poland and Turkey. In other countries it is represented by the regional management and the METRO team.

POST MALL LAB: REDESIGNING SHOPPING MALLS FOR THE POST-CORONA ERA

PROF. I. VTR. SABINE KRIEG, PETER BEHRENS SCHOOL OF ARTS (PBSA)
OF THE HOCHSCHULE DÜSSELDORF (HSD)
WITH THE SUPPORT OF HANS HÖHENRIEDER M.A.

Das Post Mall Lab an der Peter Behrens School of Arts (PBSA) der Hochschule Düsseldorf ist ein semesterübergreifendes Research-&-Development-Projekt unter der Leitung von Prof. i. Vtr. Sabine Krieg, Prof. Bernhard Franken, Prof. Dr. Rainer Zimmermann und Prof. Philipp Teufel, das sich mit möglichen Transformationen des Auslaufmodells Shopping Mall beschäftigt. Im Post Mall Lab arbeiten Studierende aus den Bachelor-Studiengängen Retail Design und Kommunikationsdesign sowie aus dem Studio Raum/Retail im Master Kommunikationsdesign.

Schwerpunkte im Bereich der Lehre im Retail Design an der PBSA sind die Entwicklung von Konzeptionen, die Förderung konzeptionellen Denkens sowie dessen Umsetzung in der räumlichen Gestaltung. Teil des Research ist dabei immer die Auseinandersetzung mit den drei Sphären Historie, Kunst und Markt.

1. Hintergrund und Hypothesen

Das Format Shopping Mall wird zurzeit durch Onlinehandel und sich verändernde Kundenbedürfnisse so stark transformiert wie zuletzt während der Jahrtausendwende durch die Verlagerung der Malls von der Peripherie in die Innenstädte. Ging es hierbei mehr um den Standort als das Format, so richtet sich der augenblickliche Wandel an die Substanz des Formats selbst. 1956 entstand mit dem Southdale Center bei Minneapolis das weltweit erste, in einem einzigen Gebäude integrierte Einkaufszentrum mit einigen wenigen Ankermietern als Frequenzbringern und komplementären

The Post Mall Lab at the Peter Behrens School of Arts (PBSA) of the University of Applied Sciences Düsseldorf is a research & development project over a number of semesters headed by Prof. i. Vtr. Sabine Krieg, Prof. Bernhard Franken, Prof. Dr. Rainer Zimmermann and Prof. Philipp Teufel that looks at possible ways of transforming obsolete shopping malls. Participants are students from the bachelor courses retail design and communication design and master students from the space and retail studio of the communication design course.

Retail design teaching at the PBSA focuses on the development of concepts, the encouragement of conceptional thinking and its realisation in spatial design. The three spheres history, art and market are integral parts of the research.

1. Background and hypotheses

The transformation that the shopping mall format is currently undergoing in response to online trade and changing customer needs is as dramatic as the last major transformation around the turn of the millennium with the relocation of malls from the periphery to the city centres. While this was more about the location rather than the format, the present transformation is changing the substance of the format. The Southdale Center near Minneapolis founded in 1956 was the world's first shopping centre integrated in a single building with a few anchor tenants as customer magnets, supplemented by other retail, service and food and drink businesses. Since the rent contains a revenue component, the over-

anderen Einzelhandels-, Dienstleistungs- und Gastronomiebetrieben. Durch die Umsatzbeteiligung an der Miete ist der Gesamterfolg der Mall auch immer der Erfolg des Centereigentümers. Dieses Format wurde seither im Detail optimiert, aber in den Grundzügen unverändert gelassen und weltweit übernommen.

Durch die zwischenzeitliche Verlagerung von insbesondere Unterhaltungselektronik- und Textilhandel ins Internet brechen zunehmend die Ankermieter weg. Die Problematik der Retail-Transformation und der urbanen Zentren wird an Shopping Malls wie in einem Brennglas sichtbar. Die Pandemie beschleunigt diese Entwicklung. Während Stadtregierungen gegen die herrschenden kleinteiligen Besitzverhältnisse und vertraglichen Bindungen ihrer Territorien kaum Ansätze zur Erhaltung lebendiger Innenstädte haben, können Shopping-Mall-Betreiber direkt auf Nutzungsmix und (halb-)öffentlichen Raum Einfluss nehmen. Design wird in dieser Phase den Unterschied zwischen Erfolg und Misserfolg ausmachen und zu einem kompetitiven Vorteil führen. Die PBSA sieht vier mögliche Strategien für den Erhalt des Geschäftsmodells Shopping Mall:

· **Erlebnis**

Shopping wandelt sich von simpler Bedarfsdeckung zum Erlebniseinkauf. Erleben wird zur Gestaltungsaufgabe. Der „Experience Factor" wird der Erfolgsfaktor für Shopping Malls. Wie bereits in den 1920er-Jahren in ersten Ansätzen geschehen, müssen Raumatmosphären geschaffen werden. Der Schlüssel sind hierbei mehr nachhaltige, emotionale Erfahrungen und weniger theatralische Kurzbespaßungen auf Freizeitparkniveau. Als Erlebnis dürfen nie einzelne Angebote allein betrachtet werden. Das Gesamtbild, das bei einem Besuch als Eindrücke mit allen Sinnen erfahren wird, ist entscheidend: Die Customer Journey ist nun die Visitor Journey.

· **Kuratierung**

Gerade der Mietermix der Malls könnte ihre Rettung sein. Anders als die Highstreet, die ihre Mieter nicht selbst bestimmen kann, ist die Mall ein kuratiertes Format. Der „Kurator" kann mit seiner Selektion einen völlig anderen Charakter von Malls erzeugen. Während das Internet die Omnipräsenz von allem bietet, kann die Mall spezialisierte Stilwelten zusammenstellen und sich damit einen besonderen und einzigartigen musealen Charakter verleihen. Die Rolle des Retail-Kurators geht dabei heute deutlich über die Konfiguration des Mietermixes hinaus und betrifft die generelle Inszenierung des permanenten und temporären Angebots entlang eines starken Narrativs.

all success of the mall is also the success of the owner of the centre. Over the years since then, some details of this format have been optimised, but the basic tenets have remained unchanged and have been emulated around the world.

As entertainment electronics and textile trade have meanwhile shifted into the internet, the malls are increasingly losing their anchor tenants. The problem of the retail transformation and of urban centres is evident in shopping malls, like through a magnifying glass. The pandemic is accelerating this trend. While city governments have hardly any ideas how to maintain lively city centres in the face of the small-scale ownership structures and contractual ties prevailing in their territories, shopping mall operators can directly influence the usage mix and (partly) public space. In this phase, design will be decisive for the difference between success and failure and will represent a competitive advantage. The PBSA sees four possible strategies for the preservation of the shopping mall as a business model:

· **Experience**

Shopping is changing from people simply seeking to cover their needs into an experience. Creating experiences is a design task. The "Experience Factor" becomes the success factor for shopping malls. As already seen to a certain extent in the 1920s, spatial atmospheres need to be created. The keys here are more sustainable, emotional experiences and less short-term theatrical fun on leisure park level. Individual offerings on their own are not sufficient to create an experience. The overall picture that is experienced on a visit to the mall with all the senses is decisive: The Customer Journey is now the Visitor Journey.

· **Curating**

The mix of tenants could save the malls. Unlike the high street which cannot dictate its tenants, the mall is a curated format. With its selection, the "curator" can completely change the character of the mall. While the internet offers the omnipresence of everything, the mall can be given a specialised style and thus a special and unique museum-like quality. Today, the role of the retail curator goes beyond simply configuring the mix of tenants. It now consists of the general staging of the permanent and temporary offering along a strong narrative.

· **Hybridisierung**

Unterschiedliche oder sogar gegensätzliche Komponenten bilden in ihrer Kombination ein Hybrid, das aus der gekannten Normativität heraussticht. Die Komponenten können nebeneinander stehen, aber auch teilweise oder ganz verschmelzen und somit direkte und indirekte Grenzen aufheben. Die traditionelle Einkaufslogik wird aufgebrochen, spannende Erlebnisräume entstehen. Besucher entdecken neue, überraschende Möglichkeiten. Die Verweildauer steigt, während sich das Angebot verbreitert und verfeinert. Erfolgreiche Hybridisierungen haben das Potenzial, zu neuen Typologien zu werden. Malls könnten eine Fusion von Formaten wie Gastronomie, Event, Pop-up, Co-Living sowie öffentlichen Angeboten verwirklichen und somit ein breites Publikum erreichen.

· **Reurbanisierung**

Nachdem die Shopping Malls vor zwanzig Jahren in die Stadtzentren gezogen sind, wird es nun Zeit, dass Öffentlichkeit in die Malls zieht. Soziale Nutzungen wie Nachbarschaftszentren und Kitas könnten die Flächen beleben. Großflächen könnten für Bildungszwecke wie Universitäten in Kombination mit studentischem Wohnen umgenutzt werden. Medizinische Nutzungen, Rehakliniken, Pflegewohnen bis Wellness könnten andere Nutzungsarten sein. Mit den sozialen Trägern und der öffentlichen Hand stünden solvente Mieter zur langfristigen Nutzung zur Verfügung. Die Reurbanisierungsstrategie ist untrennbar verbunden mit den derzeitigen Diskursen in der weltweiten Stadtentwicklung: Green City, Smart City, 15-Minute-City.

2. Projektdesign der Beispiele

Die oben geschilderten Hypothesen werden an der PBSA am Beispiel existierender Shoppingcenter untersucht, verfeinert und gestalterisch ausgeformt. Die Konzepte orientieren sich an den Ergebnissen des Research und berücksichtigen die oben geschilderten empirischen und theoretischen Vorgaben. Sie richten sich auf die Optimierung des Bestehenden, haben aber auch eine Transformation des Centers zum Gegenstand.

Ziel des R-&-D-Projekts ist a) eine Reflexion des gesellschaftlichen und technologischen Wandels und sein Einfluss auf das Einkaufsverhalten allgemein, den stationären Einzelhandel und die Center im Besonderen sowie b) die Hybridisierung von verschiedenen Sphären und Typologien und c) die Entwicklung von möglichen Handlungsoptionen und Lösungen für eine neue Generation zukunftsfähiger Malls nach dem Ende der Shopping Mall.

· **Hybridisation**

Different or even contradictory components can be combined to form a hybrid which stands out from the familiar norm. The components can be next to one another or be partially or wholly merged with one another and dissolve direct and indirect boundaries in the process. The traditional shopping logic is interrupted, replaced by exciting themed spaces. Visitors discover new and surprising possibilities. The length of dwell increases as the offering is broadened and refined. Successful hybridisations have the potential to become new typologies. Malls could realise a fusion of formats such as gastronomy, events, pop-ups, co-living as well as public offers and thus reach a broad audience.

· **Re-urbanisation**

It is twenty years since the shopping malls moved into the city centres. It is now time for public life to move into the malls. Social uses such as neighbourhood centres and day care nurseries could bring them back to life. Large areas could be repurposed for educational facilities like universities in combination with student accommodation. Other types of usage include healthcare facilities, rehabilitation clinics, nursing homes through to spas. Social services institutions and the public sector would be solvent tenants interested in long-term arrangements. The re-urbanisation strategy is an integral part of the current discussions in the worldwide urban development: Green City, Smart City, 15-Minute-City.

2. Project design of the examples

The hypotheses described above are being examined, refined and translated into designs at the PBSA with reference to an existing shopping centre. The concepts are guided by the results of the research and take into account the empirical and theoretical requirements listed above. Although they aim to optimise the existing structures, this will in fact involve the transformation of the centre.

The objectives of the R&D project are a) a reflection of the social and technological change and its influence on shopping behaviour in general, on bricks-and-mortar retailing and the shopping centres in particular, b) the hybridisation of the various spheres and typologies and c) the development of possible courses of action and solutions for a new generation of future-proof malls after the end of the shopping centre as we know it.

Fig. 1: bikebase

Fig. 2: Luftkur

Fig. 3: Wunderkammer

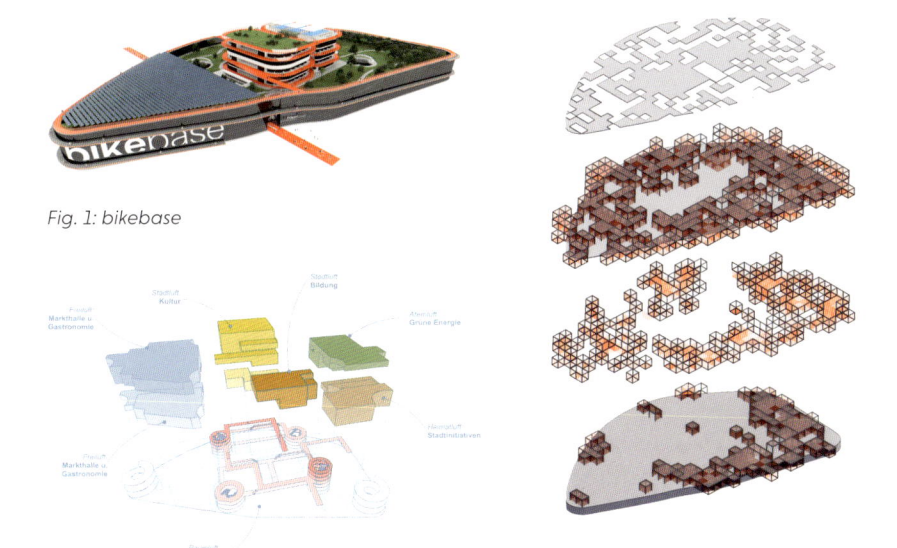

(1) Im Projekt „bikebase" erhält die Mall durch den Radweg, der das Gebäude durchläuft, eine neue räumliche wie konzeptionelle Struktur. (2) „Luftkur" bildet neuartige Raum- bzw. Luftstrukturen, die mit unterschiedlichen neuen Nutzungen gefüllt werden. (3) „Wunderkammer" schafft durch eine Grid-Struktur neue, flexible Raumaufteilungen, die verschiedene Angebote zu Hybriden verschmelzen lassen. (1) In the project "bikebase", the mall is given a new spatial and conceptional structure by the cycle path running through the building. (2) "Luftkur" creates novel structures in the space within and above that can serve various new purposes. (3) With its grid structure, "Wunderkammer" divides the space into new flexible segments merging different uses into hybrids.

Die Ergebnisse sind als Zwischenstand zu betrachten. Das Gesamtprojekt bleibt – gerade vor dem Hintergrund des aktuell rasanten Wandels – fortlaufend Gegenstand der Forschung an der PBSA. Die Projekte „bikebase" und „Luftkur" wurden jeweils von einem/einer Studierenden aus dem Studio Raum/Retail im Master Kommunikationsdesign, das Projekt „Wunderkammer" von einem Projektteam aus einer Master-Studierenden und zwei Studierenden aus dem Bachelor Retail Design entwickelt.

Alle drei Projekte beschäftigen sich mit der Mall „Limbecker Platz" am Rand der Fußgängerzone in der ehemaligen Industriestadt Essen. Inmitten des Ruhrgebiets ist auch hier seit Jahren der Strukturwandel durch den Ausstieg aus dem Kohlebergbau zu beobachten, der zuvor das Gebiet durchgehend prägte. Kultur, Natur und Wohnen profitieren vielerorts von dieser Entwicklung innerhalb des alten „Charmes". Der Einzelhandel hingegen kämpft hier besonders um erfolgreiche Strategien und damit um ein positives Image der Innenstädte.

bikebase / Hans Höhenrieder

Mit bikebase wird die Mall in Essen in ein Zentrum moderner Stadtmobilität transformiert und fügt sich so in aktuelle Megatrends und den Wachstumsmarkt Fahrrad ein. Das Gebäude öffnet sich für Fahrräder und wird somit Teil des alltäglichen öffentlichen Lebens der Stadt. Lokales Publikum wird die Mall wieder mit mehr Leben füllen, während die Strahlkraft auf regionaler Ebene ebenso neu entfacht wird. Der Radweg – das Herzstück von bikebase – verbindet die einzelnen Etagen und erzeugt als zentrales Gestaltungselement neue, spannende Raumformen und -Aufteilungen.

The results are an interim status. The overall project remains a constant part of the research at the PBSA, particularly in view of the current rapid transformation phase. The projects "bikebase" and "Luftkur" were developed by master students from the space/retail studio of the communication design degree course, while the "Wunderkammer" project was developed by a team consisting of one master student and two students from the bachelor course Retail Design.

All three projects relate to the "Limbecker Platz" mall on the edge of the pedestrian zone in the former industrial city of Essen. At the heart of the Ruhr area, the city has been undergoing a structural transformation since the discontinuation of coal mining which used to dominate this area. Culture, nature and living benefit in many places from this development within the old "charm". Retailing, on the other hand, is struggling to find successful strategies and thus a positive image for the inner cities.

bikebase / Hans Höhenrieder

bikebase makes the mall in Essen into a centre of modern city mobility and thus fits well into the current megatrend and in the growth market surrounding the bicycle. The building is open for bikes and thus becomes part of the city's everyday public life. Locals will fill the mall with life again, while the regional appeal will be rekindled. The cycle path – the centrepiece of bikebase – combines the various levels and as a central design element generates new spaces and divides up existing ones anew.

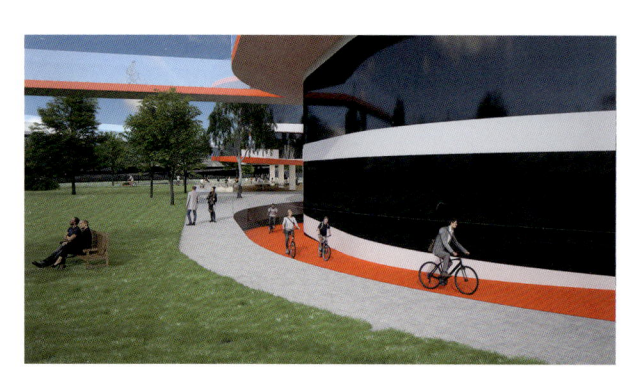

Der kuratierte und durchgebrandete Angebotsmix ist in seiner Struktur klar am Narrativ orientiert. Er spricht unterschiedliche Zielgruppen an und sorgt durch ständigen Wandel für immer neue Entdeckungsreisen. Zwischen Fahrradwerkstätten, Multichannel-Store oder wechselnden Innovationsausstellungen innerhalb der Geschosse sowie einem Park und studentischem Wohnen auf der heruntergesetzten Dachebene findet hier die Zukunft der Stadtgesellschaft statt: bikebase ist Katalysator und Leuchtturm der fahrradfreundlichen Stadt Essen und führt die Stadt in eine klimafreundliche und nachhaltige Zukunft.

Luftkur / Franziska Stasch

Der Kurort soll Raum an die Stadt und ihre Bewohner:innen zurückgeben, die Stadtmitte in einen lebenswerten, zukunftsfähigen und gesunden Ort wandeln. Luft in die Stadt bringen. Frischluft, Atemluft, Freiluft, Stadtluft, Heimatluft und Raumluft. Ein Ort, an dem Stadt, Menschen und Raum sich öffnen und verbinden.

Die bestehende innere Raumstruktur der Mall wird aufgebrochen und ein großer Luftraum entsteht. Der neu gewonnene Freiraum wird nunmehr nicht horizontal in Etagen erschlossen, sondern in einzelnen „Stadtbausteinen" vertikal. In den Bausteinen versammeln sich Dienstleistungen, Retailer und Institutionen, die sich thematisch vereinen. Stadtluft versammelt etwa Rathaus, Bürgerzentrum, Theaterprobenräume, Seminarräume der Universität und eine Bibliothek.

The curated and branded mix of offerings is clearly structured by the narrative. It appeals to different target groups and, through constant change, ensures ever new journeys of discovery. Between bike workshops, multi-channel stores or changing innovation exhibitions on the different floors as well as a park and student accommodation on the lowered roof level, the future of urban society takes place here: bikebase is the catalyst and lighthouse of the bike-friendly Essen and leads the city into a climate-friendly and sustainable future.

Luftkur (climatic spa) / Franziska Stasch

The climatic health resort is designed to give back space to the city and its inhabitants, transforming the city centre into a future-proof and healthy place with a high quality of life. It is to be a breath of fresh air for the city, providing breathing air, open air, city air, the air of home and room air. A place in which the city, people and space open up and connect with one another.

The existing inner spatial structure of the mall is broken up and a large air space is created. This new open space is now not developed horizontally by floor, but vertically in individual "urban building blocks". Services, retailers and institutions are combined in the themed building blocks. City air, for example, brings together the city hall, civic centre, theatre rehearsal rooms, university seminar rooms and a library. Breathing air, on the other hand, contains the green energy

Mit ihrem städtischen Fahrradweg fügt sich die „bikebase" in tägliche Wege der Bürger:innen ein. Die oberste Ebene wird dabei zum großen Stadtgarten (l. o.). „Luftkur" erschließt die neu geschaffenen Räume individuell und abwechslungsreich (l. u.). In der „Wunderkammer" fallen Raumgrenzen größtenteils weg: Die Wechselwirkungen der hybriden Bereiche erzeugen ein spannendes Gesamtbild (r.).
With its urban cycle path, "bikebase" becomes a part of people's daily businesses. The roof level transforms into a spacious city park (top left). "Luftkur" opens up the new spaces in an individual and diverse manner (bottom left). The "Wunderkammer" largely rids itself of spatial divisions, thus creating hybrid areas which enter an exciting interplay of impressions (right).

Die Atemluft hingegen beinhaltet den grünen Energiesektor mit dem Fokus auf erneuerbaren Energien, aber auch Retailer aus den Bereichen Outdoor, Equipment und Erlebnis. Der Negativraum, der sich zwischen den Modulen aufspannt, soll vielfältig für die Bürger:innen, die Stadt, Kunst und Kultur sein. Ein vielfach bespielter Raum, der Platz für Entfaltung inmitten der Stadt bietet.

Wunderkammer / Janna Jakobs, Svenja Krach, Niklas Riechmann

Die Vision des Projekts ist es, eine Fusion unterschiedlicher Bereiche wie zum Beispiel Kunst, Kultur oder Bildung zu erzeugen und damit ein holistisches und erstaunliches Konzept zu erschaffen.

Im Herzen des Ruhrgebiets soll eine Post-Shopping-Mall in Form einer durch Parameter bestimmten, geöffneten und in ein Raster geteilten Wunderkammer wachsen, die sich den Bedürfnissen der Besucher:innen anpassen kann. Durch das Raster und die damit verbundenen Kammern können geschlossene Studios, aber auch Freiräume flexibel unterteilt werden und so in kurzer Zeit eine völlig neue Form erzeugen. Dadurch gehen die verschiedenen Nutzungskonzepte fließend ineinander über und die hybriden Flächen können frei nach den Bedürfnissen der dort verkehrenden Menschen gestaltet werden.

Auf diese Weise entsteht eine lebendige und mit Wissen gefüllte Wunderkammer aus unterschiedlichen Disziplinen, die einen Platz zum Austausch und Teilen bietet. Die Post-Shopping-Mall wird zu einer großen, abstrakten Form der Wunderkammer und schafft damit ein holistisches, zukunftsorientiertes und überraschendes Erlebnis.

sector with a focus on renewable energies, but also retailers from the outdoor, equipment and experience sectors. The negative space that emerges between the modules is to be used in many different ways for the citizens, the city, art and culture. A multi-purpose space that offers room for development in the heart of the city.

Wunderkammer (panoptika) / Janna Jakobs, Svenja Krach, Niklas Riechmann

The vision of the project is to combine different areas such as art, culture or education and thus to create a holistic and astonishing concept.

In the heart of the Ruhr area, a post-shopping mall is to grow in the form of an open panoptika or chamber of curiosities determined by parameters and divided into a grid, which can adapt to the needs of the visitors. Through the grid and the chambers connected to it, closed studios, but also open spaces can be flexibly subdivided and transformed in a short space of time. In this way, the various concepts of use merge smoothly into one another and the hybrid spaces can be freely designed according to people's desires.

The result is a lively and knowledge-filled panoptika of different disciplines that offers a place for exchange and sharing. The post-shopping mall becomes a large, abstract form of the chamber of curiosities, creating a holistic, future-orientated and surprising experience.

NIVEA
Creme
ohne Konservierungsstoffe
HAIR CARE & STYLING
ERSTE
Creme de la Creme
NIVEA
90's
Ausbau der Dachmarke
In den 90er Jahren wurde NIVEA durch weltweit einheitliche Namen, Produkte und Verpackungen zur globalen Marke ausgebaut. NIVEA Familien, wie Visage, deo, soft, Vital und NIVEA Bath Care entstanden in dieser Zeit. Die große internationale Werbekampagne "Blue Harmony" rückte Werte wie Liebe, Freundschaft, Vertrauen, Ehrlichkeit, Glück und Sicherheit in den Vordergrund.
BLUE HARMONY
PRODUKT Neuheit
Revolutionäre Anti-Falten Pfleg
1998 entwickeln die Forscher eine Creme mit dem hauteigenen Wirkstoff Q10

COMPONENTS

34

46

50

50

38

42

34

46

38

42

50

34

38

42

50

GOT2B COSMETIC COUNTER

LOCATION GERMANY **CLIENT** GOT2B (HENKEL BEAUTY CARE AT HENKEL AG & CO. KGAA, DUSSELDORF) **CONCEPT / DESIGN** ARNO GMBH, WOLFSCHLUGEN **PHOTOGRAPHS** PETER MUNTANION, REUTLINGEN

Unter dem Motto „Make-up is what you make of it" intensiviert die Marke got2b die Zusammenarbeit mit ihrer anvisierten Zielgruppe. Das neue Make-up-Portfolio umfasst ein Sortiment, das nicht nur für die Community, sondern zusammen mit ihr entwickelt wurde. 60 junge Menschen haben sich in die Entwicklung der neuen Produktlinie von Henkel Beauty Care mit ihren persönlichen Routinen und Anforderungen eingebracht.

Under the motto "Make-up is what you make of it", the brand got2b has intensified its relationship to its designated target group. The new make-up portfolio includes an assortment which was not only created for the community but in collaboration with it. 60 young people contributed to the development of the new product line of Henkel Beauty Care with their personal routines and needs.

COMPONENTS   GOT2B COSMETIC COUNTER

Um den Prozess und die Ergebnisse dieser innovativen Zusammenarbeit zu präsentieren, war eine besonders aufmerksamkeitsstarke Kosmetiktheke gefordert. Den Markenauftritt für die neue Produktkategorie im Handel realisierte der Henkel-Konzern mit der ARNO Group aus Wolfschlugen. Das Familienunternehmen mit über 85-jähriger Tradition bietet Instore-Retail-Experience von der Konzeptentwicklung bis zur Montage und verfügt zudem über eine hauseigene Abteilung für den Prototypenbau.

In order to present the process and results of this innovative collaboration, the cosmetics counter needed to be particularly attention grabbing. The brand appearance for the new product category in retail outlets was realised by the Henkel group in collaboration with the ARNO Group from Wolfschlugen. The family-run business with a tradition of more than 85 years offers Instore Retail Experience from the development of the concept through to the installation and even has an in-house department for the construction of prototypes.

Die got2b-Kosmetiktheke erzielt durch das 3D-Logo sowie die austauschbaren, beleuchteten Grafiken im Header eine besondere Fernwirkung. Der große Spiegel mit dem speziellen Designelement in Form eines Mundes ist ein Eyecatcher. Zahlreiche LEDs leuchten – unterstützt von der Lichtführung im Rahmen – die Theke detailliert aus und setzen das Make-up-Sortiment in Szene. Die schwarzen Einsätze, die aus bis zu 80 Prozent recyceltem Material bestehen, sollen ihr einen edlen Touch verleihen. Ein weiteres Highlight ist der RGB-Farbwechsel mit integriertem Bewegungssensor: Bei näherem Herantreten stellt sich die Lichtfarbe auf ein angenehmes Weiß um, damit sich die Konsument:innen in einem möglichst natürlichen Umgebungslicht betrachten können.

With its 3D logo and exchangeable, illuminated graphics in the header, the got2b cosmetic counter attracts attention from afar. The big mirror with the special design element in the form of a mouth is a real eyecatcher. Numerous LEDs supported by the directed lighting in the frame illuminate the counter and display the make-up assortment to great effect. The black inserts, which are made of up to 80 percent recycled material, give it a high-class touch. Another highlight is the RGB colour changer with integrated movement sensor: As the customer approaches, the light colour changes to a pleasant white so that they can look at themselves in as close to natural light as possible.

COMPONENTS   GOT2B COSMETIC COUNTER   37

Im Rahmen des auf dem Instagram-Kanal von got2b live übertragenen Launch-Events wurden die Kosmetiktheke enthüllt und die Lieblingsprodukte der Co-Kreatoren präsentiert. Neben den Markenbotschaftern waren prominente Moderatoren und Gäste in Berlin dabei. Deutschlandweit wurden über 1.000 Exemplare der Kosmetiktheke „ausgerollt".

The cosmetic counter was revealed in a live broadcast of the launch event on the Instagram channel of got2b and the favourite products of the co-creators were presented. In addition to brand ambassadors, the event in Berlin was attended by prominent hosts and guests. More than 1,000 cosmetic counters have been rolled out across Germany.

MAMMUT WINDOW CAMPAIGN

LOCATION GLOBAL **CLIENT** MAMMUT SPORTS GROUP AG, SEON **CONCEPT / DESIGN / GRAPHICS** DESIGNPLUS GMBH, STUTTGART **PHOTOGRAPHS** MAMMUT SPORTS GROUP AG, SEON (ZURICH POP-UP SPACE); DESIGNPLUS GMBH, STUTTGART (MUNICH STORE MBS)

Seit mehr als 160 Jahren produziert die Mammut Sports Group AG Sportbekleidung für Menschen, die sich den widrigen meteorologischen Launen der Natur entgegenstellen. Vielleicht ist es gerade diesem besonderen Blick auf die Elemente zu verdanken, dass das Schweizer Unternehmen sich in einem besonderen Maß dem Erhalt unseres Planeten verpflichtet fühlt.

For more than 160 years, Mammut Sports Group AG has been producing sportswear for people exposed to the adverse meteorological vagaries of nature. Perhaps it is this special relationship with the elements which explains the Swiss company's extreme commitment to preserving our planet.

COMPONENTS   MAMMUT WINDOW CAMPAIGN

Ein Anliegen, das über Produktionsmethoden und Materialauswahl hinausgeht und sich seit Mitte 2020 mit Unterstützung der Brand-Retail-Agentur Designplus aus Stuttgart auch konsequent in der Gestaltung der Schaufenster fortsetzt. Zur Jahresmitte 2020 begann das Team mit der Gestaltung eines komplett neuen Schaufensterkonzepts. Vor allem sollte sich das System problemlos an den saisonalen Kollektionswechsel anpassen lassen und dabei gleichzeitig höchste Anforderungen an Langlebigkeit und Nachhaltigkeit erfüllen.

A concern that goes beyond the production methods and choice of materials. Since mid-2020 it has also been continued systematically in the design of the shop windows. With the support of the Stuttgart-based brand-retail agency Designplus, the team commenced with the design of a completely new shop window concept. It was particularly important that the system could be easily adapted to the seasonal change of collection and satisfied the highest standards of durability and sustainability.

Schon die ersten Skizzen zeigten, dass die Lösung sich aus der Reduktion auf Wesentliches entwickeln würde. Das Ergebnis ist ebenso einfach wie wandelbar: Zentrale Elemente sind variable Autopole, höhenverstellbare Klemmschienen, wie man sie aus Fotostudios kennt. Diese können in jedem Schaufenster und auf jeder Fläche flexibel positioniert werden. Durch horizontale und vertikale Präsentationsflächen ist eine optimale Anpassung an verschiedene Produkte und Verkaufsflächen möglich. Die Kombinationsmöglichkeiten des Systems mit farbigen Auflagen, pointierten Lichtelementen und wechselnden Hintergrundmotiven sind nahezu unbegrenzt, die Materialen robust, sodass eine lange Nutzungsdauer über viele Kampagnen hinweg garantiert ist. Die Integration digitaler Elemente als Bewegtbild, das über an den Autopolen befestigte Screens zugespielt wird, ist ebenfalls variabel zu handhaben.

The very first sketches already showed that the solution would be developed from a reduction to the bare essentials. The result is as simple as it is versatile: The central elements are variable autopoles, height-adjustable clamping rails, like those we know from photo studios. These can be flexibly positioned in every shop window and in any space. Thanks to the horizontal and vertical presentation areas, they can be adjusted to perfectly fit the various products and sales areas. The combination possibilities of the system with coloured covers, carefully placed lighting elements and changing background motifs are virtually endless, the materials are robust so that a long, useful life for several campaigns is guaranteed. Digital elements in the form of videos shown on screens attached to the autopoles can also be integrated in a variable manner.

COMPONENTS   MAMMUT WINDOW CAMPAIGN

Das Konzeptionsteam von Designplus hat damit ein System realisiert, das die Haltung der Marke Mammut konsequent nach außen spiegelt: Langlebige Materialien treffen auf innovatives Design – beides auf das Notwendigste reduziert. „Hinter unseren Aktionen steckt kein Marketingtrend, sondern eine von jeher verinnerlichte Haltung und Verbundenheit zur Natur unseres Planeten", so Grit Ostermayer, Head of Point of Experience der Mammut Sports Group AG.

The concept team of Designplus has thus realised a system which clearly transports the attitude of the Mammut brand: Long-lived materials meet innovative design – both reduced to the bare essentials. "Our actions are not part of a marketing trend but of an internalised attitude and a commitment to the natural world", explains Grit Ostermayer, Head of Point of Experience of Mammut Sports Group AG.

HARRODS SHOP WINDOW DISPLAY FOR LG DISPLAY

LOCATION LONDON, UK   **CLIENT** LG DISPLAY, SEOUL   **CONCEPT / DESIGN** D'ART DESIGN GRUPPE, NEUSS/SEOUL
OTHERS MILLINGTON ASSOCIATES, LONDON (REALISATION)   **PHOTOGRAPHS** D'ART DESIGN GRUPPE, NEUSS

Die Schaufenster des Luxuskaufhauses Harrods im noblen Stadtviertel Knightsbridge sind zu jeder Jahreszeit ein „Must-see". Mit über 330 Abteilungen auf einer Verkaufsfläche von zirka 90.000 Quadratmetern gehört das mondäne Kaufhaus zu den meistfrequentierten Sehenswürdigkeiten Londons.

Zehn der exponiert gelegenen Schaufenster mit jeweils 40 Quadratmetern hat sich LG Display aus Seoul für die Präsentation seiner neuen OLED-Technologie ausgesucht. Für das Unternehmen entwickelte die ebenfalls in Seoul vertretene D'art Design Gruppe eine interaktive Schaufenstergestaltung mit hohem Aufmerksamkeitsgrad.

The shop window of the luxury department store Harrods in the posh Knightsbridge district are a "must-see" at any time of year. With more than 330 departments on a sales area of around 90,000 square metres, the elegant store is one of London's most frequently visited sights.

For the presentation of its new OLED technology, LG Display from Seoul chose ten of the most prominent shop windows, each about 40 square metres in size. D'art Design Gruppe, which is likewise represented in Seoul, developed an interactive shop window design aimed to attract a high degree of attention.

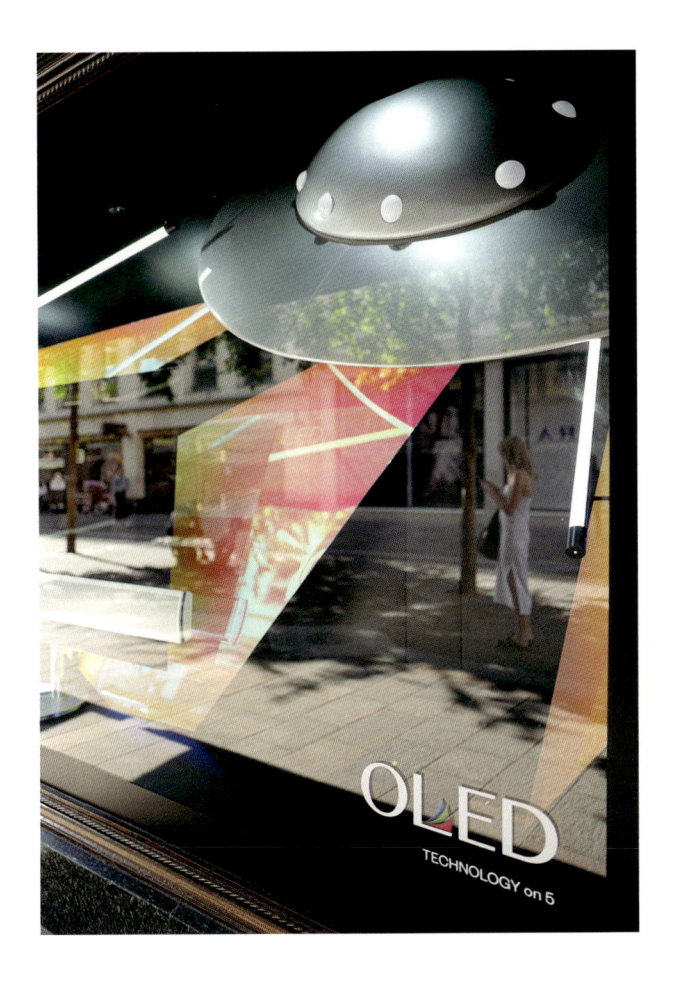

COMPONENTS   HARRODS SHOP WINDOW DISPLAY FOR LG DISPLAY

The brief was to showcase the special product features of the innovative new display. Translated into an abstract form, these features were visualised and staged so as to allow passersby to experience them. A particular challenge for the creatives was that comparable products of other manufacturers which also use the new technology in their products had to be displayed in the windows alongside the LG products. With this rather complicated situation as their starting point the designers came up with a humorous concept: UFO – "Technology from out there" is the slogan and also the main visual motif for the displays which are 'so good that even the competition has installed them'. Around the UFO key visual, D'art Design developed a retro-futuristic scenario which is to be found – staged in different ways – across all ten shop windows. The UFOs, which were realised particularly lovingly from brushed metal, seemed to be floating in the shop windows. Pulsating lights brought the scenes to life.

Es galt, die besonderen Produkteigenschaften der innovativen Displays hervorzuheben. Diese wurden abstrahiert, visuell umgesetzt und für die Passanten erlebbar inszeniert. Eine besondere Herausforderung für das Kreativteam war es, dass neben LG-Produkten teilweise auch vergleichbare Fabrikate anderer Hersteller in den Flächen ausgestellt werden mussten, die die neue Technologie ebenfalls in ihre Produkte einbauen. Aus dieser etwas komplizierten Situation haben die Gestalter ein humorvolles Konzept entwickelt: UFO – „Technology from out there" steht als Motto und als visuelles Leitmotiv für die Displays, die so gut sind, dass sie sogar von der Konkurrenz verbaut werden. Aus dem UFO-Keyvisual haben hat D'art Design ein retrofuturistisches Szenario entwickelt, das als verbindendes Motiv über alle zehn Schaufensterflächen hinweg immer wieder neu inszeniert wird. Besonders liebevoll wurden die UFOs aus gebürstetem Metall realisiert, die in den Fenstern zu schweben scheinen und durch pulsierende Beleuchtung die Szenen lebendig machen.

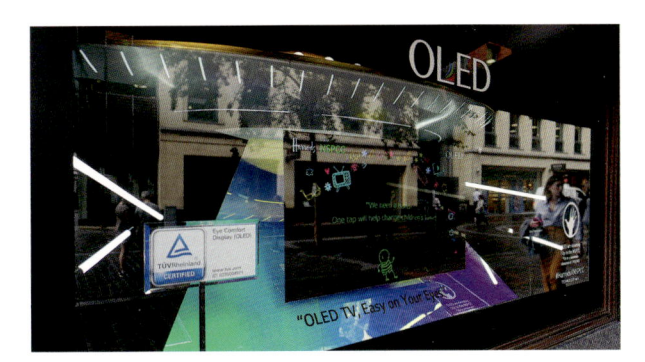

Die zahlreichen Passanten werden durch einen Touchpoint, der mittels Berührung die Bildinhalte auf den Displays verändert, interaktiv in die „außerirdische" Schaufensterinstallation eingebunden. Zugleich wurde durch jede Interaktion automatisch ein Betrag an eine gemeinnützige Stiftung zur Unterstützung von Kindern ausgelöst.

The numerous passersby are interactively incorporated in the "extra-terrestrial" shop window installation by means of a touchpoint. By touching it, they could thus change the images on the displays. But that was not all: With every interaction an amount was automatically donated to a children's charity.

COMPONENTS   HARRODS SHOP WINDOW DISPLAY FOR LG DISPLAY

DRUCK-SPÄTI

LOCATION STUTTGART, GERMANY   **CLIENT** DATEN & DRUCK OPTIPLAN GMBH, STUTTGART
CONCEPT / DESIGN / GRAPHICS RAUMKONTAKT GMBH, KARLSRUHE   **PHOTOGRAPHS** RAUMKONTAKT GMBH, KARLSRUHE; DATEN & DRUCK OPTIPLAN GMBH, STUTTGART

Ein fester Bestandteil der Berliner Kiezkultur sind die 24/7 geöffneten Kleinstläden, für die sich der Begriff „Späti" (Spätkauf) etabliert hat. Ob als Mini-Supermarkt, Zeitungsverkauf oder Getränkeshop, ist der typische Späti ein Treffpunkt von Nachbarn und Nachtschwärmern. Durch das meist improvisierte Shopdesign und die Fülle der Warenpräsentation auf kleinstem Raum wurden die Spätis zum kultigen Markenzeichen des wiedervereinigten Berlins.

Berlin's neighbourhood mini-shops that are open around the clock are referred to as "Späti", derived from the German word for late (spät). Whether a small supermarket, newspaper kiosk or off-licence, the typical Späti is a meeting place for neighbours and revellers alike. Thanks to their usually improvised shop design and the sheer volume of goods crammed into the smallest of spaces, the Spätis have become a trendy trademark of the reunited Berlin.

COMPONENTS   DRUCK-SPÄTI

Die Verknüpfung von 24/7 auf der einen und viel Persönlichkeit auf der anderen Seite ließ bei den Kreativen der Karlsruher Werbeagentur raumkontakt die Idee des Druck-Spätis entstehen. Anlass war die pandemiebedingte Einschränkung der persönlichen Übergabe von Druckprodukten. Ursprünglich für die Abholung außerhalb der Öffnungszeiten gedacht, wurde die Einführung eines Abholautomaten für das Unternehmen Daten & Druck eine wichtige Ergänzung der Dienstleistung.

The combination of 24/7 on the one hand and loads of character on the other were the inspiration for the idea of the Druck-Späti dreamt up by the creatives of the Karlsruhe advertising agency raumkontakt in response to the restrictions on personally handing over printed products due to the pandemic. Originally conceived for pick-ups outside opening hours, the introduction of a collection station in the style of a vending machine for the firm Daten & Druck has become an important addition to their services.

Der technisch versierte Digitaldruckanbieter aus Stuttgart legt viel Wert auf die persönliche Beratung seiner Kundschaft. Daher sollte die Abholung der Drucksachen mehr als nur eine anonyme Notwendigkeit sein und zum persönlichen Erlebnis werden. Die Übergabe erfolgt mit Codezugang und überrascht nicht nur durch das betont freche Design. Für die Interaktion mit den Nutzerinnen und Nutzern wird der Automat regelmäßig mit originellen Magneten zum Mitnehmen bestückt, die gleichzeitig als Werbung dienen. Um mit den Empfänger:innen der Druckprodukte im Gespräch zu bleiben, befindet sich zudem bei jeder Abholung ein kultiges Geschenk im Fach als Überraschung.

Die Idee, den Stuttgarter Abholautomaten mit dem Charme des Berliner Spätis zu verknüpfen, hat für ein gutes Echo gesorgt. Mittlerweile zieht sich der betont schräge Auftritt in Verbindung mit frechen Sprüchen über ganze Werbekampagnen, T-Shirts und Social-Media-Kanäle. Der kultige Druck-Späti entpuppt sich als willkommene Abwechslung im Alltag und ist zu einem beliebten Fotomotiv geworden.

COMPONENTS   DRUCK-SPÄTI 49

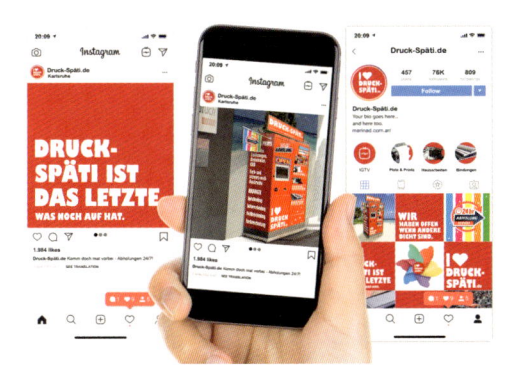

The technically-minded digital print provider from Stuttgart attaches great importance to the personal consultation of their customers. They therefore wanted the collection of the printed materials to be a personal experience rather than an anonymous necessity. The handover requires a code to be keyed in and the cheeky design of the collection station is not the only surprise. When customers pick up their products, the machine also contains original magnets which serve both as interaction with the clientele and as advertising. To keep in contact with the recipients of the printed matter, a cool gift is to be found in each compartment as a surprise.

The idea of combining the Stuttgart collection station with the charm of the Berlin Späti has been well received. Meanwhile, the crazy machine is to be found combined with sassy slogans in whole advertising campaigns, on t-shirts and in social media channels. The cool Druck-Späti has turned out to be a welcome change from the humdrum of everyday life and has become a popular motif for photos.

NIVEA HAUS

LOCATION BERLIN/HAMBURG, GERMANY **CLIENT** BEIERSDORF HAUTPFLEGE GMBH, HAMBURG **CONCEPT / DESIGN** NEST ONE GMBH, HAMBURG **LIGHTING** LICHT 01 LIGHTING DESIGN, HAMBURG **PHOTOGRAPHS** OLIVER TJADEN, DUSSELDORF

Vor über 15 Jahren eröffnete die Beiersdorf AG das erste NIVEA Haus in bester Lage am Hamburger Jungfernstieg. Mit dem in Deutschland noch neuen Konzept der Kurzzeit-Wellness bekam die Marke ein eigenes Zuhause. Die neuen NIVEA-Stores gehen noch einen Schritt weiter: Als Symbiose des digitalen und physischen Retails werden sie zu einem Ort der „phygitalen" Kundenkommunikation.

More than 15 years ago, Beiersdorf AG opened the first NIVEA Haus in a top location on Hamburg's Jungfernstieg. As the new short-term spa trend began to take hold in Germany, the brand got a home of its own. The new NIVEA stores go a step further: As symbiosis of digital and physical retail, they have become a place of "phygital" customer communication.

COMPONENTS   NIVEA HAUS

Die Hamburger Strategie- und Kreativagentur NEST ONE stellt bei der Neuauflage das Kundenerlebnis in den Mittelpunkt. Durch die Kombination von Treatments und Produkten mit einer lebendigen Markenkommunikation und einem haptisch wertigen, warmen Interior auf Basis des Interior-Design-Konzepts von Matteo Thun entsteht ein vielschichtiges Erlebnis mit Wohlfühlfaktor. Die Touchpoints in den Stores sind entlang einer klaren Customer Journey angeordnet. Zentrales Element ist eine großformatige LED-Wall, die bereits vom Schaufenster und Eingang aus sichtbar ist. Hier werden Video- und Kampagneninhalte sowie Highlight-Produkte großformatig inszeniert. Diese Inhalte werden flexibel über einen Medienserver angepasst, sodass Online- und In-Store-Kommunikation synchron laufen können.

In their design of the reloaded concept for the NIVEA Haus, Hamburg's strategy and creative agency NEST ONE focused firmly on the customer experience. Through the combination of treatments and products with a lively brand communication and a haptically valuable interior based on the interior design concept of Matteo Thun, they created a multi-layered experience with a feel-good factor. The touchpoints in the stores are arranged along a clear-cut customer journey. The central element is a large-scale LED wall which is already visible through the shop window and from the entrance. Video and campaign contents as well as highlight products are showcased here. This content is adjusted flexibly via a media server that allows the synchronisation of online and in-store communication.

Als zentrales Element der Aktivierungszone werden das Thema Nachhaltigkeit und Zero-Waste-Kosmetik in konkreten Angeboten von Refill-Stationen und Produkten erlebbar. Durch die In-Store-UV-Analyse können die Kund:innen ihren Hauttyp analysieren lassen und real überprüfen, wie gut sie sich gegen die Sonne schützen. Dieses wird unkompliziert in Form eines Selbsttests an einem Screen mit UV-Kamera ermöglicht. Die Selbsterfahrung wird durch den digitalen Skin Guide mit Fotoanalyse auch an einem anderen Punkt der Customer Journey erlebbar.

In the activation zone, customers can experience the topic of sustainability and zero waste cosmetics at refill stations and test the product offerings. The in-store UV analysis offers customers the opportunity to have their skin type analysed and find out how well they protect themselves from the sun. A screen with UV camera makes self-testing easy. The direct experience continues in another part of the customer journey with a digital skin guide including photo analysis.

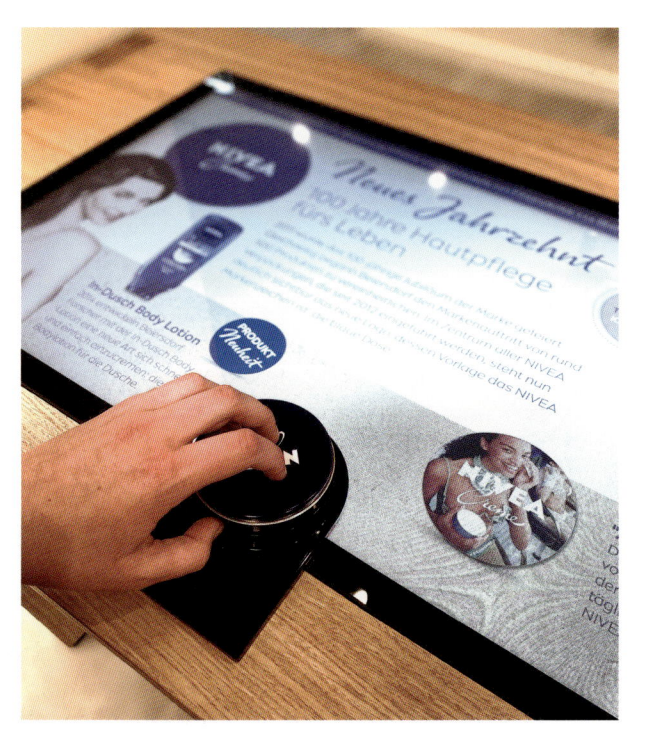

COMPONENTS   NIVEA HAUS

Was 1911 als Nivea-Creme begann, ist heute eine große Markenfamilie mit über 500 Produkten. Diese Entwicklung und das Design werden dem Kunden in einem interaktiven Heritage Table nahe gebracht. Über einen „Dial" kann die Markengeschichte durchsurft werden und am Dosenautomaten wird die ikonische blaue Metalldose, mit individuellen Covern versehen, zum ganz persönlich gestalteten Produkt zum Mitnehmen.

What started in 1911 as Nivea cream, is now a huge brand family consisting of more than 500 products. At an interactive Heritage Table, customers can find out more about the development and design. They can dial through the brand history while the tin dispenser invites them to customise the iconic blue metal tin as a personal souvenir with an individual cover.

FASHION
CIRCUS

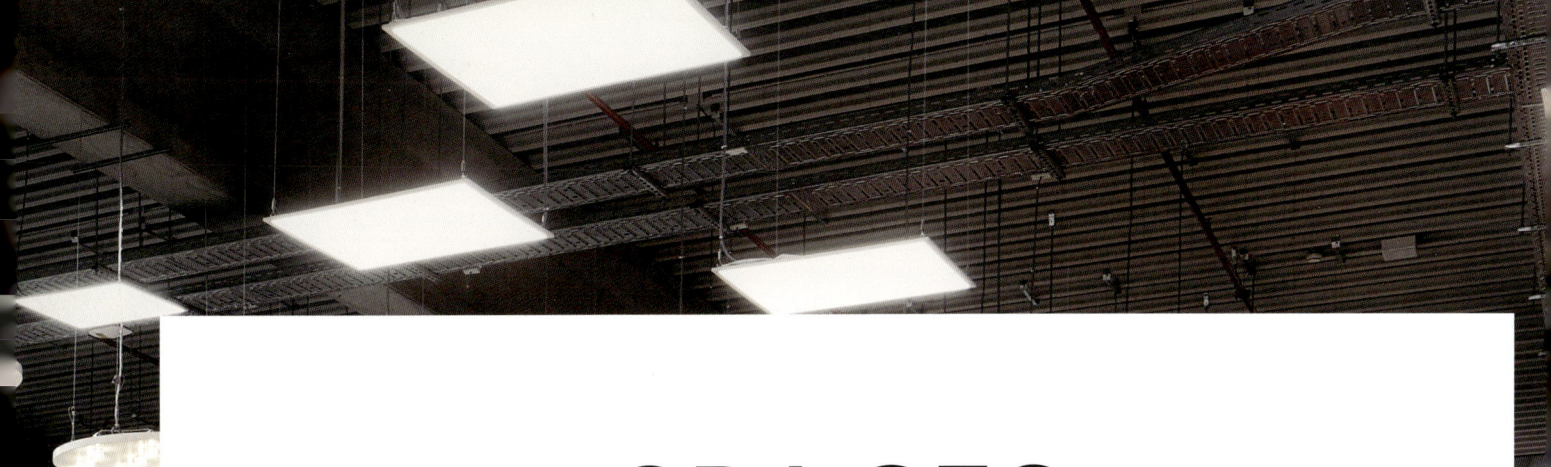

SPACES

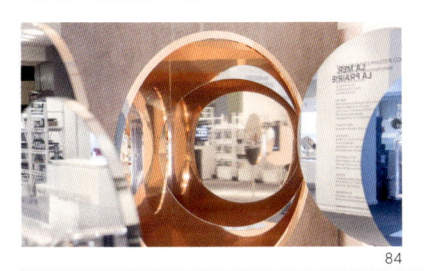

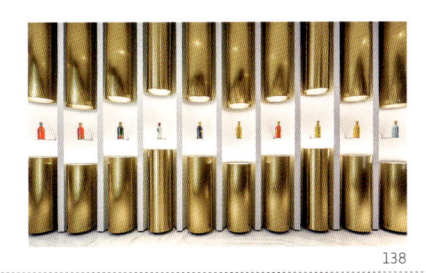

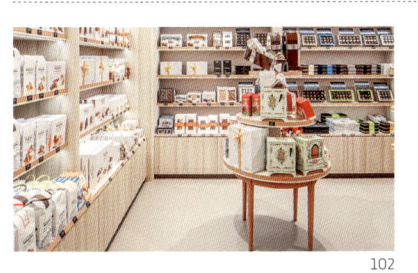

148	134	98
56	76	122
84	138	94
116	72	112
102	68	106

SARA SHOWROOM

LOCATION DUBAI, UAE **CLIENT** SARA GROUP, DUBAI **CONCEPT / DESIGN** RK GULF LLC, DUBAI
GRAPHICS ANSORG GMBH, MÜLHEIM A. D. RUHR **PHOTOGRAPHS** SARA GROUP, DUBAI

In Dubai sind innerhalb weniger Jahrzehnte immer wieder städtebauliche Akzente der Superlative entstanden. In kaum einer anderen Stadt der Welt ändert sich das Stadtbild so rasant wie in der Metropole am Persischen Golf. Wo es früher nichts außer sandigem Wüstenboden gab, setzen heute markante Hochhäuser weithin sichtbare Zeichen. Als Touristenmagnet bietet Dubai heute mit exklusiven Einkaufswelten und luxuriösen Übernachtungsmöglichkeiten vielfältige Erlebnisse.

Within the space of just a few decades, amazing architectural highlights have been added to Dubai's cityscape. Indeed, the appearance of hardly any other city in the world changes as rapidly as in the metropolis on the Persian Gulf. What used to be nothing more than flat sandy desert, is now home to a series of striking skyscrapers, landmarks that are visible from a huge distance. In today's Dubai with its exclusive shopping worlds and luxurious hotel accommodation visitors are guaranteed a diverse experience.

SPACES   SARA SHOWROOM

Das Eintauchen in die Welt der hochwertigen Innenausstattung bietet der Flagship Showroom der SARA Group, der vom Beleuchtungsexperten Ansorg in eine glamouröse Lichtszenerie getaucht wurde. Die 1967 gegründete SARA Group hat sich zum führenden Großhändler für luxuriöse Bäder, Gastronomie und Küchenausstattungen im arabischen Raum entwickelt. Der Kundenstamm reicht von der gehobenen Retail-Branche bis hin zu 5-Sterne-Hotels.

Die Spezialisten von Ansorg entwickelten zu Projektbeginn eine lichtplanerische Gesamtkonzeption, die über die koordinative Begleitung aller Lichtgewerke bis hin zur finalen Ausrichtung aller Leuchten umgesetzt wurde. Während in der Empfangshalle und auf den Verkaufsflächen eine einheitliche Ausleuchtung vorherrscht, konnte an der Fensterfront eine erheblich höhere Beleuchtungsstärke realisiert werden, um die Außenwirkung an der Hauptverbindungsstraße in Dubai, der Sheikh Zayed Road, hervorzuheben.

Those interested in high-quality interior design are advised to visit the flagship showroom of SARA Group, which has been bathed in a glamourous light atmosphere by lighting expert Ansorg. Founded in 1967, SARA Group has evolved into the leading wholesaler for luxurious bathrooms as well as equipment and furnishings for bars, restaurants and kitchens in the Arab region. The clientele ranges from the premium retail business through to 5-star hotels.

At the beginning of the project, the specialists from Ansorg developed an overall concept for the light planning which was subsequently realised from the coordination of all lighting trades through to the final adjustment of all the lights. While the light of the foyer and the sales floor is essentially uniform, a considerably higher illumination level was achieved at the window façade in order to heighten the external impact on the main connecting road in Dubai, Sheikh Zayed Road.

Über zwei Zugänge in der zylinderartigen Glaskonstruktion im Eckgebäude gelangen die Gäste in das Foyer mit kreisförmig präsentierten Exponaten. Bei der Inszenierung von Highlight-Flächen wurde auf eine naturgetreue Farbwiedergabe der hochwertigen Keramik und den Glanz der Armaturen Wert gelegt. Durch die verwendete Reflektortechnik mit verschiedenen Ausstrahlwinkeln konnten eine stimmungsvolle Grundbeleuchtung sowie auch das pointierte Setzen von Highlights realisiert werden.

In abgetrennten, Separee-ähnlichen Bereichen werden den Besuchern und Besucherinnen Bade- und Wellness-Szenerien präsentiert, die in der boomenden Wüstenmetropole ein ruhiges Oasen-Erlebnis bescheren.

SPACES   SARA SHOWROOM

Via two entrances in the cylindrical glass structure in the corner building, guests make their way into the entrance zone that contains a circular presentation of exhibits. When staging the highlight spaces, it was important to ensure a natural rendering of the colours of the high-quality ceramic goods and the shine of the fittings. The reflector technique with various radiation angles created an atmospheric basic illumination and also allowed highlights to be placed with effect.

In discrete areas with the flair of private rooms, visitors can view the bathroom and spa scenarios and enjoy a tranquil oasis experience in the booming desert metropolis.

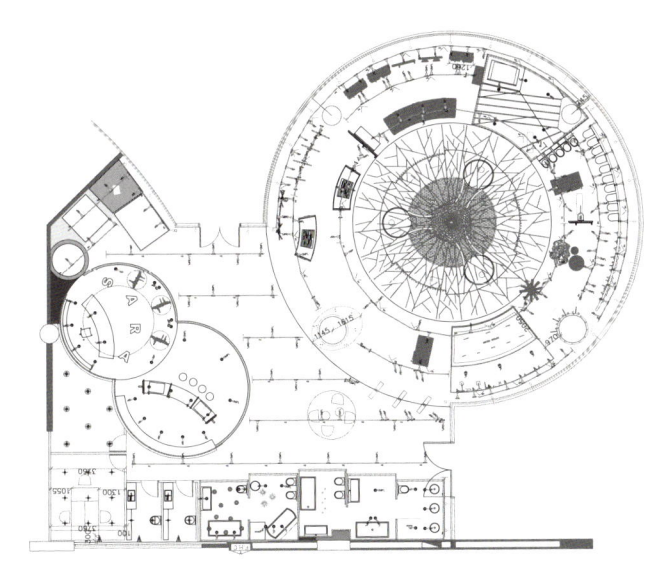

OCCHIO STORE MILAN

LOCATION MILAN, ITALY **CLIENT** OCCHIO GMBH, MUNICH **CONCEPT / DESIGN** 1ZU33 ARCHITECTURAL BRAND IDENTITY, MUNICH **GRAPHICS** MARTIN ET KARCZINSKI GMBH, MUNICH **LIGHTING** OCCHIO GMBH, MUNICH **OTHERS** CONDUK GMBH, EPPAN (GENERAL CONTRACTOR / SHOPFITTING) **PHOTOGRAPHS** CHRISTOPH PHILADELPHIA, MUNICH

Der Corso Monforte im Herzen der Designmetropole Mailand wird in der Dunkelheit zu einer illuminierten Flaniermeile. Auf der sogenannten „Straße des Lichts" präsentiert Occhio seit April 2021 seine Kompetenz und das komplette Produktsortiment zur Gestaltung von Räumen mit Licht. Der Occhio Store Milano ist das erste Flagship-Konzept außerhalb Deutschlands und bildet einen wichtigen Meilenstein auf dem Weg der zunehmenden Internationalisierung des Münchner Unternehmens.

After dark, Corso Monforte at the centre of the design metropolis Milan is transformed into an illuminated promenade. Since April 2021, Occhio has been presenting its competence and the whole product assortment for the design of spaces with light on what is referred to as the "Street of Lights". The Occhio Store in Milan is the first flagship concept outside Germany and marks an important milestone as the Munich-based company continues its internationalisation drive.

SPACES   OCCHIO STORE MILAN

1zu33 Architectural Brand Identity developed a multi-functional concept that builds on the visual language of the existing stores. The prize-winning studio of Hendrik Müller and Georg Thiersch has played a decisive role in shaping the spatial appearance of Occhio. For the designers from Munich it is important to develop long-term strategies in order to continuously nurture customer relationships.

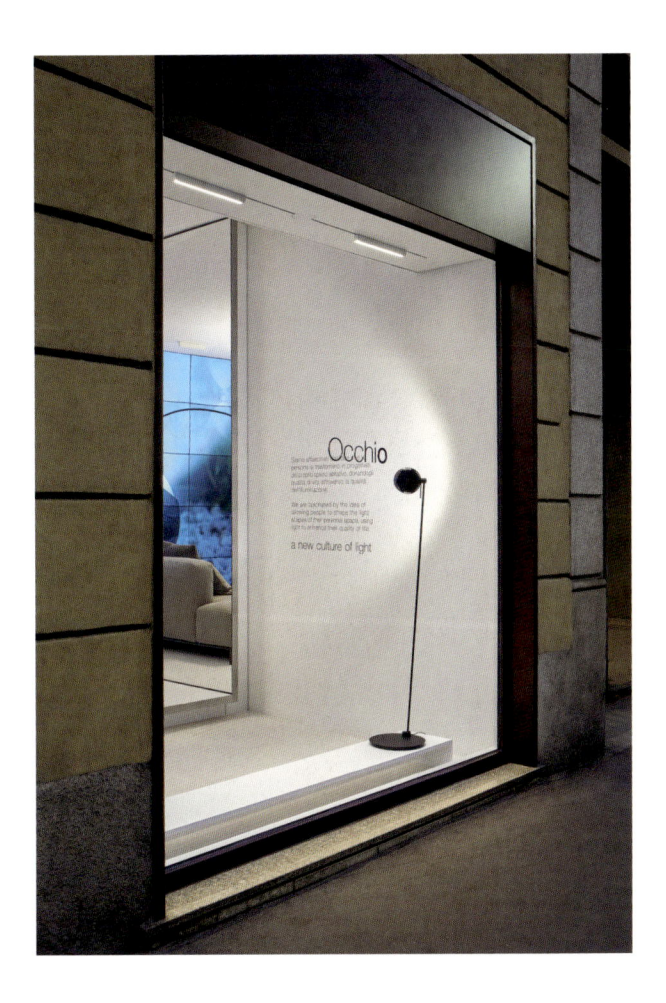

1zu33 Architectural Brand Identity hat ein multifunktionales Konzept entwickelt, das auf der visuellen Sprache der bereits existierenden Stores aufbaut. Das vielfach mit hochkarätigen Awards ausgezeichnete Studio von Hendrik Müller und Georg Thiersch hat das räumliche Erscheinungsbild von Occhio nachhaltig geprägt. Den Münchner Gestaltenden ist es ein Anliegen, langfristige Strategien zu entwickeln, um kontinuierliche Kundenbeziehungen zu pflegen.

Raum und Material bilden im Occhio Store die physischen Ebenen zur Integration der ebenso puristisch wie zeitlos anmutenden Produktwelt des 1999 von Axel Meise gegründeten Unternehmens. Auf rund 120 Quadratmetern wurden verschiedene Bereiche geschaffen, die zur Erkundung und zum Erleben der Wirkung von Licht und Lichtqualität im Raum einladen. Die „Welcome Area" empfängt die Besucher:innen in einer warmen Atmosphäre mit einem kommunikativen Beratungstisch. Die beeindruckende „Stage" ist eine erhöhte Showbühne und mehrdimensionale Videowall, die mit raumvergrößerndem Spiegel einen kaleidoskopischen Effekt entstehen lässt. Dieser Bereich dient zudem als Light Lab, in dem Lichtwirkung erfahrbar gemacht wird. Im „Arsenal" werden die Leuchtenfamilien in einem eigens dafür entwickelten Möbelsystem vorgestellt. Interessierte können hier eine individuell auf ihre Bedürfnisse abgestimmte Leuchte konfigurieren.

„In Mailand, der internationalen Metropole des Designs, setzen wir ein Zeichen für Lichtkultur und laden Besucher ein, ihrer Individualität durch Licht Ausdruck zu verleihen. Unser neuer Store ist zudem unser Lichtkompetenz-Hub im südeuropäischen Raum", so Axel Meise, Gründer und Gestalter von Occhio.

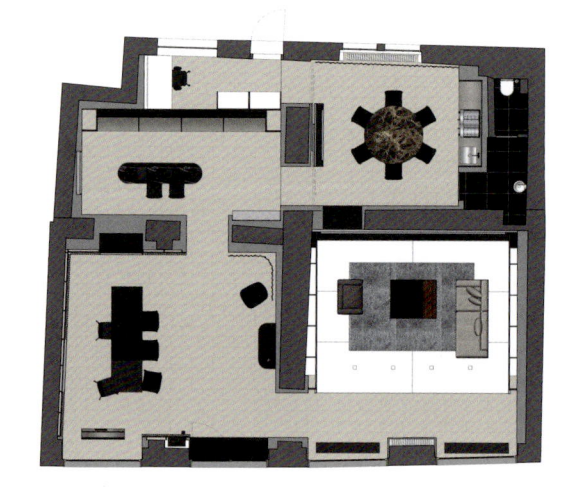

SPACES   OCCHIO STORE MILAN

In the Occhio Store, space and material form the physical level for the integration of the purist and timeless product world of the company that Axel Meise founded back in 1999. On around 120 square metres, various areas have been created that invite visitors to explore and experience the effect of light and light quality in a spatial context. The "Welcome Area" receives them in a warm atmosphere with a communicative consultation table. The impressive "stage" is an elevated platform with a multidimensional video wall which uses space-enlarging mirrors to create a kaleidoscope effect. This area also serves as a Light Lab in which light effects can be experienced. In the "Arsenal", the lighting families are introduced in a specially designed furniture system. Here, potential customers can configure individual lights tailored precisely to their requirements.

"In Milan, the international metropolis of design, we showcase lighting culture and invite visitors to express their individuality through light. Our new store is also our light competence hub in the southern European area", explains Axel Meise, Occhio's founder and designer.

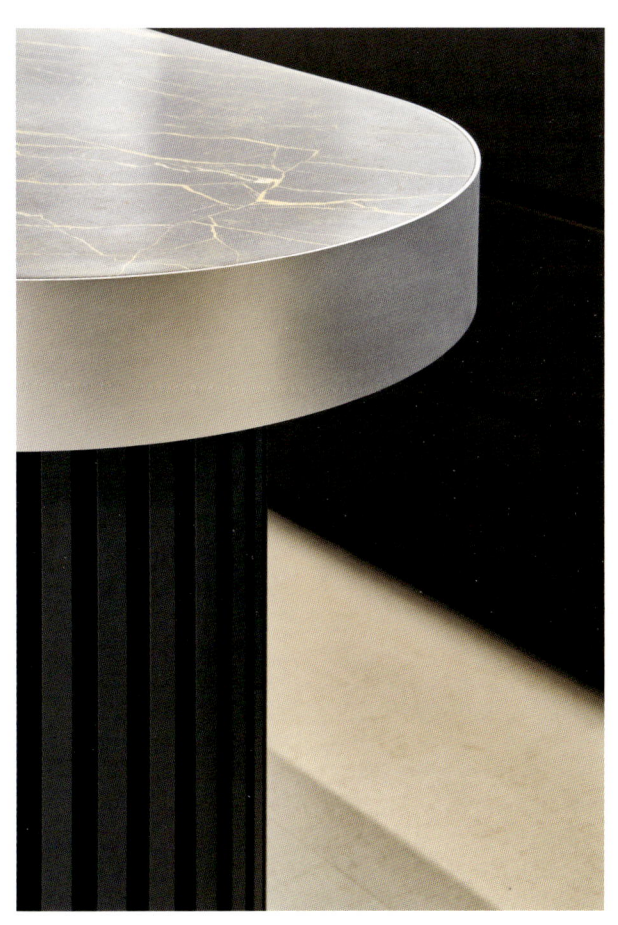

STEFFL VIENNA

LOCATION VIENNA, AUSTRIA   **CLIENT** KAUFHAUS STEFFL BETRIEBS AG, VIENNA   **CONCEPT / DESIGN** BLOCHER PARTNERS, STUTTGART   **LIGHTING** ELAN BELEUCHTUNGS- UND ELEKTROANLAGEN GMBH, COLOGNE   **OTHERS** GANTER INTERIOR GMBH, WALDKIRCH (SHOPFITTING SPORTS DEPARTMENT)   **PHOTOGRAPHS** PATRICIA PARINEJAD, BERLIN; CLEMENS BEDNAR, VIENNA

Der Name, der in Anlehnung an den Stephansdom – von den Wienern liebevoll „Steffl" genannt – entstanden ist, hebt die besondere Verwurzelung des Traditionskaufhauses in Wien hervor. Bis heute lädt das Kaufhaus Steffl in der prominenten Kärntner Straße neben den Boutiquen namhafter Labels aus aller Welt zum Flanieren ein.

Mit der Neugestaltung der Sport- und dem Umbau der Kinderabteilung konnten die Innenarchitekten von blocher partners die gewachsene Tradition des Hauses mit innovativem Retail Design fortschreiben.

Inspired by St. Stephen's Cathedral which the Viennese refer to affectionately as "Steffl", the name underscores the deep-rooted relationship of the heritage department store to Vienna. To this day, Kaufhaus Steffl located in the well-known Kärntner Street alongside the boutiques of prestigious labels from around the world invites shoppers to take a stroll.

With the redesign of the sport department and refurbishment of the children's department, the interior architects from blocher partners continued the evolved tradition of the store with innovative retail design.

SPACES   STEFFL VIENNA

Sobald die Besucherinnen und Besucher über die Rolltreppen im Atrium das vierte Geschoss erreichen, tauchen sie in die mit Alu- und Lochblechmaterialien, Granit und Plexiglas gestaltete neue Sportabteilung ein. Sondermöbel markieren die Highlight-Flächen und nehmen mit ihrer handwerklichen Verarbeitung und Materialität, wie zum Beispiel Zirbenholz, lokale Bezüge auf.

Once the visitors reach the fourth floor via the escalator from the atrium, they are immersed in the sport department with a design of aluminium and perforated sheet metal, granite and Perspex. Special furniture elements mark the highlight zones and the way they are crafted, and the materials used to create them, such as stone pine, draw local references.

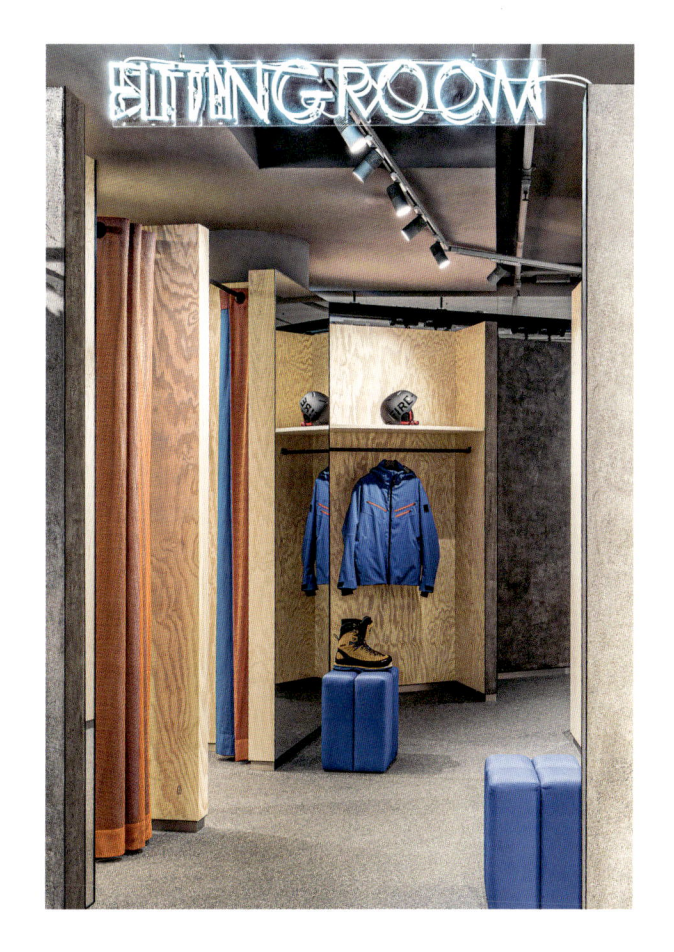

Das Spiel mit Kontrasten charakterisiert auch die anderen Ebenen: Um das Shoppingerlebnis zu erweitern und vertiefende Informationen zu vermitteln, wird die Warenpräsentation mit neuen Medien überlagert. Auf dem sogenannten „Inspiration Island" sind an der flexiblen Deckenschiene nicht nur Waren abgehängt, sondern auch Monitore, die beidseitig mit inspirierenden Inhalten bespielt werden. In der Mitte der Verkaufsfläche wurde eine spielerische Workshop-Area mit großem Tisch und einem Frame gestaltet. Je nach Bedarf kann dort Ware oder eine Leinwand für Events montiert werden. Die Rückwand des Kassenbereichs wurde aus spiegelndem Edelstahl gefertigt und im Nachhinein mit einem intensiven Farbverlauf von Orange zu Blau lackiert. Der anregende Shoppingtrip kann schließlich in der Sky Bar mit Dachgarten und einem atemberaubenden Blick auf den Stephansdom seinen Ausklang finden.

Auf einem Teil des heutigen Steffl-Areals komponierte Wolfgang Amadeus Mozart in seinem letzten Lebensjahr die „Zauberflöte" und das Requiem. Eine Gedenktafel erinnert daran. Mit dem Umbau des Kaufhauses, das seit 1961 unter dem Namen Steffl dort ansässig ist, wird nun die Stadtgeschichte Wiens fortgeschrieben.

SPACES   STEFFL VIENNA

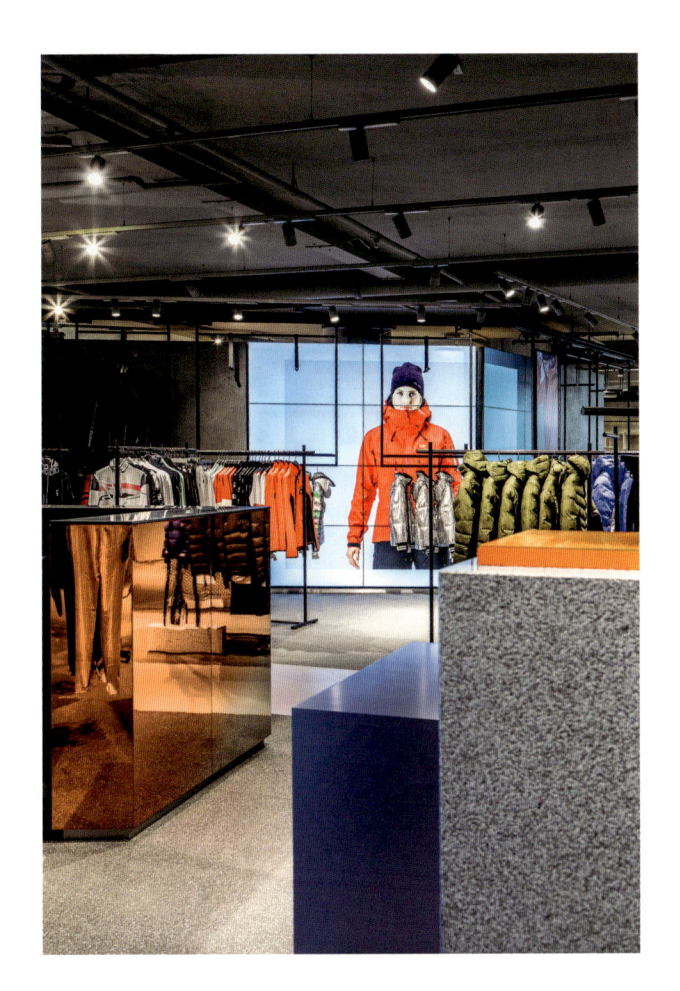

The play with contrasts also characterises the other levels: To expand the shopping experience and to convey more in-depth information, the goods presentation is superimposed with new media. On the aptly named "Inspiration Island", not only goods are suspended from the flexible ceiling tracks, but also monitors which present inspiring content from both sides. At the centre of the shop floor, a playful workshop area has been created with a large table and a frame. As needed, either goods can be presented here, or a screen installed for events. The backdrop of the cash desk area is made of reflective stainless steel that was subsequently painted with intense colour gradients from orange to blue. After an inspiring shopping trip, customers can wind down in the Sky Bar with roof garden and a breathtaking view of St. Stephen's Cathedral.

In the last year of his life, Wolfgang Amadeus Mozart composed The Magic Flute and The Requiem on part of today's Steffl areal. This is commemorated by a plaque. With the refurbishment of the store, that has resided here under the name Steffl since 1961, the history of the city of Vienna is continued.

BOBO'S BIKESHOP

LOCATION STUTTGART, GERMANY   **CLIENT** BOBO'S BIKESHOP, STUTTGART
CONCEPT / DESIGN / GRAPHICS / MEDIA BARTHOLOMAE DESIGN, STUTTGART   **PHOTOGRAPHS** MATTHIAS SOMBERG, STUTTGART

„Irgendwann sagst du dir: ‚Ich mach das jetzt' – und aus Hobby wird Beruf", beschreibt Nikolas „Bobo" Betzler seinen Weg zum eigenen Bikeshop. Seine erste kleine, urige Fahrradwerkstatt eröffnete er im Stuttgarter Stadtteil Degerloch. Dort hat er sich mit seinen Kollegen einen beträchtlichen Kreis an Stammkunden aufgebaut, denen sie mit ihrer Kompetenz und ihrer Leidenschaft rund ums Fahrrad weiterhelfen.

"At some point, you just say to yourself: 'I am going to do it now – turn my hobby into my career'", is how Nikolas "Bobo" Betzler describes his journey to owning his own bike repair shop. He opened his first small, old-worldly bicycle workshop in Degerloch, a district of Stuttgart. With his colleagues, he built up a substantial clientele, who they were able to help with their competence and passion for everything to do with bikes.

SPACES BOBO'S BIKESHOP

69

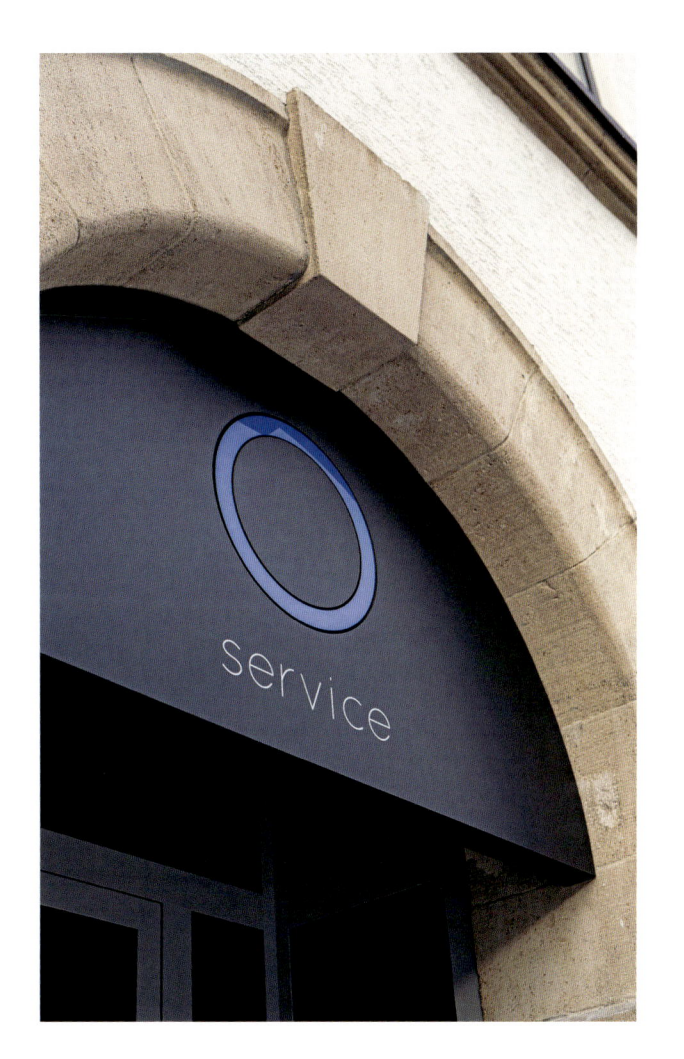

Mit dem wachsenden Erfolg seines Konzepts fragte Bobo die Gestalter von Bartholomae Design nach einer neuen Visitenkarte, um „professioneller" wahrgenommen zu werden. Dabei blieb es nicht: Es folgte ein komplettes Corporate Design, das inzwischen neben Bobos Auto auch die neue Werkstatt im Zentrum des Stadtteils umfasst. Der neue Standort liegt im Erdgeschoss eines stattlichen Geschäftshauses in bester Lage, mit großen Schaufenstern und ausladenden Sandsteinbögen. Darin lag die Herausforderung für die Gestalter: Das in den letzten Jahren von schicken Boutiquen genutzte Ladenlokal sollte in eine Werkstatt verwandelt werden, die den authentischen Charakter des ersten Standorts weiterführt.

As the success of is concept grew, Bobo asked the designers from Bartholomae Design for a new business card, so that he would be perceived more "professionally". But that wasn't the end of their collaboration: There followed a full corporate design, which meanwhile extends not only to Bobo's car, but also to the new workshop in the centre of the city district. The new shop is on the ground floor of an imposing business property in a top location, with large shop windows and sweeping sandstone arches. And precisely that was the challenge for the designers: The store that had previously housed elegant boutiques needed to be transformed into a workshop which continued the authentic character of the first location.

Zu diesem Charme trugen maßgeblich die Mechaniker bei mit ihrer für alle gut einsehbaren Arbeit. Daraus folgte der Entschluss, den Protagonisten gleich eine offene Bühne zu spendieren. Die Bühnenkonstruktionen sind mit Gummimatten ausgelegt, was zu einem leichten Gummigeruch führt, der in einer Fahrradwerkstatt aber gerne wahrgenommen wird. Da die Mitarbeiter nicht „ausgestellt" werden sollten, wurde entschieden, die großen Schaufenster vollflächig zu folieren. Von außen wird durch die Folierung eine gewisse Neugier bei den Passanten geweckt, während das gedämpfte Tageslicht im Innenraum die konzentrierte Werkstattatmosphäre betont. Hinter dem CI-blauen Tresen nimmt eine symmetrische Installation aus Laufrädern das Thema Fahrrad sichtbar auf.

Auch vor dem umgestalteten Ladengeschäft wurde an die Kundschaft gedacht: Eine urige Holzbank mit gummigedippten Füßen wurde vor der Werkstatt platziert und bietet eine coronakonforme Sitzgelegenheit für die wartenden Bike-Enthusiasten.

SPACES   BOBO'S BIKESHOP

Much of this charm had been made up by the mechanics whose work had been visible for all to see. With this in mind, the designers decided to give the main "characters" an open stage. The stage constructions are covered with rubber mats, lending the place a slight smell of rubber which for many is a pleasant association with a bike workshop. But because the employees were not to be put "on display", it was decided to cover the large shop windows with foil. From the outside, the foliation arouses the curiosity of passers-by, while the muted daylight on the inside emphasises the focused workshop atmosphere. Behind the counter in CI blue, a symmetrical installation of various wheels picks up the bicycle theme.

The area outside the refurbished shop was also designed with the customers in mind: a rustic wooden bench with rubber-dipped feet has been placed in front of the workshop and offers corona-compliant seating for waiting bike enthusiasts.

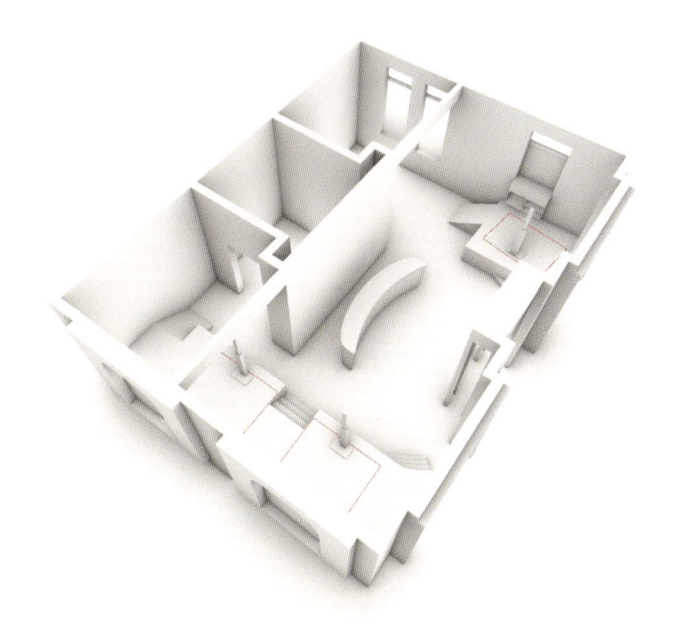

SALLYS WELT FLAGSHIP STORE

LOCATION MANNHEIM, GERMANY **CLIENT** SALLYS SHOP GMBH & CO. KG, SULZ AM NECKAR **CONCEPT / DESIGN / LIGHTING** BRUST+PARTNER GMBH, BAD SCHÖNBORN **GRAPHICS / MEDIA** SALLYS SHOP GMBH & CO. KG, SULZ AM NECKAR **PHOTOGRAPHS** MAXIMILIAN HEINSCH FOTOSCHMIEDE, WAGHÄUSEL; ELISABETH SAMURA, FRAU HOLLA MARKE & CONTENT GMBH, BAD SCHÖNBORN

Die gebürtige Badenerin Sally gründete im Jahr 2012 während ihres Studiums auf das Grundschullehramt ihren eigenen YouTube-Kanal „Sallys Welt" und veröffentlicht dort seither regelmäßig Rezeptideen. Heute besitzt sie einen der größten Back- und Kochkanäle Europas und hat mittlerweile bereits fast 1,94 Mio. Abonnenten.

Born in Baden in southwest Germany, Sally founded her own YouTube channel called "Sallys Welt" back in 2012 while she was still studying to be a primary school teacher. Since then she has been publishing recipe ideas there regularly. Today, she has one of the biggest baking and cookery channels in Europe and has nearly 1.94 million subscribers.

SPACES   SALLYS WELT FLAGSHIP STORE

Die Zielsetzung der Planerinnen und Planer von Brust + Partner aus Bad Schönborn war es, mit dem Flagship Store die On- und Offlinewelt zu verbinden. Der Store sollte sich deutlich vom klassischen Einzelhandel unterscheiden und zu einem persönlichen „best place" werden. Mit der Original-Sally-Küche, die eins zu eins im Shop nachgebaut wurde, sollen sich die Gäste fühlen, als wären sie bei Sally persönlich zu Hause.

Auf 330 Quadratmetern verbinden die Gestalter heimelige Wohnzimmeratmosphäre mit spannendem Eventcharakter. Hinter dem Schaufenster wurde eine große Videowall mit Ausrichtung zur Straße verbaut sowie im ganzen Store Monitore von der Decke abgehängt. Offene Deckenelemente und individuell einstellbare Lichtspots führen durch den Store und setzen die entsprechenden Warengruppen gekonnt in Szene. Die rollbaren Warenwägen können zur Seite geschoben werden, wodurch die Verkaufsfläche im Handumdrehen zur Eventlocation mit freiem Blick auf die Studioküche mutiert. In modularen Regal-Stecksystemen können die Produkte flexibel und nach Themen sortiert präsentiert werden. Die Farbwelt ist identisch mit Sallys Welt im Internet, sofort zu erkennen an den grünen Teppichläufern oder etwa den vertraut wirkenden pinkfarbenen Akzenten.

The goal of the designers Brust + Partner from Bad Schönborn was to use the flagship store to combine the online and offline worlds. Very different from the classic retail outlet, the store was to become a personal "best place". By carefully replicating the original Sally kitchen in the shop, they wanted customers to feel like guests, as if they were at home with Sally.

On 330 square metres, the designers have combined cosy living room atmosphere with exciting event character. Behind the shop window, a large video wall facing the street was installed and monitors are suspended from the ceiling through the store. Open ceiling elements and individually adjustable spots assist navigation through the store and shed the best possible light on the various groups of goods. At the drop of a hat, the wheeled goods carts can be pushed to one side, transforming the shop floor into an event location with a clear view of the studio kitchen. The products can be presented flexibly in the modular plug-and-play shelving system and sorted by topic. The colour palette is identical to that seen in Sallys Welt on the internet, instantly recognisable from the green carpets or the familiar, pink-coloured highlights.

LIMITED
EDITION
WILLKOMMEN

SALLYS KERAMIK
GESCHIRRSET
„MIX & MATCH"
GEFU

SPACES SALLYS WELT FLAGSHIP STORE

Saliha „Sally" Özcan entwickelt ihre Produkte selbst und lässt sie von anderen herstellen, vom Produkt bis zur Verpackung erfolgt alles in Eigenregie. Dabei achtet sie auf faire Löhne, Arbeitssicherheit und die Einhaltung der Umweltstandards. Ihr Engagement wurde vielfach ausgezeichnet, so unter anderem 2016 vom Land Baden-Württemberg mit dem Landespreis für junge Unternehmen. Der erste physische Store in Mannheim soll nun ein Ort der analogen Begegnung für alle Koch- und Backbegeisterten werden.

Saliha "Sally" Özcan develops her products herself and has them produced by others, but she has control of the whole process from the product through to the packaging, paying special attention to fair wages, occupational safety and compliance with environmental standards. For her commitment, she has already received several prizes, for instance the state prize for young companies from the state of Baden-Württemberg. The first physical store in Mannheim is to become a place of analogue encounters for all cooking and baking enthusiasts.

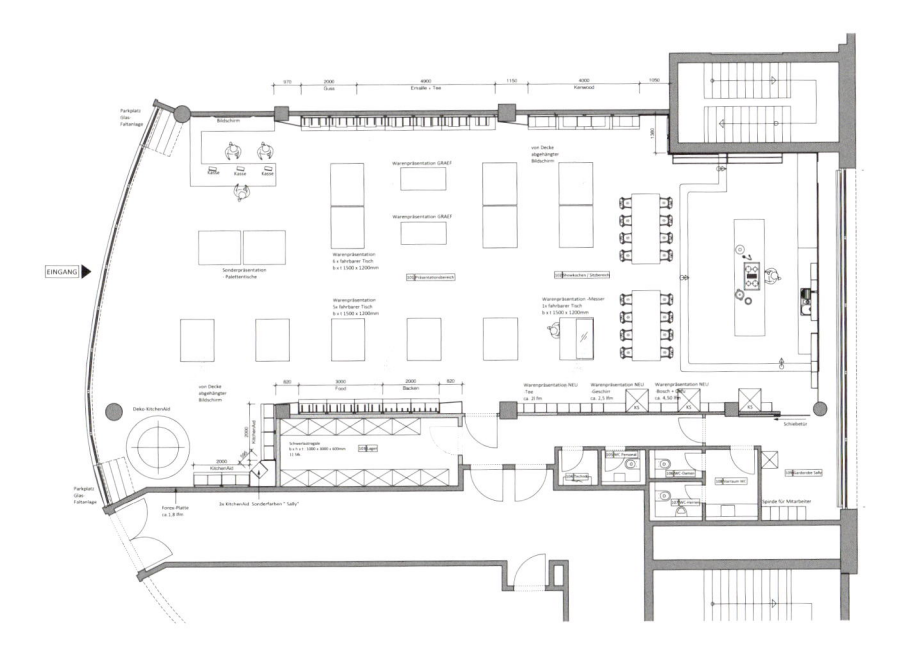

TOD'S STUDIOS

LOCATION MILAN, ITALY   **CLIENT** TOD'S S.P.A., CASETTE D'ETE   **CONCEPT / DESIGN** GWENAEL NICOLAS | CURIOSITY INC., TOKYO   **LIGHTING** EFFETO LUCE S.P.A., MACERATA; MLD LAB, MILAN   **PHOTOGRAPHS** ALESSANDRA CHEMOLLO, VENEZIA

Durch die gekonnte Kombination traditioneller Handwerkskunst mit Innovation hat sich die Tod's Group zu einem Symbol italienischer Lebensart entwickelt. Auf der renommierten Via Montenapoleone in Mailand hat Tod's nun ein experimentelles Shopkonzept eröffnet, das von Filmstudios mit ihren ständig wechselnden Storys und Szenen inspiriert ist.

By skilfully combining arts and crafts traditions with innovation, the Tod's Group has become a symbol of the Italian lifestyle. On the famous Via Montenapoleone in Milan, Tod's has now launched an experimental shop concept, inspired by film studios with their constantly changing stories and scenes.

Der Franzose Gwenael Nicoals hat auf rund 1.000 Quadratmetern Fläche ein Labor für Ideen und Inhalte installiert, das den Namen seines Tokioter Büros reflektiert: Curiosity – Neugier, die seiner Lebensphilosophie und Arbeitsweise entspricht. Tod's Studios hat er als Galerie konzipiert, deren Stil sich fortlaufend weiterentwickelt. Sie besteht aus einem Raum, der auf vielfältige Weise genutzt werden kann, sich physikalisch jedoch mehr an der Interaktivität des Digitalen und der Idee des Omnichannel Retails orientiert. Der Hauptbereich des Studios bietet Platz für die verschiedenen Kollektionen unter einem weiträumigen skulpturalen Deckensystem, in das die Beleuchtung und die wechselnden Präsentationsflächen integriert sind. Die Kollektionen werden sorgfältig wie eine Auswahl an Kunstgegenständen in kräftigen, prägnanten Holzrahmen an den Wänden positioniert. Passend zu den jeweiligen Kollektionen und ihren Themen können die Stücke „zusammengetragen" und bewegt werden. Die Besucher:innen sind eingeladen, von einer Sammlung zur nächsten zu flanieren.

On the roughly 1,000 square-metre space, Frenchman Gwenael Nicolas has installed a laboratory for ideas and content which reflects the name of his Tokyo office: Curiosity, encapsulating his philosophy of life and the way he works. He designed Tod's Studios as a gallery that will evolve over time. It is a space that can be used in many different ways, indeed the physical space is closer to the interactivity of the digital world and the idea of omnichannel retail. The main studio area is open to the different collections, under a large and sculptural ceiling system that integrates all lighting and flexible displays. The collections are displayed on the walls like a selection of crafted pieces carefully presented in strong, iconic frames. These pieces can be "curated" and moved, depending on the collection and themes of the collections. Visitors are invited to browse from one collection to another.

Tod's Produktbibliothek steht für die außergewöhnliche Handwerkskunst der Marke. Streng im Einklang mit dem genetischen Bauplan von Tod's DNA gemahnt sie an deren Ursprünge in den 1920er-Jahren, als Dorino Della Valle beschloss, in seiner Heimatstadt in der mittelitalienischen Region der Marche mit der Produktion einer neuen Schuhmarke zu beginnen.

The brand's outstanding craftsmanship is manifested in Tod's library. It contains the codes that make up Tod's DNA, which dates back to the 1920s, when Dorino Della Valle decided to start a new shoe manufacturing business in his native town in the central Italian region of Marche.

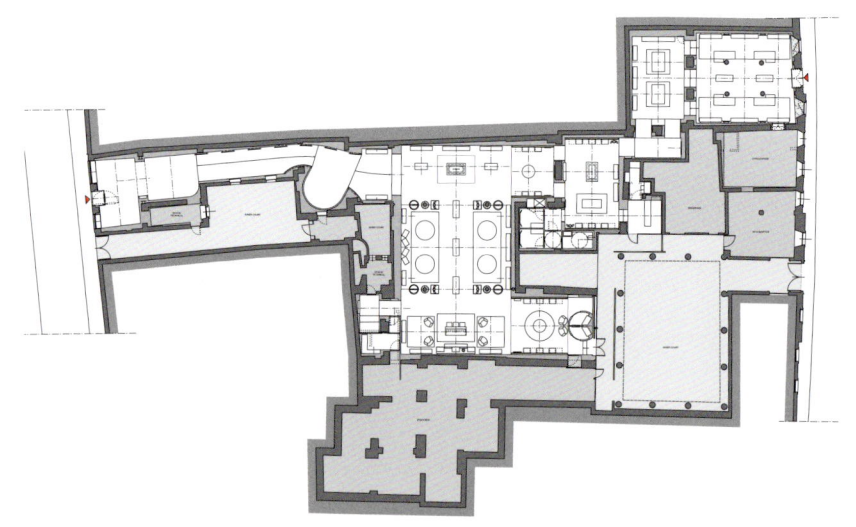

In den 1970ern brachte die Markteinführung des patentierten „Gommino" Tod's an die Spitze des internationalen Erfolgs. Mit seiner von 133 Gumminoppen überzogenen Sohle ist der Mokkasin zum bis heute bekannten Symbol für das Unternehmen geworden. Anders als industriell gefertigte Sneaker, die durch Limitierungen verknappt werden, stehen die handgefertigten Produkte für nachhaltige Handwerkskunst. In den Mailänder Tod's Studios treffen die traditionellen Werte des Unternehmens auf zukunftsweisendes Retail Design.

In the 1970s, the launch of the patented "Gommino" transported Tod's to the pinnacle of international success. The moccasin with 133 rubber pebbles on its soles has become a long-lasting symbol for the company. Unlike industrially produced sneakers, the supply of which is kept artificially low through limitations, the handcrafted products stand for sustainable craftmanship. In Tod's Studios in Milan, the traditional values of the company meet future-orientated retail design.

BRAUKUNSTHAUS ZILLERTAL BIER

LOCATION ZELL AM ZILLER, AUSTRIA **CLIENT** ZILLERTAL BIER, ZELL AM ZILLER **CONCEPT / DESIGN** HOLZER KOBLER ARCHITEKTUREN, ZURICH **GRAPHICS** HIMMEL. STUDIO FÜR DESIGN UND KOMMUNIKATION, SCHEFFAU **MEDIA** MELANIE HOLLAUS, VIENNA; GEORG LENDORFF, ZURICH; AGNIESZKA KRUCZEK, BERLIN; GÜNTHER ZECHBERGER, HALL IN TIROL **IDEA** MARTIN LECHNER / PHILIPP GEIGER (DIRECTION), ZELL AM ZILLER **CURATION** MARTIN LECHNER, ZELL AM ZILLER; ANDREAS BRAUN, LANS; PHILIPP GEIGER, ZELL AM ZILLER; TRISTAN KOBLER, ZURICH **PHOTOGRAPHS** ZILLERTAL BIER, ZELL AM ZILLER; HOLZER KOBLER ARCHITEKTUREN, ZURICH

Ludwig Jobst, ein direkter Vorfahr der heutigen Eigentümer von Zillertal Bier, erwarb 1678 das Recht, Bier und Branntwein herzustellen, und war damit der erste „freie" Bierbrauer Tirols. Im Rahmen eines multimedial inszenierten Rundgangs haben die Besucher:innen im BrauKunstHaus die Gelegenheit, mehr über die Geschichte des Familienunternehmens und zu den Bräuchen in der Region zu erfahren.

Ludwig Jobst, a direct forefather of today's owner of Zillertal Bier, acquired the right to produce beer and spirits in 1678 and was Tyrol's first "free" beer brewer. Visitors to BrauKunstHaus have the opportunity to take a tour to find out more about the history of the family-run business and regional customs.

SPACES   BRAUKUNSTHAUS ZILLERTAL BIER

Mit dem Neubau der Brauerei am Ortsrand von Zell am Ziller wurde auch der Grundstein für das BrauKunstHaus gelegt. Die rund 5.000 Quadratmeter Ausstellungs- und Verkaufsfläche auf drei Etagen wurden von Holzer Kobler Architekturen konzipiert und umgesetzt. Das inhaltliche und gestalterische Konzept entstand in enger Zusammenarbeit mit dem Auftraggeber sowie Film- und Multimediaschaffenden. Die Verankerung am Ort und das Bekenntnis zu Regionalität spiegeln sich in der narrativen Ebene ebenso wider wie in den verwendeten Materialien. So wird beispielsweise das Gauder Fest thematisiert, Österreichs größtes Frühlings- und Trachtenfest, das von jeher eng mit Zillertal Bier verknüpft ist. Der Rundgang folgt dem Anbau wertvoller Rohstoffe über die einzelnen Veredelungsschritte bis hin zum Verkauf. Auch wird der Brauprozess mithilfe einer aufwendigen Videoinstallation als „Blick ins Innere" der Kessel gezeigt.

The foundation stone for the BrauKunstHaus was laid in conjunction with the construction of the new brewery on the outskirts of Zell am Ziller. The roughly 5,000 square-metre exhibition and sales area over three floors was designed and realised by Holzer Kobler Architekturen. The content and design concept was evolved in close collaboration with the client and a number of film and multimedia creators. The local roots and the commitment to regionality are reflected at the narrative level and in the materials that have been used. One theme is the Gauder Fest, Austria's biggest spring and traditional costume festival, which has long-standing associations with Zillertal beer. The tour traces the cultivation of high-quality raw materials via all steps involved in the refining process through to the sale. The brewing process itself is also shown with the help of an elaborate video installation that allows visitors to get a "view inside" the boilers.

Neben dem Design der multimedialen Inszenierung planten Holzer Kobler auch die Servicebereiche mit Bar, Seminarraum und den 285 Quadratmeter großen Shop. Die Verkostung der Bierspezialitäten bildet den Abschluss des Rundgangs durch die Ausstellung, der mit einem Besuch des angeschlossenen BrauKunstHaus Shops endet. Dort werden neben Bierspezialitäten auch Artikel rund um den Biergenuss und Produkte aus der Region angeboten.

In addition to the design of the multimedia production, Holzer Kobler also designed the service areas with bar, seminar room and the 285 square-metre shop. The tasting of the beer specialities forms the culmination of the tour through the exhibition which ends with a visit to the adjacent BrauKunstHaus shop. On sale: beer specialities next to all kinds of items related to the enjoyment of beer and other regional products.

SPACES   BRAUKUNSTHAUS ZILLERTAL BIER

Die Besonderheit, dass die Brauerei seit rund 350 Jahren in Familienbesitz ist, wird durch audiovisuell „wiederauflebende Familienmitglieder" verschiedener Generationen thematisiert, die über Monitore und Lautsprecher zu den Besucherinnen und Besuchern sprechen. Sie begrüßen, geben Wissenswertes über die Bierbraukunst preis und vergleichen die heutige Zeit mit der ihrigen.

To celebrate the fact that the brewery has been owned by the same family for around 350 years, an audio-visual presentation brings family members back to life who address the visitors via speakers and monitors. They welcome their guests, share interesting facts about the art of beer brewing and compare our times with theirs.

LONGINES
POP-UP INSTALLATION

LOCATION ALSTERHAUS HAMBURG / KADEWE BERLIN, GERMANY   **CLIENT** COMPAGNIE DES MONTRES LONGINES, FRANCILLON S.A., SAINT-IMIER   **CONCEPT / DESIGN** DFROST RETAIL IDENTITY, STUTTGART
PHOTOGRAPHS ULRICH SCHAARSCHMIDT FOR DFROST RETAIL IDENTITY, STUTTGART

Eine Mondphasenuhr simuliert die Bewegung des Mondes in Relation zur Erde. Zunächst erscheint der Erdtrabant nur als kleiner Anschnitt auf dem Zifferblatt, später rückt er weiter vor, bis er in seiner runden Darstellung den Vollmond anzeigt. Ein magisches Umfeld zwischen Realität und Illusion hat DFROST für die „Moon Phase Collection" des Schweizer Uhrenherstellers Longines geschaffen.

A moon phase watch simulates the movement of the moon in relation to the Earth. At first, the Earth trabant appears as just a small sliver on the face of the watch, later it moves on until it ultimately shows the rounded form of the full moon. For the "Moon Phase Collection" of the Swiss watchmaker Longines DFROST has created a magical setting somewhere between reality and illusion.

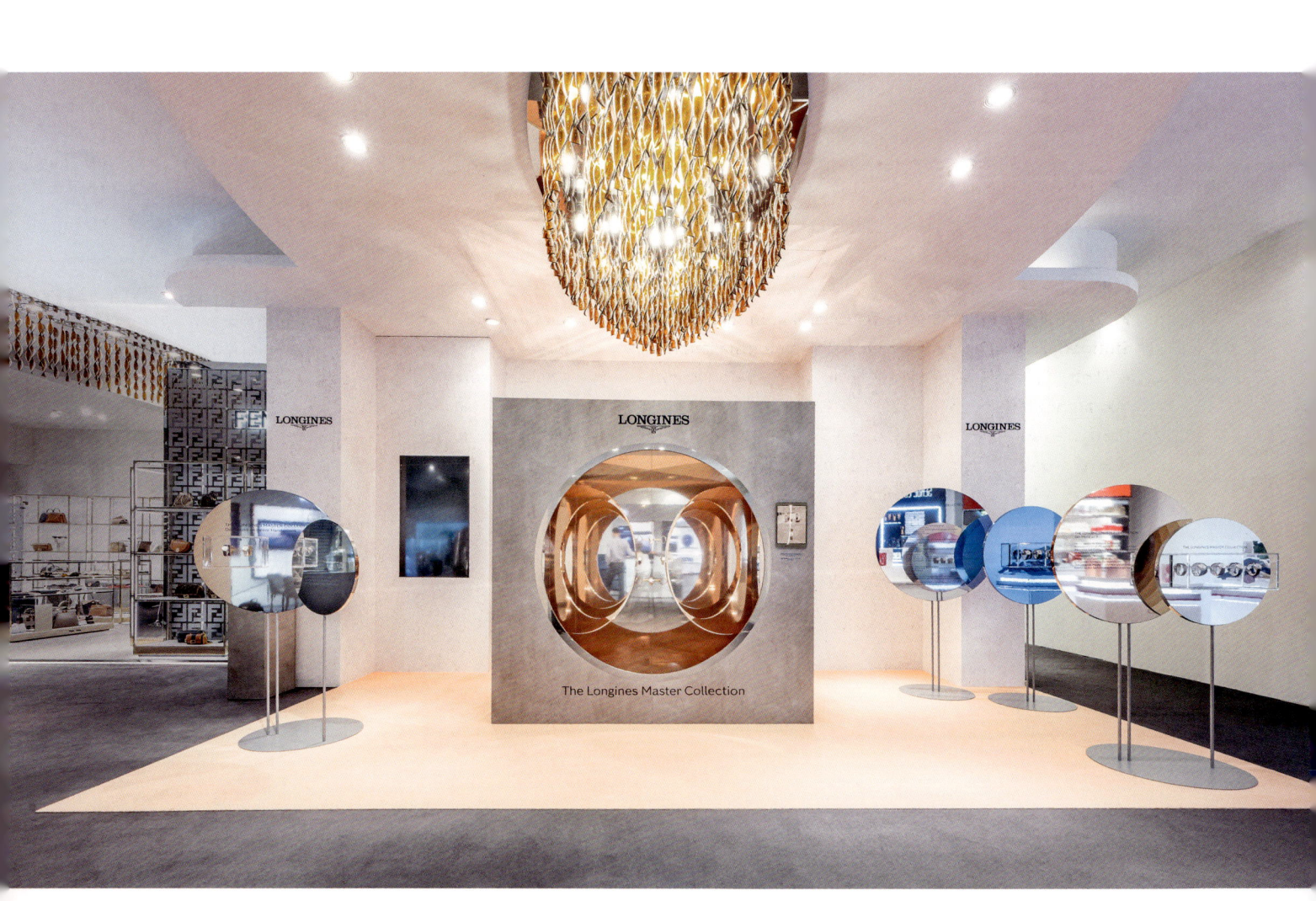

SPACES   LONGINES POP-UP INSTALLATION

Für Standorte in den klassischen Premium-Warenhäusern KaDeWe in Berlin und Alsterhaus in Hamburg haben die Stuttgarter Experten für Retail Identity eine Installation entwickelt, die das Thema der Mondphasen im Produktkontext aufgreift. Ein kompakter Würfel mit runden Öffnungen zieht die Aufmerksamkeit der Kundinnen und Kunden auf sich. Die Gestaltung der Außenfläche soll an die Oberfläche und das fahle Licht des Mondes erinnern. Das Innere des Kubus ist vollständig verspiegelt, sodass sich je nach Perspektive des Betrachtenden verschiedene Reflexionen ergeben, die eine jeweilige Verbindung zu den Mondphasen herstellen.

For locations in the classical premium department stores KaDeWe in Berlin and Alsterhaus in Hamburg, the Stuttgart-based experts for retail identity developed an installation which picks up the theme of the phases of the moon and places it in the context of the product. A compact cube with round openings attracts the attention of the customers. The design of the outside of the cube is reminiscent of the surface and dim light of the moon. The mirrored inside of the cube allows various reflections depending on the perspective of the observer which create a connection to the respective lunar phases.

Die Produkte befinden sich im Inneren des Würfels und können durch verschiedene Öffnungen entdeckt werden. Über ein integriertes interaktives Element lässt sich das Wissen zu den Mondphasen vertiefen. Um den magischen Kubus herum wurden separate Präsentationselemente angeordnet, die sich in Form und Farbe ebenfalls auf das Thema der Mondphasen beziehen. Wie auf dem Zifferblatt der Uhren überlagern sich auch hier getönte Spiegelflächen, auf denen sich Informationen zu den ausgestellten Produkten befinden. Weitere Informationen und Inhalte zu den Produkten des Unternehmens, das heute zur Swatch Group gehört, können via QR-Code auf dem Smartphone aufgerufen werden, um eine möglichst nahtlose Customer Journey zu gewährleisten.

The products are located inside the cube and can be discovered through various openings. Via an integrated interactive element, customers can also find out more about the phases of the moon. Separate presentation elements arranged around the magic cube likewise reference the phases of the moon in terms of form and colour. Like on the face of the watches, here too tinted mirrored surfaces are used as a backdrop for the information about the products on display. Further information and content about the products of the company, which today belongs to Swatch Group, can be accessed on the smartphone via a QR code, thus ensuring as seamless a customer journey as possible.

SPACES   LONGINES POP-UP INSTALLATION   87

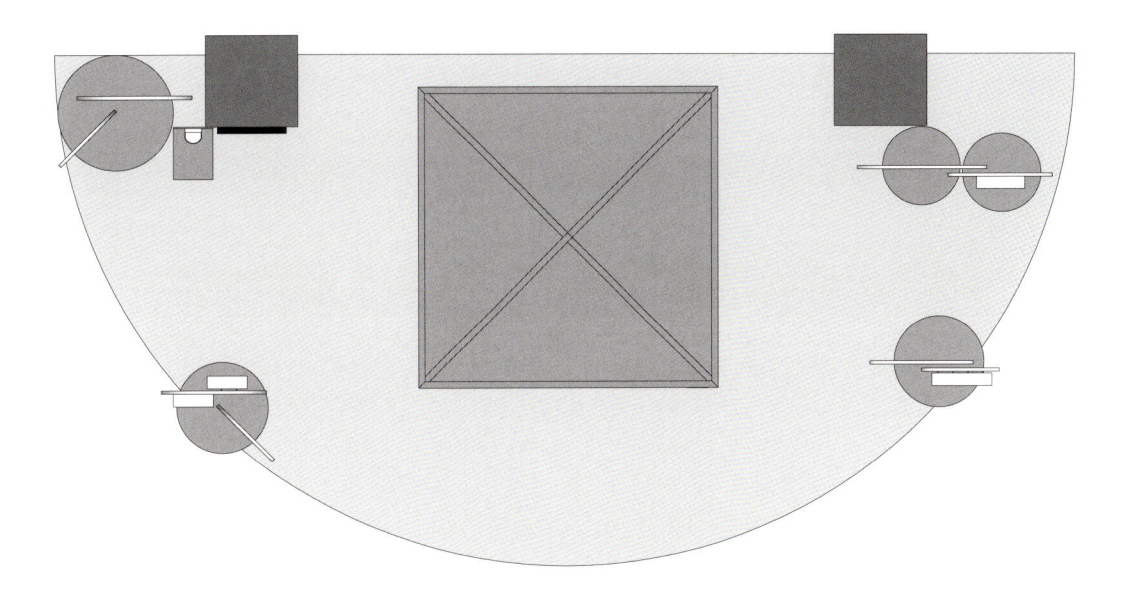

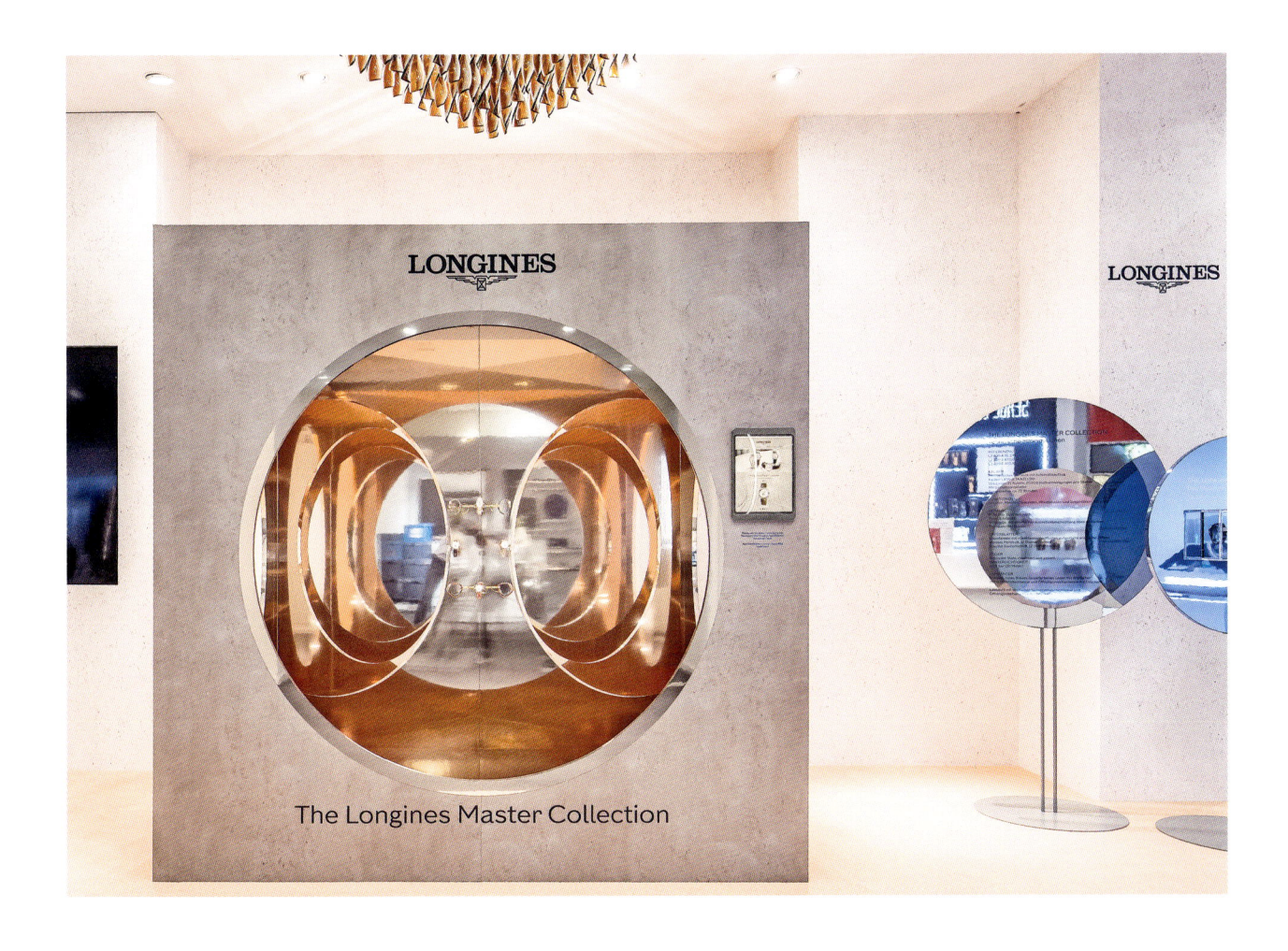

The Longines Master Collection

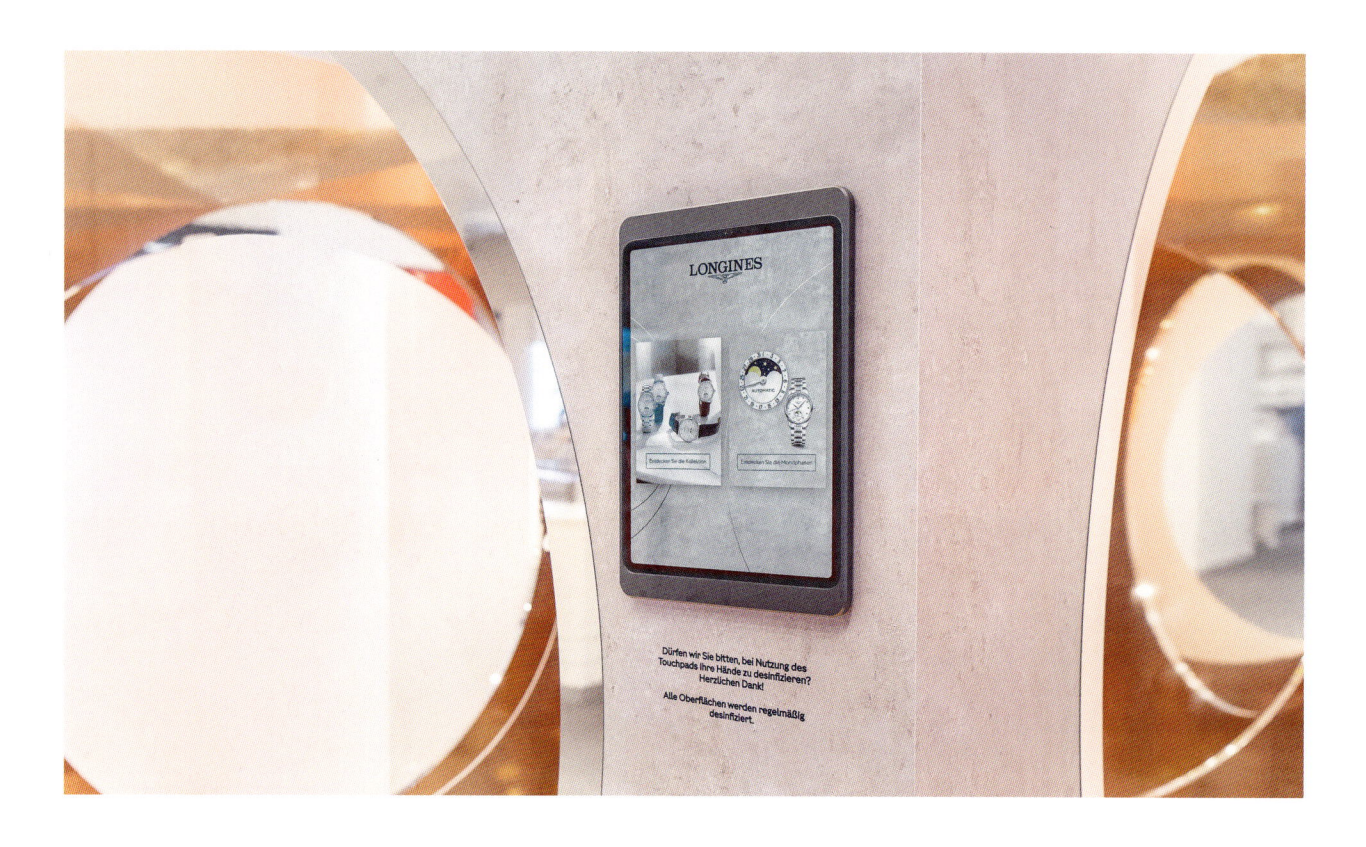

Dürfen wir Sie bitten, bei Nutzung des
Touchpads Ihre Hände zu desinfizieren?
Herzlichen Dank!

Alle Oberflächen werden regelmäßig
desinfiziert.

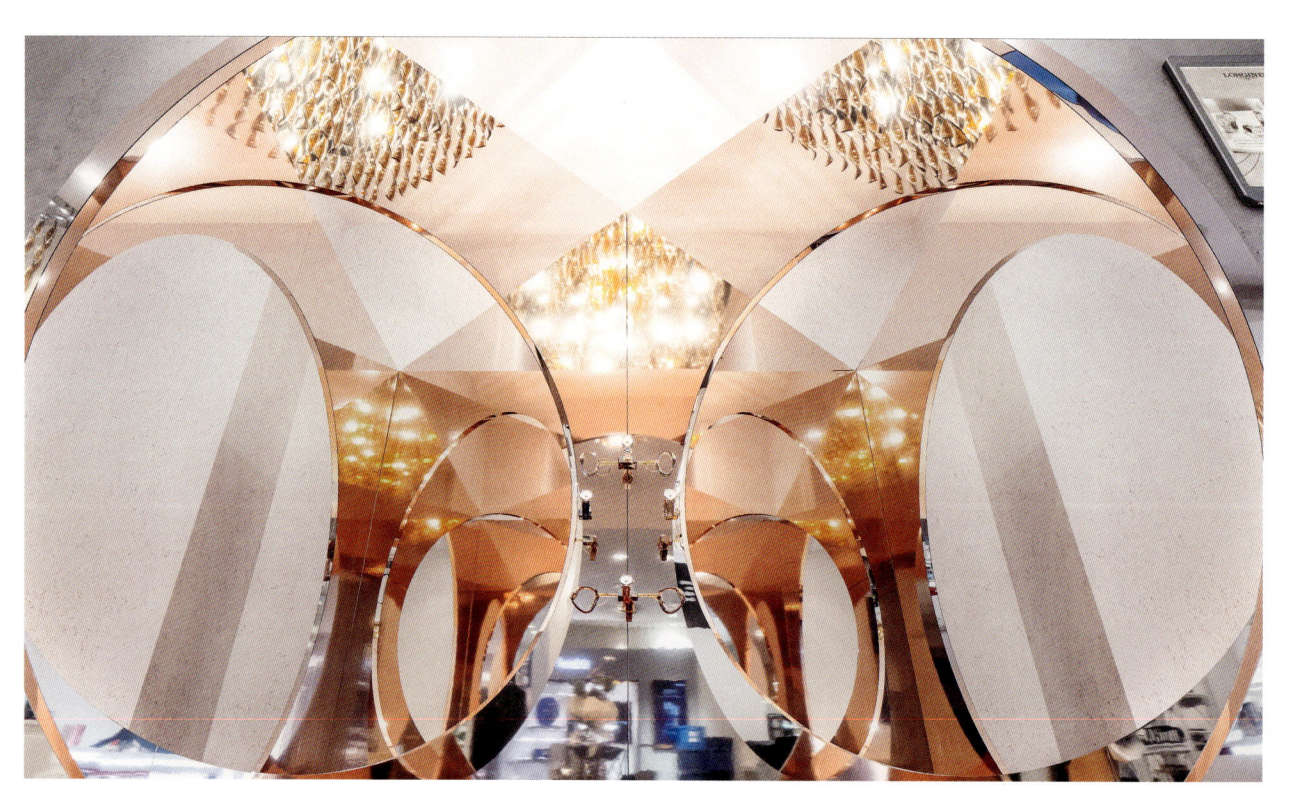

„Just an Illusion" – Das raffinierte Storytelling nimmt die anspruchsvolle Kundschaft mit auf eine Reise in die faszinierende Welt der Zeitmessung. Bereits seit seiner Gründung im Jahr 1832 misst Longines die Zeiten bei internationalen Sportmeisterschaften. Diese Expertise wurde nun in einen „Zeit"-gemäßen und durchaus instagramtauglichen Raum überführt.

"Just an Illusion" – The sophisticated storytelling takes the discerning clientele on a journey into the fascinating world of time measurement. Since its foundation in 1832, Longines has been stopping the time at international sport championships. This expertise has now been transferred into an instagrammable space in keeping with the "times".

SCHTONY OPTIK

LOCATION KIEL, GERMANY **CLIENT** SCHTONY OPTIK GMBH, KIEL **CONCEPT / DESIGN** HEIKAUS ARCHITEKTUR GMBH, STUTTGART **PHOTOGRAPHS** HP-STUDIOS, HAMBURG

Einfach mal „was Einzigartiges" machen, lautete die Aufgabenstellung für die gestalterische Umsetzung des Optikfachgeschäfts Schtony in der Kieler Innenstadt. Das Ladenlokal befindet sich in einem geschichtsträchtigen Gebäude. Das Geschäftshaus Thöll an der Holstenstraße / Hafenstraße wurde 1908 nach einem Entwurf des Architekten Johann Theede gebaut und nach einigen Kriegsschäden stark verändert wieder instand gesetzt.

Quite simply "something unique" was the brief for the design of the dispensing optician Schtony Optik in Kiel's city centre. The shop is located in a building with a history. The commercial building Thöll on Holstenstrasse / Hafenstrasse was built in 1908 on the basis of a design by architect Johann Theede and refurbished after some war damage in a very new guise.

SPACES SCHTONY OPTIK

Der typische „Kieler Stil" sollte in den Materialien und im Flair des neuen Ladenlokals spür- und erkennbar sein. Zur Umsetzung dieses Konzepts standen dem HEIKAUS-Team lediglich fünf Wochen Bauzeit für 85 Quadratmeter Fläche zur Verfügung. Inhaber Stefan Haase wünschte sich eine einladende Atmosphäre mit wirkungsvollen Präsentationselementen für seine Korrektions- und Sonnenbrillenkollektionen. Nach umfangreichen Sanierungsarbeiten begann der Innenausbau, der Transparenz und Offenheit mit optimaler Warenpräsentation und „diskretem" Raum zur Beratung und Untersuchung kombiniert. Die hohe Einsehbarkeit im Schaufensterbereich lädt Passantinnen und Passanten dazu ein, den Verkaufsraum für sich zu entdecken.

The typical Kiel style should be noticeable and recognisable in the materials and in the flair of the new shop. The HEIKAUS team had a mere five-week construction period for the 85 square-metre space to achieve this. Owner Stefan Haase wanted an inviting atmosphere with effective presentation elements for his collections of corrective spectacles and sunglasses. After extensive restructuring measures, the interior construction commenced, combining transparency and openness with optimum goods presentation and "discrete" spaces for consultation and testing. The high degree of visibility in the shop window area invites passersby to explore the sales room.

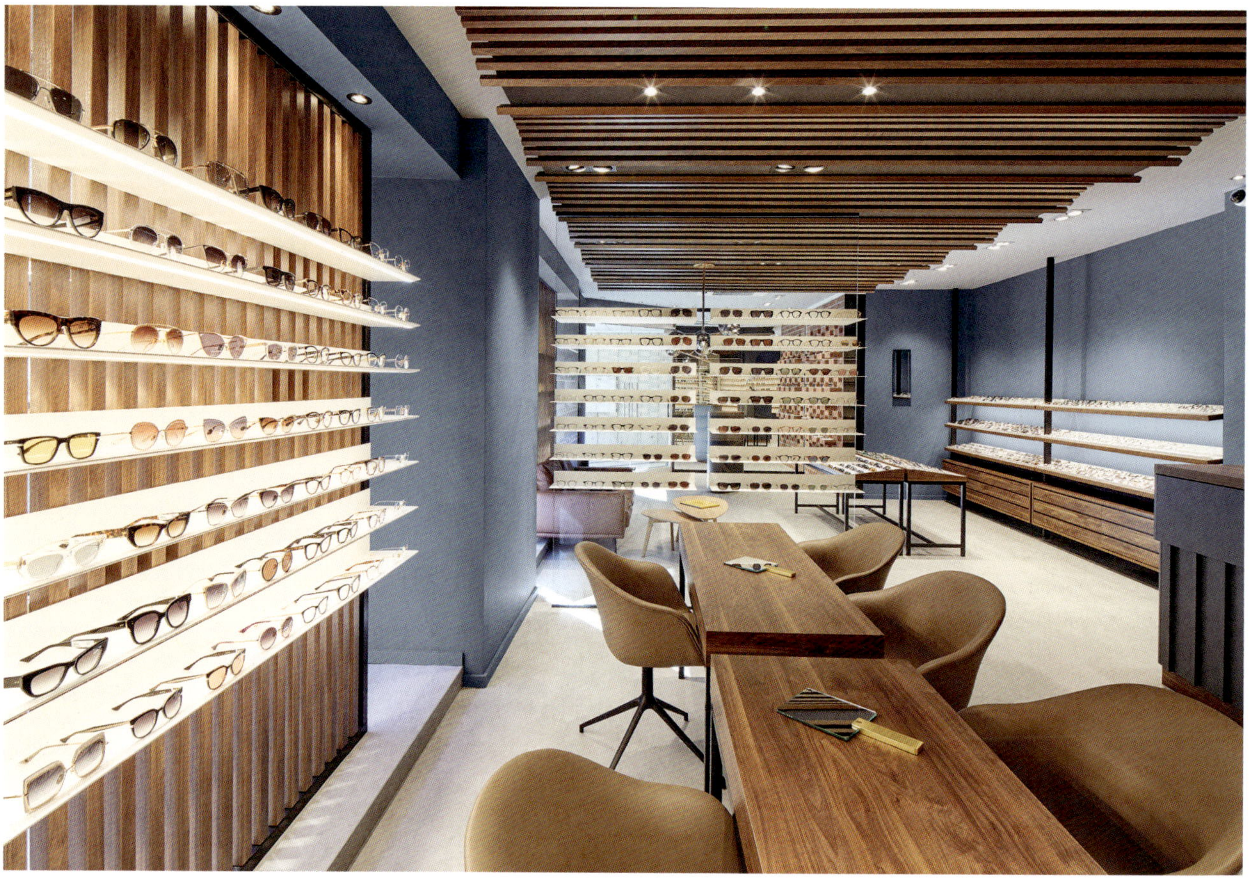

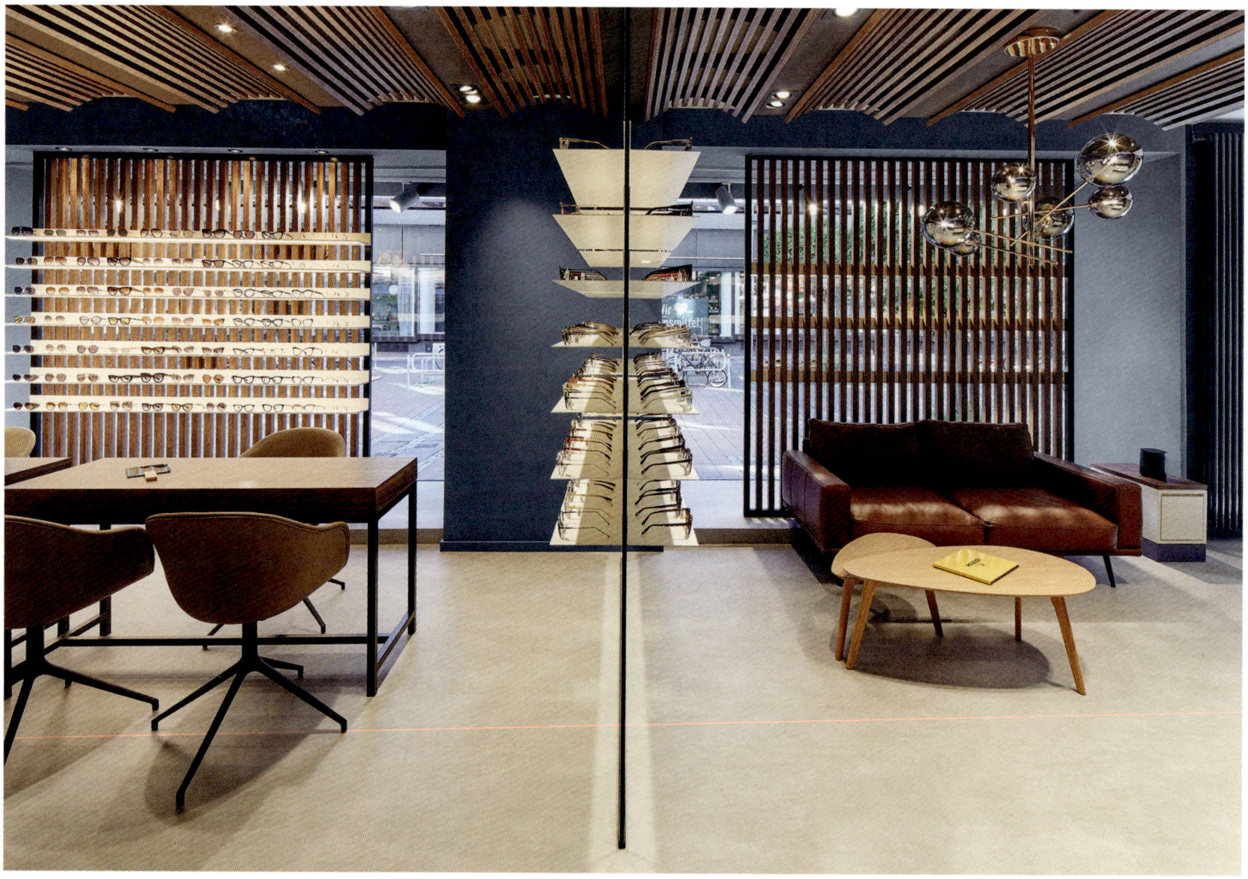

SPACES   SCHTONY OPTIK

Im Innenraum greift eine wellenförmige Nussbaumlattung an der Decke die historischen Gewölbe des traditionsreichen Geschäftshauses auf. Regionaltypische Materialien wie roter Ziegel, dunkler Nussbaum, Glas, Metall und Beton bestimmen die Anmutung des neuen „Heimathafens". Die Brillen werden auf offenen Ziegelwänden und hölzernen Laden präsentiert, die an die Geschichte des früheren Teekontors erinnern. Die gesamte Farb- und Materialkombination wirkt warm und zugleich nordisch frisch, mit großzügig viel Raum zum Erkunden der Produkte. Dafür sorgen auch die filigran möblierten Beratungseinheiten und ein einladender Loungebereich am Eingang.

Der Name „Schtony" basiert auf einer wahren Familienbegebenheit: Wenn Stefan Haase und sein Bruder Tony früher von ihrer Mutter gerufen wurden, fasste sie die Namen gleich zusammen, sodass daraus nur noch „Schtony" entstand. Und diesen Namen erhielt dann auch das eigene Geschäft.

Inside, wave-like walnut battening on the ceiling is a reference to the historical vaulting of the heritage building. Materials typical for the region like red bricks, dark walnut wood, glass, metal and concrete create the flair of the new "home port". The glasses are presented on open brick walls and wooden shelves which are reminiscent of the history of the tea house. The whole colour and material combination has a warm and yet at the same time fresh north German effect, with plenty of room to explore the products. The delicately furnished consultation units and the inviting lounge area near the entrance contribute to this experience.

The shop's name "Schtony" stems from a true family story: When their mother used to call Stefan Haase and his brother Tony when they were children, she put both their names together, becoming "Schtony".

MARKTKAUF GELSENKIRCHEN

LOCATION GELSENKIRCHEN, GERMANY   **CLIENT** EDEKA HANDELSGESELLSCHAFT RHEIN-RUHR GMBH, MOERS
CONCEPT / DESIGN KINZEL ARCHITECTURE, SCHERMBECK   **GRAPHICS** ALEX KINZEL ARCHITECT M.A., SCHERMBECK
LIGHTING BAERO GMBH & CO. KG, LEICHLINGEN   **OTHERS** FLIESEN VILLEROY & BOCH GMBH, METTLACH (FLOORING)
PHOTOGRAPHS GUIDO LEIFHEIM, BECKUM

Zur Marktkauf Einzelhandelsgesellschaft Rhein-Ruhr gehören über 30 Standorte mit Warengruppen von Lebensmitteln über Haushaltswaren bis hin zu Sportartikeln. Mit einem hohen Absatzvolumen sind die Märkte ein wichtiger Partner kleinerer und mittlerer Produzenten in ihrem jeweiligen Einzugsgebiet.

Marktkauf Einzelhandelsgesellschaft Rhein-Ruhr operates more than 30 stores across the region with goods ranging from food to household goods and sports equipment. Their high volume of sales make the supermarkets an important partner of smaller and mid-sized producers in their respective catchment area.

Die Architektin Valentina Kinzel entwickelt und realisiert seit 2011 Retail-Konzepte von der Planung bis zur schlüsselfertigen Übergabe. Nach einer Bauzeit von nur sieben Monaten bei laufendem Betrieb bietet der im März 2021 wiedereröffnete Marktkauf in Gelsenkirchen eine komplett neu organisierte Verkaufsfläche von rund 8.500 Quadratmetern. Nach dem Betreten des Marktes empfängt die großzügig gestaltete Obst- und Gemüseabteilung, die über die ganze Breite von einer hölzernen Fachwerkkonstruktion überspannt wird, die Kundschaft. Nicht nur die Holzkonstruktion, sondern auch die kräftige grüne Farbe, die weißen Fliesen und die von der Decke hängenden Pflanzen wecken Assoziationen zur Frische der Produkte.

Since 2011, architect Valentina Kinzel has been developing and realising retail concepts from the planning through to the turnkey handover. After a construction period of just seven months during regular operations, the Marktkauf in Gelsenkirchen that was reopened in March 2021 offers a completely reorganised shop floor of around 8,500 square metres. Upon entering the supermarket, customers are greeted by the generously dimensioned fruit and vegetable department, which is roofed in its entirety by a timber truss construction. Not only the wooden structure, but also the strong green colour, the white tiles and the plants hanging from the ceiling arouse associations with the freshness of the products.

Im Bereich der Frischetheke wurden die Blende und Wände ebenfalls mit der weiß glänzenden Fliese versehen. Hinter den Theken bilden Glasbausteine als Raumtrenner einen transluzenten Effekt: Die bis unter die Decke gestapelten Elemente werden von farbigen Leuchtstäben eingerahmt, deren Lichtakzente sich in der Decke spiegeln. Die angrenzende Molkereiabteilung bildet mit dunklen Überbauten und schwarzer Lamellenoptik einen Kontrast zu der hell gestalteten Frischetheke und durch die Betonung jeder Sortimentsgruppe mit Highlightregalen entsteht eine klare Raumgliederung. Die großen schwarzen Schriftzüge bilden einen gut ablesbaren grafischen Kontrast zu den hochglänzenden weißen Fliesen. Das Thema der jeweiligen Abteilung wird durch passende Grafiken an den Regalen und Wänden widergespiegelt.

The front panel of fresh produce counter and the walls are likewise covered with the shiny white tiles. Behind the counters, glass bricks serve as partitions with a translucent effect: The elements, which are piled up to the ceiling, are framed by coloured light sticks, creating a play of lights on the ceiling. The adjacent dairy department with its dark top structures and black slatted optic contrasts with the brightly designed fresh food counter. Thanks to the highlight shelves featuring each group of products, the space is clearly organised. The big black letters form an easy-to-read graphic contrast to the glossy white tiles. The theme of each department is reflected in matching graphics on the shelves and walls.

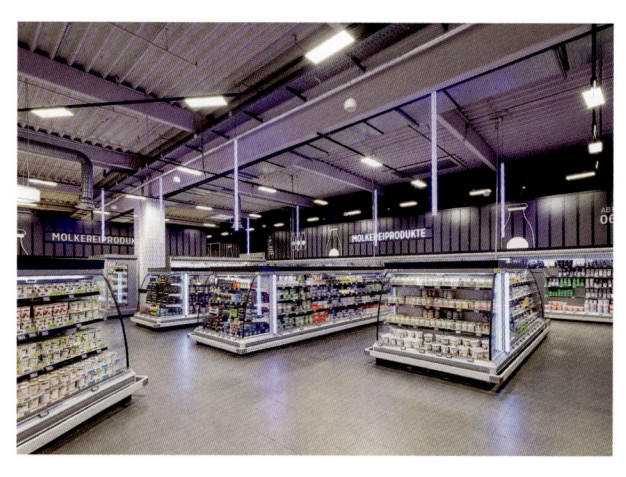

SPACES   MARKTKAUF GELSENKIRCHEN

Bei der Neugestaltung des Marktes mitten im Herzen der Metropolregion Rhein-Ruhr lag der Schwerpunkt für Kinzel Architecture auf der Verbesserung der Orientierung im Markt, was mit klaren Linien und prägnanter Grafik erfolgreich umgesetzt wurde und zum Erlebnisfaktor des Einkaufs maßgeblich beiträgt.

In their redesign of the market in the heart of the metropolitan Rhine-Ruhr region, the focus for Kinzel Architecture was on improving orientation in the market. This was achieved with clear lines and striking graphics, helping to enhance the shopping experience.

MONDENERO

LOCATION DUSSELDORF, GERMANY   **CLIENT** LEONARDO GROUP GMBH, DUSSELDORF
CONCEPT / DESIGN / GRAPHICS / LIGHTING / MEDIA HOLGER WEDDIGE, NEUSS
PHOTOGRAPHS PHILIPP KREMER, DUSSELDORF

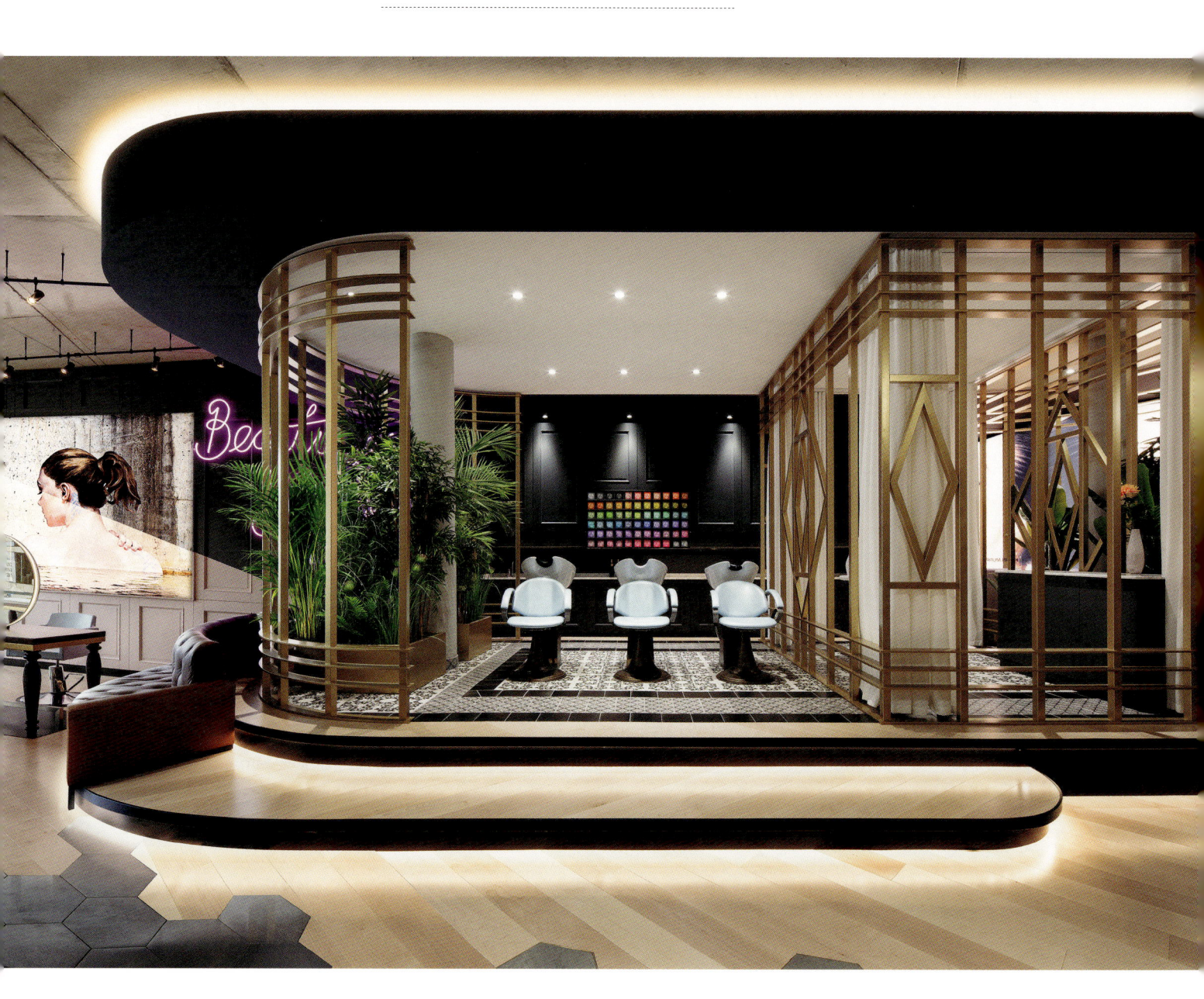

Am markanten KÖ-Bogen in Düsseldorf hat Beate Katzalis mit ihren Partnern ein hybrides Store-Konzept eröffnet, das neue Wege für den innerstädtischen Handel aufzeigt. Unter einem gemeinsamen Dach bilden hier Verkauf, Handel und Dienstleistung eine erlebnisreiche Adresse. Kooperationspartner des innovativen Mix sind ein Mobilfunkanbieter, der hier einen Store integriert hat, sowie ein Barbershop mit verschiedenen Beauty-Zonen im ersten Stock.

At the KÖ-Bogen complex in Dusseldorf, Beate Katzalis and her partners have opened a hybrid store concept that demonstrates a new approach to city-centre retailing. Selling, commerce and service under a shared roof make this an exciting place. The cooperation partners of the innovative mix are a mobile communications provider, which has integrated a store here, as well as a barber shop with various beauty zones on the first floor.

Herzstück des Mondenero ist ein elegantes Café mit raumgreifender Bar, in der sowohl Kaffee, Drinks, Patisserie und Snacks als auch Mode vom gleichnamigen Label angeboten werden. Unter der hohen Decke gruppieren sich, wie in einer komfortablen Hotellobby, klassische Ledercouches mit kleinen Tischen. Die Servicebereiche sind nicht räumlich abgetrennt, sondern frei stehend und offen in den Innenraum integriert, und das Erdgeschoss wird durch eine vertikale Skulptur im Treppenhaus mit dem ersten Stock verbunden. Reminiszenzen an die „Goldenen" 1920er-Jahre prägen den gesamten Innenraum und kommen auch beim Fahrstuhl zum Einsatz. Der Barbershop und das Beauty-Konzept der ersten Etage spielen indessen mit kontrastierenden Gestaltungselementen, die als typisch männlich oder typisch weiblich wahrgenommen werden. Die eher maskuline Atmosphäre mit rauem Beton, klaren Linien, Holz, Leder und Stahl wird punktuell von femininen Elementen in Gold und mit filigranen Mustern unterbrochen. Vieles ist in Schwarz gehalten, der CI-Farbe des Unternehmens, dessen Name aus einer Symbiose der französischen und italienischen Sprache hervorgeht.

At the heart of Mondenero is an elegant café with a large bar, in which coffee, drinks, patisserie and snacks as well as fashion from the label of the same name are on offer. Under a high ceiling, groups of classical leather couches and small tables give it the ambiance of a comfortable hotel lobby. The service areas are not separated off but stand alone, openly integrated in the interior, and the ground floor is connected to the first floor by a vertical sculpture in the stairwell. The whole interior, even the lift, is reminiscent of the golden twenties of the last century. The barber shop and beauty concept on the first floor play with contrasting design elements which are perceived as typically male or typically female. The generally masculine atmosphere with rough concrete, clear lines, wood, leather and steel is interrupted by a series of feminine elements in gold and with delicate patterns. Black, the CI colour of the company, dominates the space. It is also part of the name which is a symbiosis of French and Italian.

Entworfen und realisiert wurde das Mixed-Use-Konzept von der Agentur für Interior Design Heilight aus Neuss. Ihre langjährige Erfahrung in der Gestaltung von angesagten Clubs und Events im subkulturellen Umfeld übertragen Bayram Avucu, Siegbert Heil und Holger Weddige in benachbarte Branchen. Mit dieser Herangehensweise haben sie die Grenzen des klassischen Retails gesprengt und wurden dafür mit einem German Design Award für Interior Architecture ausgezeichnet.

The mixed usage concept was designed and realised by the interior design agency Heilight from Neuss. The agency's many years of experience with the design of trendy clubs and events in the subcultural environment are transferred by Bayram Avucu, Siegbert Heil and Holger Weddige into adjacent sectors. With this approach, they have broken down the borders of conventional retail and received a German Design Award for interior architecture for their pioneering work.

SPACES   MONDENERO

LÄCKERLI HUUS

LOCATION BASLE, SWITZERLAND **CLIENT** LÄCKERLI HUUS, FRENKENDORF **CONCEPT / DESIGN / GRAPHICS / LIGHTING** DIOMA AG, BERNE **PHOTOGRAPHS** TOBIAS SIEBRECHT PHOTOGRAPHY, ZURICH

Bei dem Schweizer Süß- und Backwarenhersteller Läckerli Huus, der unter anderem das Original Basler Läckerli herstellt, setzt man ganz auf die Präsentation der Ware. Gemäß der Unternehmensphilosophie werden keine digitalen Elemente in den Ladengeschäften eingesetzt. Dafür kommen Wandsegmente mit eigens entwickelter Tapete und Bilderrahmen sowie klassische Etagèren und Glasglocken für die Degustation zum Einsatz.

At the Swiss sweets and cookies manufacturer Läckerli Huus, which produces the original Basel Läckerli (the Swiss word for such treats!), the presentation of the goods is paramount. In line with the corporate philosophy, no digital elements are used in the shops. Instead, wall segments with specially designed wallpaper and picture frames are to be found along with classical etageres and glass domes for the tasting.

SPACES LÄCKERLI HUUS

2007 übernahm Miriam Baumann als ausgebildete Lebensmittelingenieurin und Unternehmerin das Läckerli Huus. Somit ist die Firma nach über hundert Jahren weiterhin ein unabhängiges Schweizer Traditionsunternehmen in Privatbesitz. Dennoch waren mit der Zeit alle bestehenden Ladengeschäfte in die Jahre gekommen. Der Wunsch des Kunden, den Altersdurchschnitt deutlich herabzusenken, war das erklärte Ziel der Neukonzeption. Die dioma ag wurde nach einem Pitch-Gewinn damit beauftragt, das gesamte Shopdesign auf modernsten Stand zu bringen.

In 2007, Miriam Baumann, a qualified food engineer and entrepreneur, took over Läckerli Huus. Thus, more than a century after its foundation, the company remains an independent Swiss heritage company in private ownership. Nonetheless, all the existing stores had become rather outdated. The desire of the client to significantly reduce the average customer age was the declared objective of the new concept. After winning the pitch, dioma ag was tasked with updating the whole shop design.

Geschäftsführer Marco Dionisio setzte von Beginn an auf eine möglichst helle und angenehme Atmosphäre, um die Schlüsselbegriffe Sympathie, Tradition, Handwerkskunst und Innovation widerzuspiegeln. Dafür mussten viele Neuerungen auf kleinstem Raum integriert werden. Dies umfasste den Kassenbereich, eine Live-Backen-Thekensituation, großzügige Wandsegmente mit Lagerschubladen für die breite Produktpalette sowie ein kleines Office im hinteren Bereich. Bei der Materialisierung wurde auf Langlebigkeit und Hygiene gesetzt. Dort wo keine Naturmaterialien eingesetzt werden konnten, haben die Gestalter darauf geachtet, die Natur nicht künstlich zu imitieren. Die Farbpalette wurde zurückhaltend zusammengestellt, um der typischen Produktpalette wie beispielsweise Rahmtäfeli, Gelée Russe, Pralinés und Truffes eine hochwertige Bühne zu bieten.

Right from the outset, general manager Marco Dionisio opted for a bright and pleasant atmosphere that reflects the key terms likeability, tradition, craftsmanship and innovation. To achieve this, many innovations had to be integrated into the smallest space. This included the check-out area, a live baking counter situation, generous wall segments with storage drawers for the wide product range as well as a small office to the rear of the shop. When choosing the materials, great store was set by durability and hygiene. Where natural materials could not be used, the designers made sure that nature was not artificially imitated. The muted colour palette was devised in order to provide a suitable stage for the typical product assortment such as cream fudge, Russian gelee, pralines and truffles.

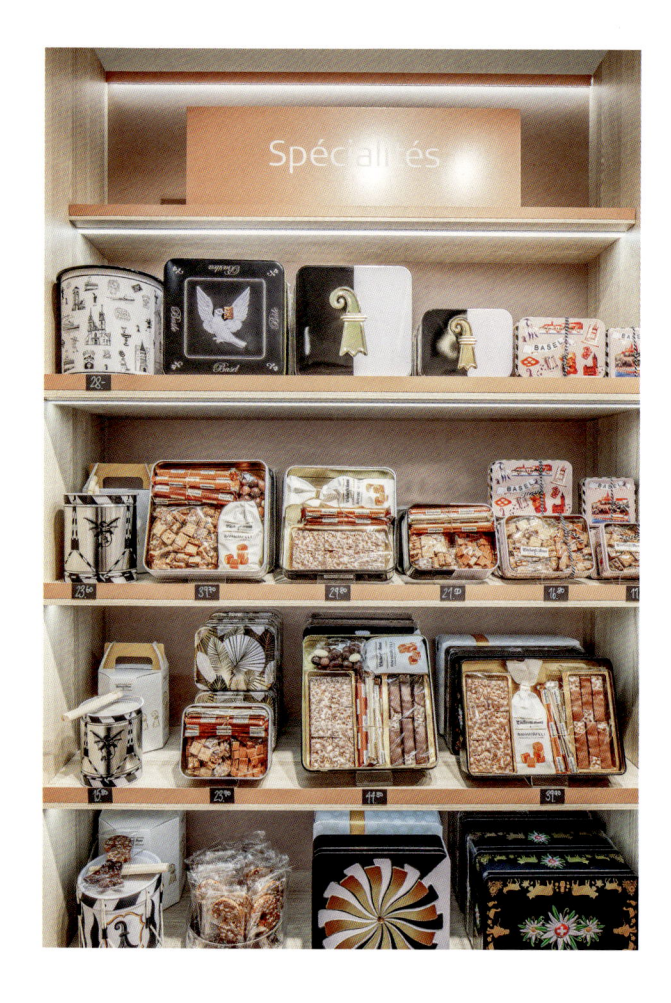

SPACES   LÄCKERLI HUUS

Durch das freundliche Entrée und die transparente Frontöffnung gewinnt die Kundschaft nun wieder an Nähe und wird zurück auf die Verkaufsfläche geholt. Der Duft des „Läckerli-Live-Backens" wird in die nahe Umgebung verströmt und weist auf die authentische Handwerkskunst im Läckerli Huus hin.

Thanks to the friendly entrance area and transparent opening at the front of the store, the desired proximity to the customers has been achieved, enticing them back to the shop floor. The fragrance of Läckerli live baking wafts out into the immediate vicinity, bearing testimony to the authentic craftsmanship to be found in Läckerli Huus.

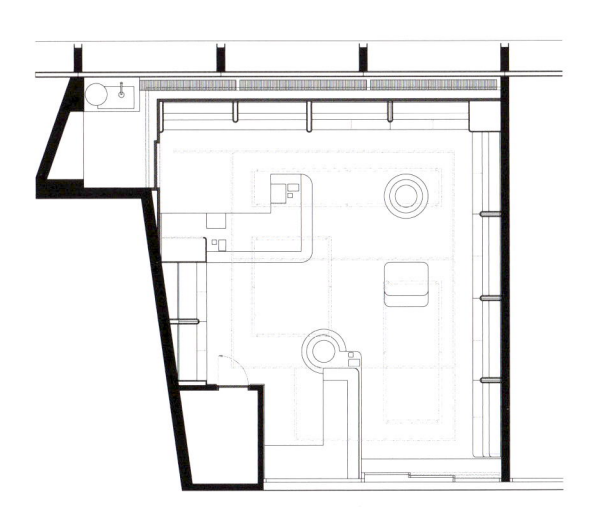

VERSACE PARIS FLAGSHIP

LOCATION PARIS, FRANCE **CLIENT** GIANNI VERSACE S.P.A., MILAN **CONCEPT / DESIGN** GWENAEL NICOLAS | CURIOSITY INC., TOKYO **LIGHTING** FLOS S.P.A., BOVEZZO (BRESCA); MLD LAB, MILAN **PHOTOGRAPHS** ALESSANDRA CHEMOLLO, VENEZIA

Der neue Pariser Versace Flagship Store befindet sich im Herzen der angesagtesten Luxus-Einkaufsmeile der Stadt. Die Rue Saint Honoré im ersten Arrondissement steht für ihre Kunstgalerien und die Modeboutiquen der Haute Couture.

Das in dieser Boutique umgesetzte neue Designkonzept des Tokioter Studios CURIOSITY inszeniert die Kunst der Mode in einem Raum, der als Leinwand für die Kollektionen fungiert und dabei sichtbar von der Versace-DNA geprägt ist. Über drei Stockwerke erstrecken sich die durch eine skulpturale Treppe aus Marmor und Messing verbundenen Ladenflächen. Grau-weißer Marmor und die unterschiedlich arrangierten geriffelten Wände erinnern an Casa Casuarina, auch bekannt als die Versace Mansion in Miami Beach, Florida, die im „Mediterranean Revival"-Stil erbaut ist.

The new Versace flagship store in Paris is located at the heart of the city's premier luxury shopping destination. Rue Saint Honoré in the first arrondissement is synonymous with art galleries and high fashion boutiques.

Designed following a new concept created by Tokyo-based Studio CURIOSITY, the boutique showcases the art of fashion in a space that becomes the canvas for the collections and an expression of Versaces's DNA. Spanning three floors, the levels of the store are connected by sculptural stairs crafted in marble and brass. A white and grey selection of marble and the fluted walls in different patterns are reminiscent of Casa Casuarina, built in Mediterranean revival style, also known as the Versace Mansion in Miami Beach, Florida.

SPACES   VERSACE PARIS FLAGSHIP

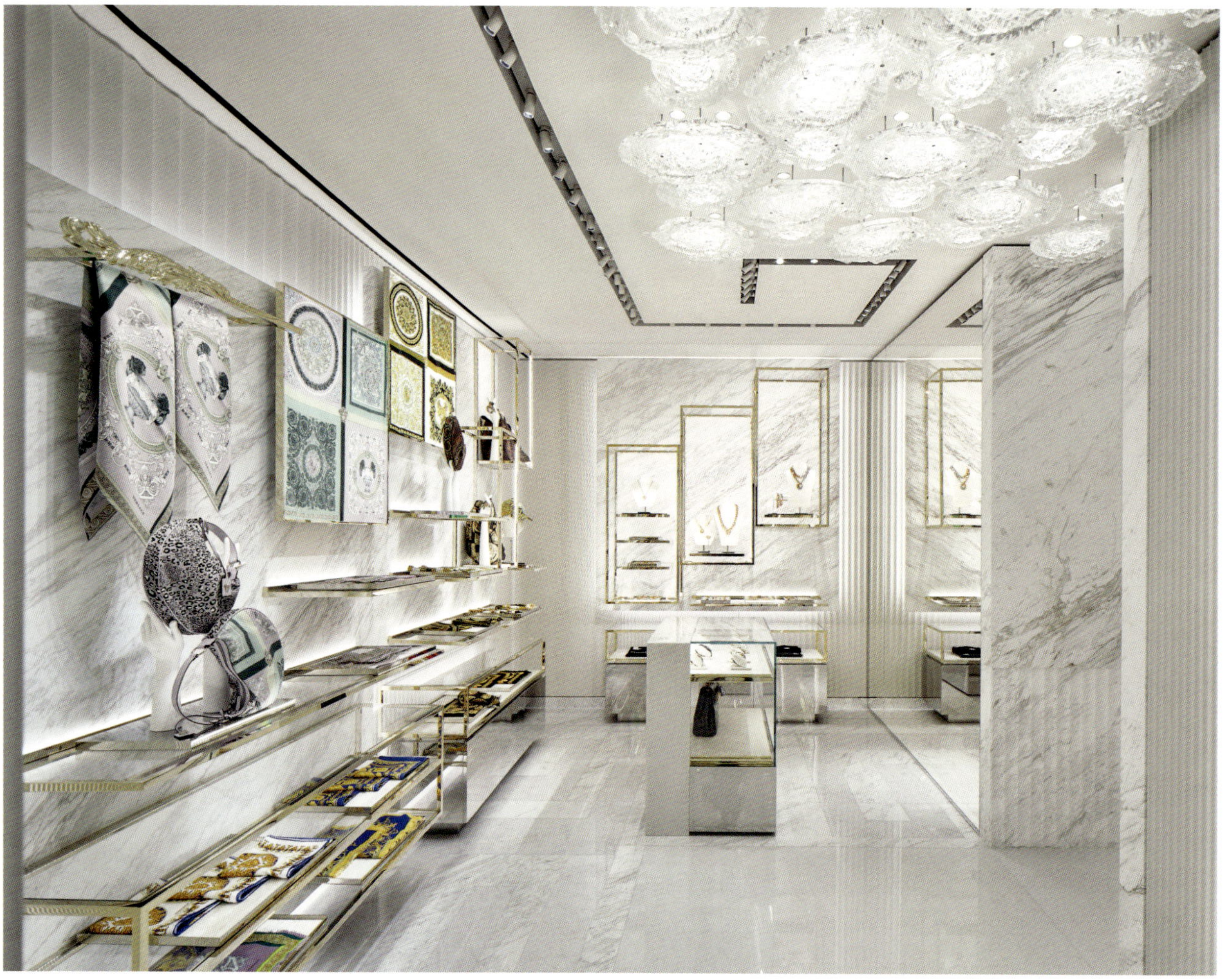

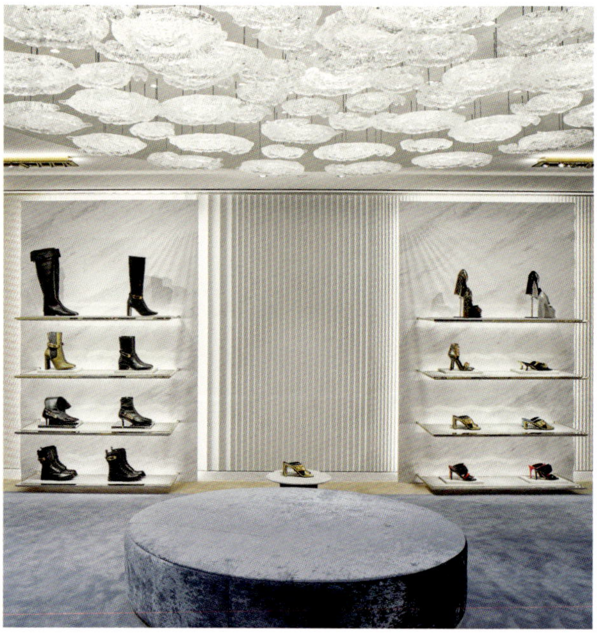

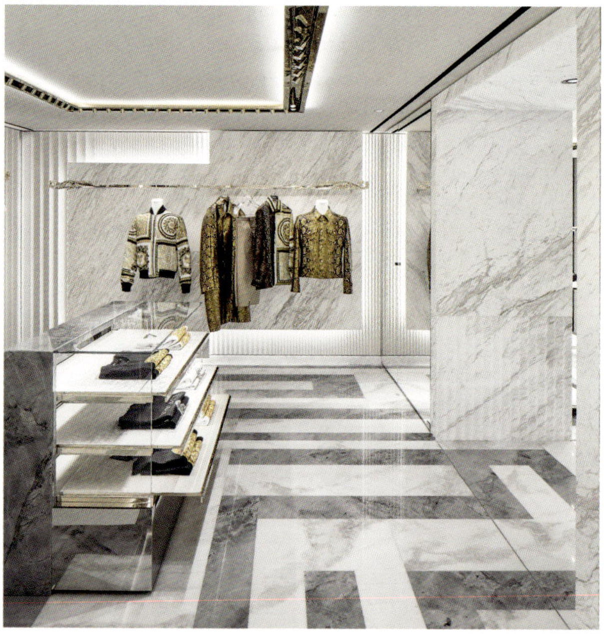

Die Kollektionen werden in sorgsam entlang des Raumes platzierten Tableaus präsentiert und lassen die Kunden die unterschiedlichen Aspekte der Marke entdecken. So stößt man beim Durchwandern der Arkaden auf eine Reihe von „Gemälden", die sich aus den verschiedenen Kollektionen zusammensetzen. Ein wahrer Blickfang ist die handgefertigte Decke aus Massivglas, die sich aus dem bekannten Barockmotiv Versaces herleitet und im Haus des berühmten Glasmachers Vistosi entstand. Der durch die Reflexionen und Lichtbrechungen im Glas hervorgerufene Effekt hat etwas Magisches und erzeugt ein reizvolles Spiel mit modernen Kunstwerken, die für den Store gestiftet wurden und das bekannte Logo der Marke, den Medusenkopf, interpretieren. Das Designkonzept findet im Dialog zwischen klassischen Elementen und abstrakter moderner Kunst einen gelungenen Abschluss.

The collections are displayed in a series of tableaux mindfully placed around the space, sequencing discovery of the different aspects of the brand. As the customers walk through the arcade, they will encounter a series of "paintings" created by the different collections. The strong feature of the space is a crafted glass ceiling elaborated from Versace's famous Baroque motif and crafted in solid glass by master glass maker Vistosi. The effect created by the reflections and refractions of the glass is quite magical and interacts beautifully with modern art pieces commissioned for the store that interpret the iconic logo, the medusa head. The dialogue between classic elements and modern abstract art rounds off the design concept.

Seit 1997 steht die in Mailand gegründete Gianni Versace S.r.l unter der künstlerischen Leitung von Donatella Versace. Die Gruppe hat ihr „Erbe" neu definiert und präsentiert sich heute in den weltweiten Fashion-Metropolen einem globalen Publikum. „Es ist ein solch erhebender Moment, in Paris, dem Herzen Europas und der Fashion-Metropole schlechthin, ein Flagship zu eröffnen. Wir sind für unsere zweite Boutique in der Stadt der Liebe nach langer Zeit in die Rue Saint Honoré zurückgekehrt", so Donatella Versace in einem Statement anlässlich der Eröffnung des neuen Flagships im Dezember 2020.

Gianni Versace S.r.l that was founded in Milan has been under the creative direction of Donatella Versace since 1997. In this time, the group has redefined its "legacy" and today presents itself in the fashion metropoles of the worlds to a global audience. "It's such an exciting moment to open a new flagship in Paris, the heart of Europe and the capital of fashion. We have returned to Rue Saint Honoré after a long time, opening a second boutique in the city of love," creative director Donatella Versace said in a statement commemorating the opening of the new flagship store in December 2020.

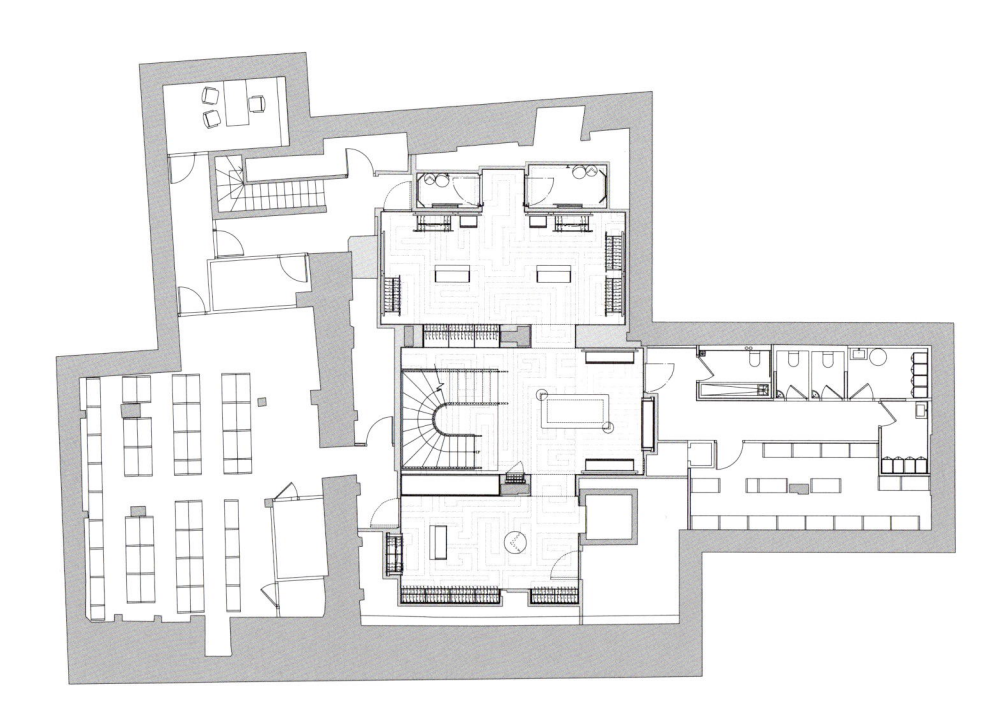

SPACES   VERSACE PARIS FLAGSHIP

GLAMBOU SHOP CONCEPT

LOCATION ALSTERHAUS HAMBURG / KADEWE BERLIN, GERMANY **CLIENT** GLAMBOU GMBH, BERLIN
CONCEPT / DESIGN DFROST RETAIL IDENTITY, STUTTGART **PHOTOGRAPHS** ULRICH SCHAARSCHMIDT FOR DFROST RETAIL IDENTITY, STUTTGART

Für die Expansion im gesamten D/A/CH-Raum suchte das junge Schmuckunternehmen Glambou ein modulares Storekonzept, um auf unterschiedliche räumliche Bedingungen effizient und unkompliziert reagieren zu können. Die Aufgabe der Stuttgarter Retail-Spezialisten DFROST war es, das bestehende Konzept weiterzuentwickeln, um die Kommunikation an allen Standorten zu vereinheitlichen.

For the expansion throughout the German-speaking countries, the young company for costume jewellery Glambou was looking for a modular store concept in order to be able to react efficiently and easily to various spatial conditions. The Stuttgart-based retail specialists DFROST were tasked with refining the existing concept in order to standardise the communication at all locations.

SPACES   GLAMBOU SHOP CONCEPT

Dabei galt es, den Wiedererkennungswert gegenüber den Kundinnen stärker herauszuarbeiten und sicherzustellen, dass die Kommunikation auf unterschiedlichen Ebenen aufeinander abgestimmt ist. Für die optimale Präsentation der Schmuckstücke lieferte DFROST auch die entsprechenden Visual Merchandising Tools.

Glambou arbeitet aus Überzeugung nicht nur mit großen Namen, sondern auch mit kleinen Ateliers und Werkstätten zusammen. Durch Partnerschaften mit Luxus-Kaufhäusern bietet es aufstrebenden Designer:innen und kleinen Familienunternehmen den Zugang zu erstklassigen Verkaufsflächen. Neben Shop-in-Shop-Konzepten und Pop-up-Stores ist das Unternehmen auch in eigenen Stores und im Onlineshop präsent.

Part of the brief was to reinforce the recognition value among the customers and to ensure that communication was harmonised across all levels. DFROST also provided the visual merchandising tools necessary for the optimum presentation of the pieces of jewellery.

For Glambou, it is a matter of conviction that they collaborate not only with the big names, but also with small studios and workshops. Thanks to partnerships with luxury department stores, the company thus offers budding designers and small family-run business access to premium sales space. In addition to shop-in-shop concepts and pop-up stores, the company also has its own stores and an online shop.

Die Gestalter entwickelten ein ikonisches Setup für den POS, das die Identität der Marke analog zu den wertvollen Produkten vermittelt. In ihm ermöglichen modulare Elemente ein unkompliziertes Reagieren auf unterschiedliche räumliche Gegebenheiten und sorgen für ein klares Brand Statement. Der Fokus liegt hierbei auf einer Ausgewogenheit zwischen der femininen Formensprache und den damit kombinierten modernen geometrischen Elementen. Der klassische Rundbogen bildet als Grundform und wiederkehrendes Element die Basis und den Rahmen für Kommunikation und Produktpräsentation. Das homogene Erscheinungsbild wird mit Add-ons aufgelockert und den jeweiligen Kampagnen angepasst. Im Ergebnis wird die Brand Glambou bis ins Detail erkennbar und kann somit auch räumlich als durchgängige und ikonische Marke wahrgenommen werden.

With this in mind, the designers developed an iconic set-up for the POS which conveys the identity of the brand by analogy to the valuable products. Its modular elements allow an uncomplicated response to the various spatial conditions and ensure a clear brand statement. The focus lies on a balance between feminine shapes in combination with modern geometrical elements. As the basic shape and recurring element the classical rounded arch creates the basis and framework for communication and product presentation. The homogenous appearance is interspersed with add-ons and can be adjusted for each campaign. In effect, the Glambou brand becomes recognisable down to the smallest detail and can thus be perceived as a well thought-through and iconic brand which is also manifested in the physical appearance.

SPACES   GLAMBOU SHOP CONCEPT

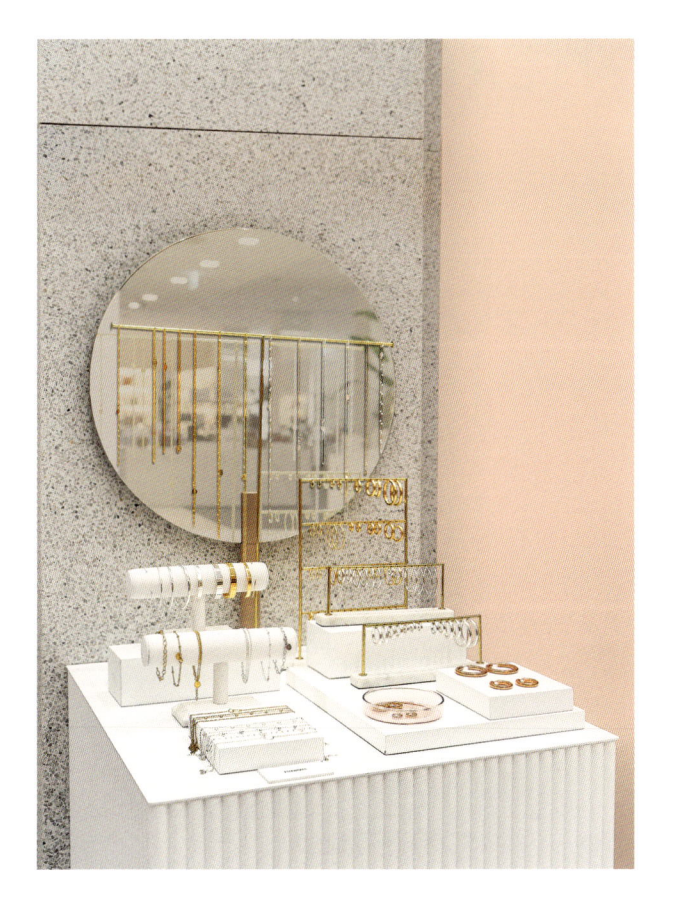

Als Markenbegleiter gestaltet DFROST für internationale Kunden den Handel der Zukunft entlang der gesamten Customer Journey. Das kuratierte Sortiment und die ikonische Formensprache des neuen Storekonzepts nimmt die Kundinnen von Glambou mit auf eine Reise des Entdeckens und Erlebens.

As brand companion, DFROST designs the future of retailing for international customers along the whole customer journey. The curated assortment and iconic spatial idiom of the new store concept takes Glambou's customers on a journey of discovery and experience.

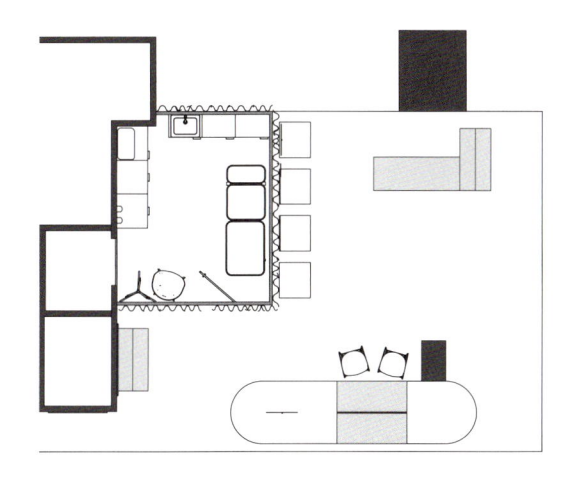

CIFI SALES CENTER WUXI

LOCATION WUXI, CHINA   **CLIENT** CIFI HOLDINGS GROUP CO. LTD., SHANGHAI   **CONCEPT / DESIGN** IPPOLITO FLEITZ GROUP – IDENTITY ARCHITECTS, STUTTGART   **PHOTOGRAPHS** EIICHI KANO, SHANGHAI

Die rasant wachsenden Metropolen in China kämpfen immer stärker mit der Verknappung von naturnahen Flächen als Lebensraum und natürlichen Ressourcen wie sauberer Luft und klarem Wasser. Als Reaktion darauf sucht die Generation der Millennials verstärkt nach Wohnstandorten, die dem Wunsch nach einem individuell gestalteten Leben im Einklang mit der Natur entgegenkommen.

The fast-growing cities in China are increasingly struggling with a shortage of space near to nature as habitat and of natural resources like clean air and water. In response to this trend, the millennial generation is increasingly seeking residential locations which take them a step closer to the desire to shape their lives individually in harmony with nature.

SPACES CIFI SALES CENTER WUXI

Der Real Estate Developer CIFI hat diese Entwicklung erkannt und spricht die kaufkräftige Klientel direkt an den zukünftigen Standorten und auf den Baustellen neuer Immobilienprojekte an. Die eigenen Sales Center sollen den Markenclaim „Building for a better life" baulich veranschaulichen. Dementsprechend sind der Bezug zur Natur, großzügige Dimensionen und Qualität in Material und Ausführung die Alleinstellungsmerkmale. Die international tätige Ippolito Fleitz Group konnte bereits mehrere Sales Center in China realisieren. Die Bauprojekte zeichnen sich durch ihre außergewöhnliche Lage und die Einbeziehung regionaler Besonderheiten aus.

Real estate developer CIFI has recognised this development and addresses the affluent clientele directly at the future locations and on the building sites of new real estate projects. Their own sales centres are a built manifestation of the brand claim "Building for a better life". The unique selling points are the proximity to nature, generous dimensions and the quality of the materials and execution. In the course of its international operations, Ippolito Fleitz Group has realised a number of these Sales Centers in China. The construction projects are characterised by their unusual location and the inclusion of special regional features.

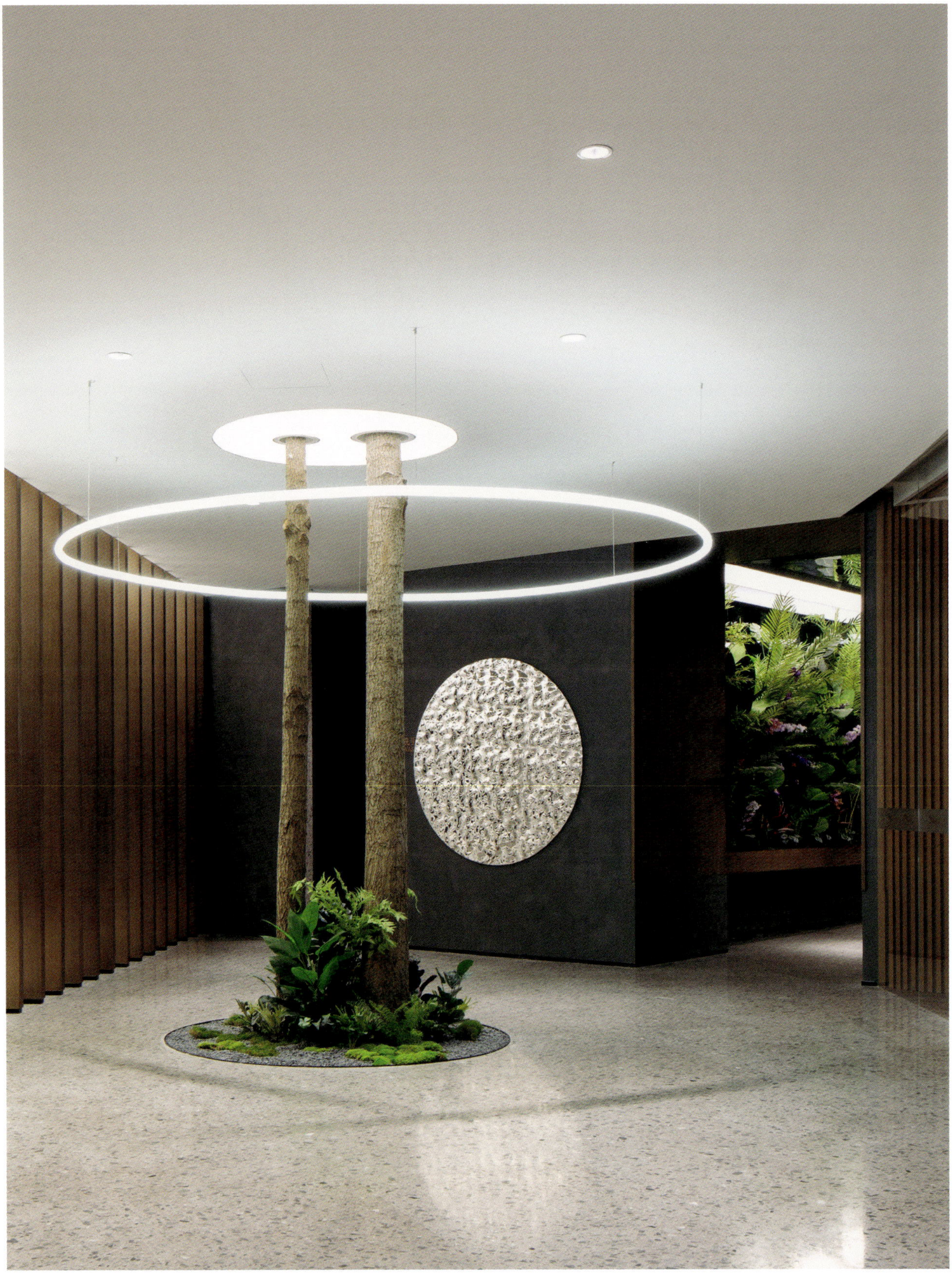

SPACES   CIFI SALES CENTER WUXI

Das jüngste Projekt in Wuxi am Taihu-See greift den lokalen Architekturtypus der „Jiangnan Mansion" auf. Um einen zentralen Hof mit klassischen Wasserelementen sind alle Räume nach einer klaren Ordnung angelegt, die sich in der Customer Journey wiederfindet. Die erste Station ist ein mit warmen Materialien ausgestatteter Kinoraum, in dem die Markenwelt von CIFI filmisch präsentiert wird. Gleich daneben befindet sich ein eigens für die Kinder der zukünftigen Eigentümer gestalteter Raum. Auf den medialen Einstieg folgt als nächstes Bild eine offene Küchenzeile, die mit einem großzügigen Tisch die soziale Bedeutung des gemeinsamen Kochens und Essens hervorhebt.

The most recent project in Wuxi on Lake Taihu picks up the local architecture of the "Jiangnan Mansion". In this style of building all the rooms are arranged in a specific way around the central courtyard with classical water features. The customer journey follows this arrangement. The first station is a cosily furnished projection room in which the brand world of CIFI is presented in a film. Next to that is a room designed especially for the children of future owners. The media-based introduction is followed by an open kitchen unit with a large table to underline the social importance of cooking and eating together.

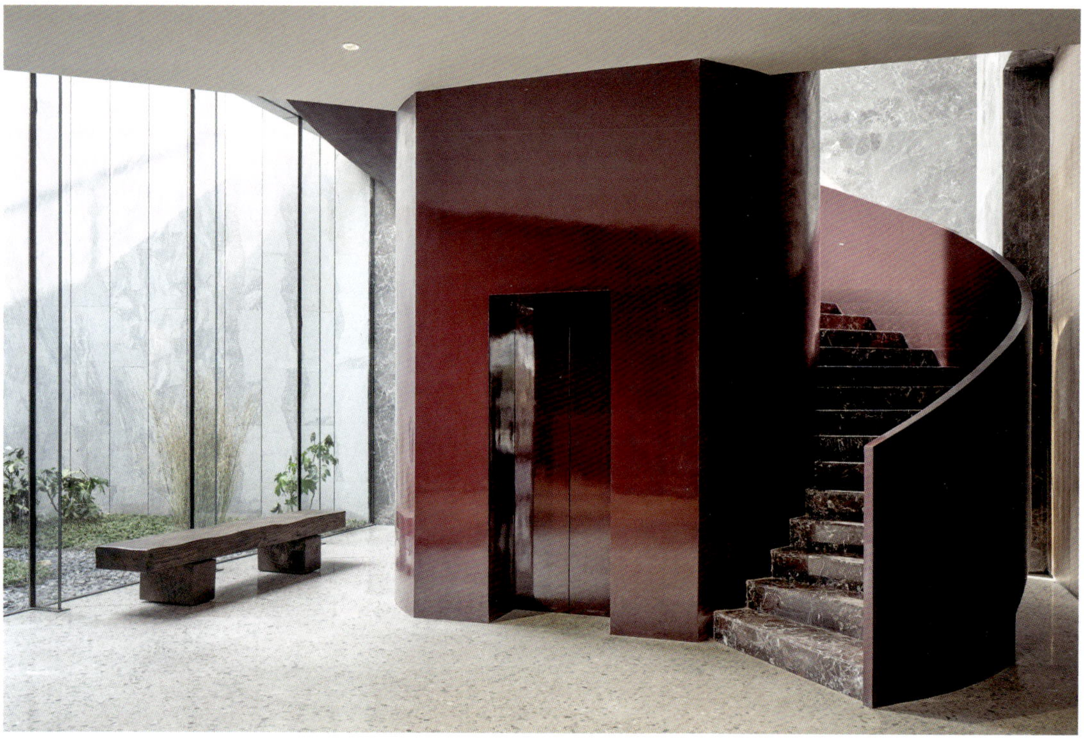

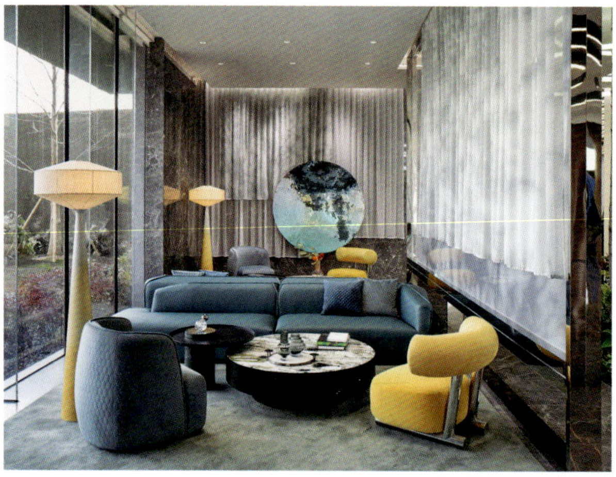

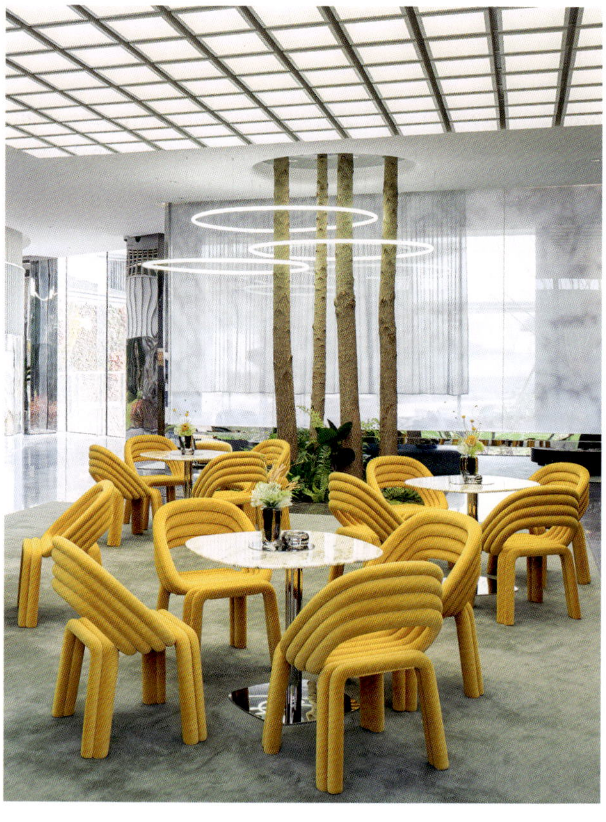

SPACES   CIFI SALES CENTER WUXI

Eine Bibliothek mit Sitzgelegenheiten bietet einen gerahmten Blick in den grünen Hof. Vorbei an einem Yogaraum werden die Gäste über eine skulpturale Wendeltreppe ins Obergeschoss mit einem Modell der zukünftigen Wohnbebauung geführt.

Auch an die Nachnutzung des Sales Center wurde gedacht: Es soll den zukünftigen Anwohnern als gemeinschaftliches Clubhaus dienen.

A library with seating offers a framed view of the green courtyard. Passing a yoga room, guests are guided via a sculptural spiral staircase to the upper floor which houses a model of the future residential development project.

The designers have also thought about the usage of the Sales Center after the project is completed: it is to be repurposed as a club house for the future residents.

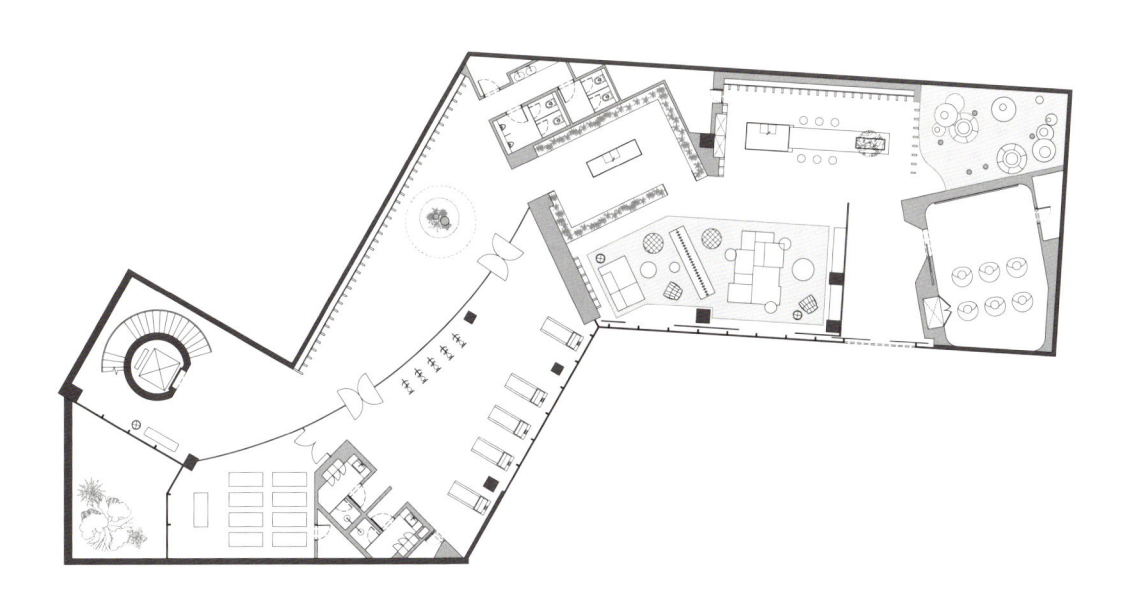

BREUNINGER SACHSENHEIM CONTENT PRODUCTION

LOCATION SACHSENHEIM, GERMANY **CLIENT** E. BREUNINGER GMBH & CO., STUTTGART **CONCEPT / DESIGN** STUDIO ALEXANDER FEHRE, STUTTGART **PHOTOGRAPHS** PHILIP KOTTLORZ FOTOGRAFIE, STUTTGART

Hybride Handelsformen führen nicht nur zu einer rasanten Veränderung des Retail Design vor Ort, sondern haben auch einen enormen Einfluss auf die damit verbundenen Arbeitswelten. Der gesamte Bereich „Hinter den Kulissen", vom Marketing über die Warenlogistik bis hin zur Foto- und Videoproduktion für den Onlinehandel, nimmt immer mehr Raum ein.

Hybrid trading forms have not only dramatically changed retail design on location, they have also had a huge impact on the associated working worlds. The whole "behind the scenes" area from marketing via fulfilment through to photo and video production for online trade is taking up an increasing amount of space.

SPACES   BREUNINGER SACHSENHEIM CONTENT PRODUCTION

Im beschaulichen Ort Sachsenheim befindet sich das Warendienstleistungszentrum der E. Breuninger GmbH & Co. mit einer Fläche von rund 80.000 Quadratmetern. Das Studio Alexander Fehre aus Stuttgart wurde mit der Gestaltung einer neuen Arbeitswelt für die Abteilung Content Production betraut. Als Kontrast zum peripheren Standort galt es, einen kreativen Raum für die junge Belegschaft zu gestalten, der die Identifikation fördert und Wertschätzung des Unternehmens ausdrückt. Analog zum Bild einer dynamischen Fashion Show gestaltete Alexander Fehre ein vom Zirkus inspiriertes Spielfeld. Die alltägliche Arbeitsdynamik vom Wareneingang der Modestücke über die Aufbereitung und das Shooting bis hin zum Auftritt im Onlineshop erinnert an eine Zirkusaufführung. Aspekte dieses Motivs werden aufgegriffen und in verschiedene Gestaltungselemente übersetzt.

The small town of Sachsenheim is home to the goods services centre of E. Breuninger GmbH & Co. with a footprint of around 80,000 square metres. Studio Alexander Fehre from Stuttgart was entrusted with the design of a new working world for the content production department. In stark contrast to the tranquil location on the periphery, they were tasked with designing a creative space for the young workforce which fosters identification with the company and expresses its appreciation. By analogy to the image of a dynamic fashion show, Alexander Fehre designed a playing field inspired by the circus. The everyday workflow from the receipt of the fashion items via preparation of the goods and the shoot itself through to the appearance in the online shop is reminiscent of a circus show. Some aspects of this motif are picked up and translated into various design elements.

Schon beim Betreten der Abteilung Content Production zieht eine strahlenförmig auseinanderstrebende Bodengrafik den Betrachtenden dynamisch in den Raum. Vorbei an einer geschwungenen Sitztreppe, umrahmt von einer wellenförmigen Wand, wird der Blick in Richtung Manege gelenkt, die das Zentrum der Arbeitswelt bildet. Die Besprechungsecke hinter Gitterelementen sowie ein samtbezogenes Sofa bilden einen Rückzugsort für den kreativen Ideenaustausch.

Upon entering the content production department, a radiating floor graphic already draws the visitor into the space. Passing curved seating steps, framed by a wave-like wall, the eye is drawn to the circus ring which forms the centre of the working world. The consultation corner behind lattice elements as well as a velvet-upholstered sofa provide a retreat for the creative exchange of ideas.

SPACES   BREUNINGER SACHSENHEIM CONTENT PRODUCTION   125

Während eigentlich die Fotoboxen für die Shootings vorgesehen sind, lässt sich auch die gesamte Arbeitswelt in Fotoproduktionen einbinden. Nicht zuletzt wegen der kulissenhaften Materialien wie etwa Kunststoff- und Spiegelfolien, Wellprofilen, Maschendraht und Estrichfarbe. Die humorvolle Hommage an den „Modezirkus" schafft Raum für spontane Kreativität und funktionale Professionalität – tatsächlich wie bei einer Fashion Show, die niemals endet.

While there are designated photo boxes for the photo shoots, the whole working world can be incorporated into the photo productions. This is facilitated not least by the availability of suitable backdrop materials such as plastic and mirrored films, corrugated sheets, wire mesh and coloured floor finish. The tongue-in-cheek homage to the "fashion circus" creates space for spontaneous creativity and functional professionalism – like at a never-ending fashion show.

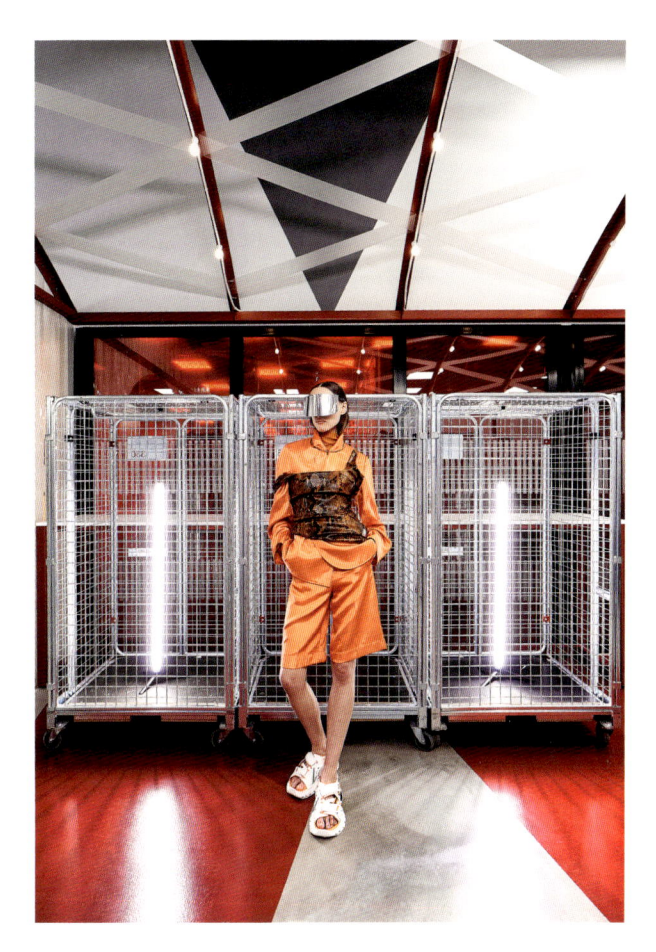

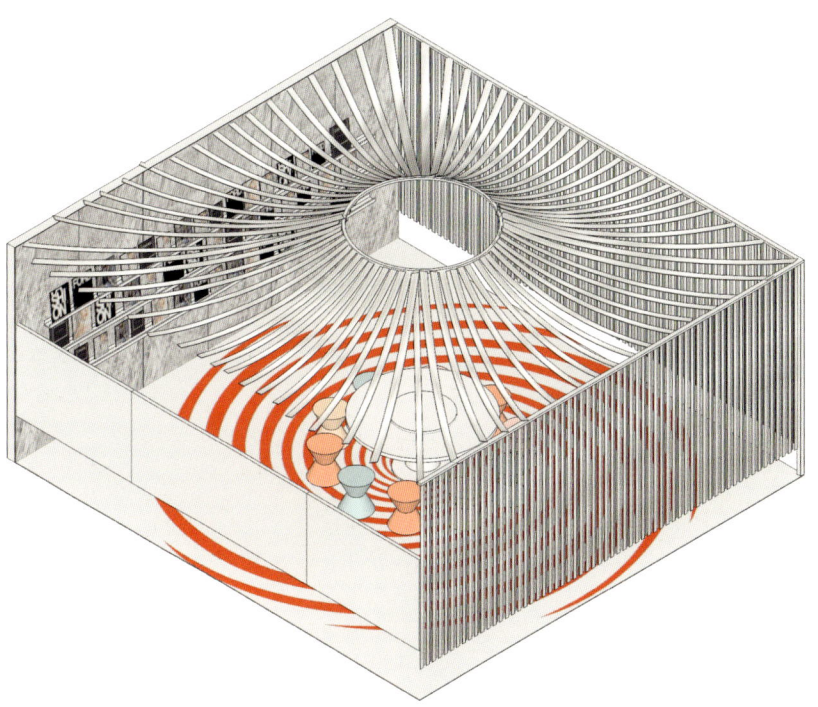

HUNGRY EYES

LOCATION STUTTGART, GERMANY **CLIENT** HUNGRY EYES THOMAS HOMMERBERG, STUTTGART **CONCEPT / DESIGN** FLORIAN SIEGEL & SEVERIN KÜPPERS, STUTTGART **GRAPHICS** JESSICA BENDER, STUTTGART (GRAPHIC & UX DESIGN) **LIGHTING** CANDELA GMBH, STUTTGART **OTHERS** WERK33 GMBH & CO. KG, VAIHINGEN; JAN SCHÄFER, STUTTGART (SHOPFITTING) **PHOTOGRAPHS** JULIA OCHS, STUTTGART; ERICH SPAHN, REGENSBURG

Der passende Leitsatz „nice to see you" grüßt in gut lesbaren Lettern auf der großzügigen Schaufensterscheibe die neue urbane Nachbarschaft in Stuttgart-West. Hier stimmen Infrastruktur und Nachbarschaft, und hier fühlt sich der staatlich geprüfte Augenoptikermeister Thomas Hommerberg wohl. Deswegen war es keine Frage, warum er seinen Optik-Store HUNGRY EYES im bevorzugten Stuttgarter Quartier eröffnet hat.

The fitting slogan "nice to see you" in easily legible letters on the generously dimensioned shop window pane greets its new urban neighbourhood in Stuttgart-West. Infrastructure and neighbourhood are a great fit for state-examined ophthalmic optician Thomas Hommerberg. It was therefore an easy decision for him to open his HUNGRY EYES opticians in the popular Stuttgart district.

SPACES   HUNGRY EYES

Eine moderne Präsentationsfläche in einem urbanen Verkaufsraum erlebbar zu machen, war die Aufgabe von Architekt Severin Küppers und Innenarchitekt Florian Siegel. Dafür entwickelten sie eine klare Sprache, die sich wie selbstverständlich in das historische Ladengeschäft aus der Jahrhundertwende mit charmanten Elementen aus den 1950er-Jahren einfügt. Entstanden ist eine räumliche Schnittstelle zwischen Innen und Außen, die der Kundschaft die Hemmschwelle nimmt und zum Eintreten einlädt.

The brief for architect Severin Küppers and interior architect Florian Siegel was to create the experience of a modern presentation space in an urban sales room. With this in mind, they developed a clear language which blended seamlessly into the historical shop from the turn of the 20th century with charming elements from the 1950s. The result is a spatial interface between inside and outside which helps potential customers to overcome their inhibitions and invites them to enter.

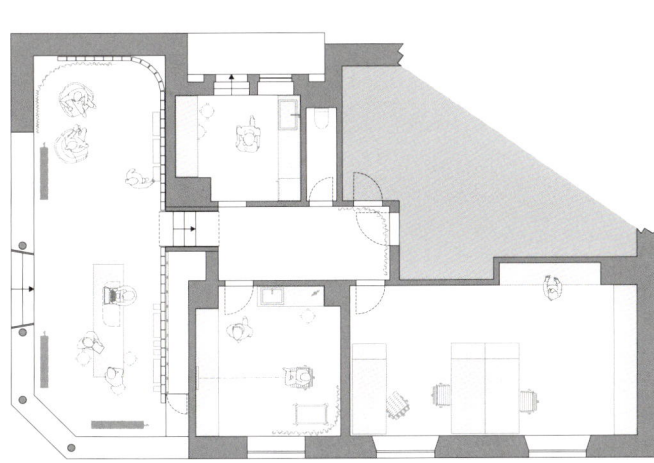

Bewusst wurden alle Schaufensterrückwände des vorigen Geschäfts entfernt, um die gesamte Ladenfläche nach außen hin sichtbar zu machen. Der Blick kann nun ungehindert auf das markante Rückgrat des Fachgeschäfts fallen. Der Kalksandstein, der eigentlich für den Schallschutz entwickelt wurde, ist hier zur flexiblen Steckwand umfunktioniert worden. Zwei Rundrohre gepaart mit einem einfachen Aluminiumtableau bilden eine wandelbare Produktpräsentationsfläche für die Brillen. Ein Tor aus Aluminium, das die gemauerte Wand unterbricht, führt in die dahinterliegende Refraktion mit dem Werkstattbereich. Hier angekommen, wird der Kunde vom unerwarteten Charme einer Stuttgarter Altbauwohnung empfangen. Dezenter Stuck und klassisches Fischgrätparkett stehen im Kontrast zu industriellen Schwerlastregalen. Partiell blieben die originalen Wand- und Deckenflächen bewusst unbehandelt, um den wohnlichen und privaten Charakter des Interieurs zu erhalten.

Im HUNGRY EYES sucht das Retail Design den Dialog mit dem lebendigen Quartier und tritt in ein harmonisches Wechselspiel zwischen urbanem Raum und Altbaucharme. Ein Ort, an dem es leichtfallen wird, den Hunger nach neuen Brillen im Stuttgarter Westen zu stillen.

SPACES   HUNGRY EYES

It was decided to remove all the walls behind the shop window from the previous shop in order to make the interior fully visible from the outside, allowing an unimpeded view of the striking backbone of the specialist store. The sand-lime brick that was initially developed for sound insulation has been repurposed into a flexible presentation wall. Two round tubes coupled with a simple aluminium tableau form a versatile product presentation surface for the spectacles. An aluminium-clad gateway leading through the brick wall forms the entrance to the examination unit for refraction with an integrated workshop. Here the customer is greeted by the unexpected charm of an old Stuttgart apartment. Delicate stucco and classic herringbone parquetry contrast starkly with the heavy-duty industrial shelving. Some of the original wall and ceiling surfaces have been left deliberately untreated in order to conserve the residential and private character of the interior.

In HUNGRY EYES, retail design seeks to enter into dialogue with a lively city district, skilfully juxtaposing urban space with the charm of the old building. A place in which it will certainly not be difficult to still the hunger for new glasses in Stuttgart-West.

BRIDGE

LOCATION ZURICH, SWITZERLAND **CLIENT** GENOSSENSCHAFT MIGROS ZÜRICH, ZURICH
CONCEPT / DESIGN / GRAPHICS / REALISATION INTERSTORE | SCHWEITZER, NATURNS
PHOTOGRAPHS TIM LOVE WEBER, BERNE

Bereits zur Gründung der Migros AG setzte Gottlieb Duttweiler das Motiv einer Brücke auf seinen ersten Produkten, Prospekten und Lieferfahrzeugen ein. Das Motiv wurde zu mehr als einem Firmenlogo, es gilt als Wahrzeichen einer Idee, zu der sich der Schweizer Verbund von Genossenschaften bis heute bekennt.

When Migros AG was founded, Gottlieb Duttweiler already chose the motif of a bridge for his first products, catalogues and delivery vehicles. The motif has become more than a company logo; it is considered to be the symbol of the idea to which the Swiss association of cooperatives is committed to this day.

SPACES BRIDGE

Mit dem Projekt Bridge konnte Interstore | Schweitzer ein neues Marktkonzept mit einem Mix aus Gastronomie und Retail realisieren. Als Innovationsplattform soll der Markt dazu dienen, neue Ideen zu testen und Akzente für den Einzelhandel der Zukunft zu setzen. Auf einer Gesamtfläche von rund 2.000 Quadratmetern, verteilt auf zwei Ebenen, bietet der Markt einen sprichwörtlichen „Brückenschlag" zwischen Frischemarkt, kreativer Gastronomie mit Produkten von lokalen Partnern und eigenen Events. Unter dem Motto „Meet Food, Meet Market, Meet People" soll der Markt zu einem neuen Treffpunkt im Herzen der Schweizer Metropole Zürich werden.

With the Bridge project, Interstore | Schweitzer has realised a new market concept with a mix of gastronomy and retail. As innovation platform, the market offers space for new ideas to be tested and to set trends for the retail business of the future. On a total area of around 2,000 square metres spread over two levels, the market provides the proverbial "bridge" between fresh produce, creative gastronomy with products from local partners and its own events. Under the motto "Meet Food, Meet Market, Meet People", the market is to become a new meeting point at the heart of the Swiss metropolis Zurich.

Außer den fest installierten Kochstationen sind alle Einrichtungselemente zu 100 Prozent flexibel und verschiebbar. Das Foodlab kann für private Veranstaltungen oder Firmenevents gebucht werden, und für die Kund:innen werden dort zudem Kochkurse angeboten. Die hohe Flexibilität macht es möglich, auf lokale, situationsbedingte und saisonale Anforderungen zu reagieren. So kann das Store-Layout je nach Anforderung schnell und kostengünstig umgebaut werden. Die Dynamik des Layouts eignet sich besonders zur Bespielung der Fläche mit Pop-ups und saisonalen Events. Auch können einzelne Abteilungen kurzfristig vergrößert oder auch verkleinert und von Bedienung auf Selbstbedienung umgestellt werden. Ein Highlight ist die über den Verkaufsflächen schwebende Brücke im Zentrum des Marktes. Sie verbindet die unterschiedlichen Ebenen und bietet einen beeindruckenden Blickfang.

With the exception of the permanently installed cooking stations, all the furnishings are completely flexible and movable. The Foodlab can be booked for private functions and company events, and cooking courses are also offered for customers. The high degree of flexibility makes it possible to respond to local, situational and seasonal requirements. The store layout can thus be changed quickly and cost-effectively to meet requirements. The dynamic layout lends itself particularly well to the staging of pop-ups and seasonal events. Individual departments can also be enlarged or downsized at short notice and converted from service to self-service. A highlight is the bridge suspended over the shopfloor at the centre of the market. A real eye-catcher, it connects the different levels.

SPACES BRIDGE

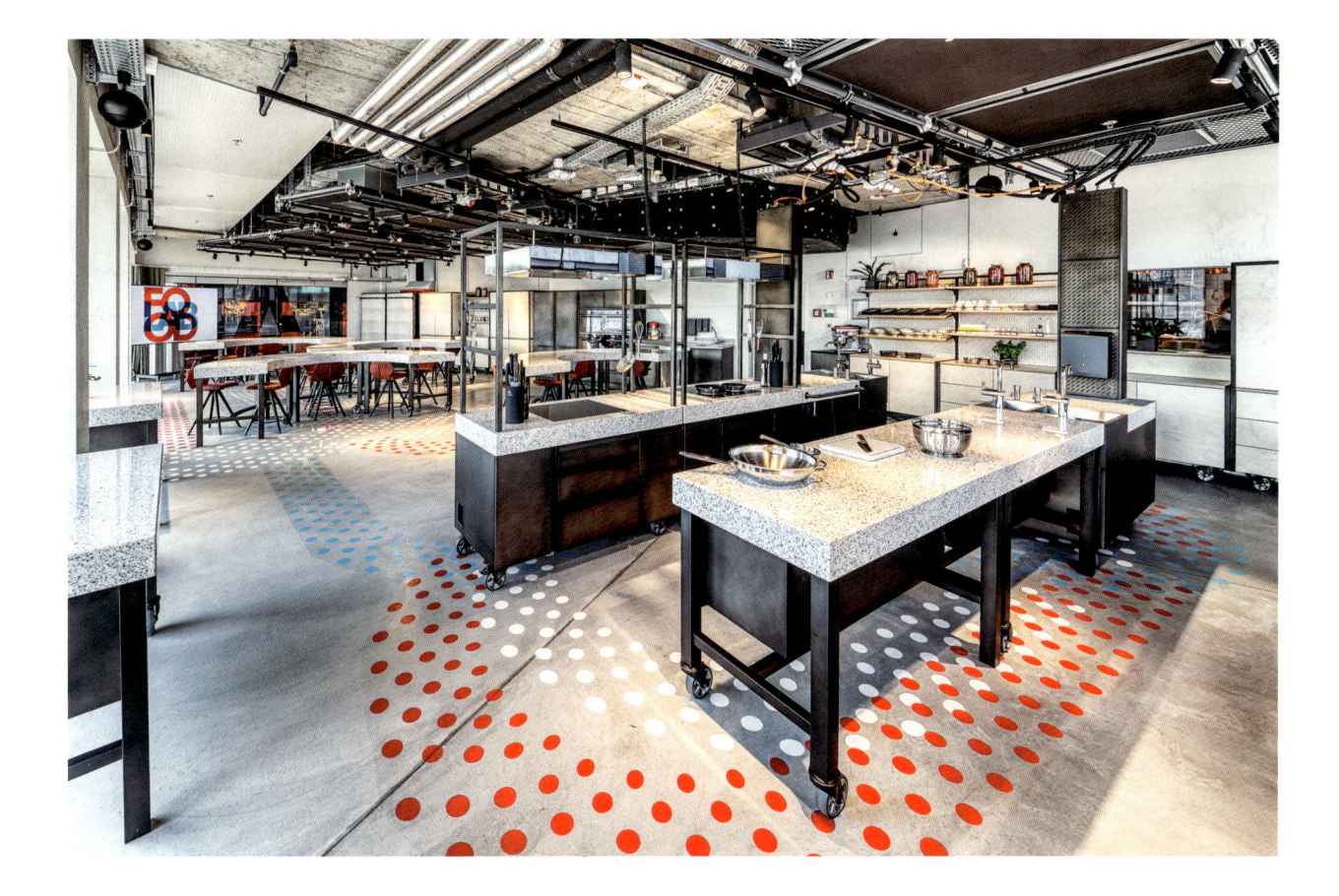

Migros Zürich eröffnete mit „Bridge" zum ersten Mal einen Markt mit eigenständigem Namen und setzt somit auch dem Unternehmensgründer Gottlieb Duttweiler, der sich als Brückenbauer zwischen Produzenten und Konsumenten verstand, ein würdiges Denkmal.

With "Bridge", Migros Zurich has for the first time opened a store with its own name, thus also creating a worthy memorial to the company's founder Gottlieb Duttweiler, who saw himself as a bridge builder between producers and consumers.

"REINVENTING LOCAL" – ALDI CORNER STORE

LOCATION SYDNEY, AUSTRALIA   **CLIENT** ALDI AUSTRALIA (ALDI SUD), MINCHINBURY
CONCEPT / DESIGN LANDINI ASSOCIATES, SYDNEY   **GRAPHICS / LIGHTING** LANDINI ASSOCIATES, SYDNEY
OTHERS MULGA THE ARTIST, SYDNEY   **PHOTOGRAPHS** CORPORATE PIXEL / KYLE FORD, SYDNEY

Mit seiner Betonung urbaner Umgebungen folgt das Design der kleinen ALDI Corner Stores dem Grundsatz, existierende Gebäude zu überarbeiten, statt neue Ladenflächen zu errichten – ein Ansatz im Einklang mit den Ansprüchen einer örtlichen, großteils nur kurz verweilenden Laufkundschaft. Das Konzept entstand aus dem landesweiten Redesign der großen Märkte unter dem Namen „Project Fresh", das in der vorigen Ausgabe von Retail Design International präsentiert wurde.

With its emphasis on urban locations, the layout of the small ALDI Corner Stores is driven by the idea to refurbish existing buildings rather than constructing new properties – an approach that is aligned to the needs of a local, largely walk-in customer base. The concept builds on the nationwide redesign of the large-format stores, called "Project Fresh", which was presented in Retail Design International's previous volume.

SPACES "REINVENTING LOCAL" – ALDI CORNER STORE

Landini Associates hatte den Auftrag, den traditionellen ALDI-Markt in ein neues Format zu übersetzen, das lokal und „anders" sein sollte, aber dennoch die unverkennbare Handschrift der deutschen Handelskette trug. Dies umfasste Benennung, Identität, Planung, Inneneinrichtung, alle Kommunikationsgrafiken im Ladeninneren sowie die Beschaffung und Organisation der Wandbemalungen. Der erste Corner Store in North Sydney demonstriert, wie die kleineren Formate in Australien umgesetzt werden sollen.

The brief to Landini Associates was to interpret the traditional ALDI supermarket into a new format that is local and different, but still belongs recognisably to the chain of the German retailer. The scope of work included naming, identity, planning, interiors, all in-store graphic communications and mural commission and direction. The first Corner Store that was realised in North Sydney shows how smaller formats will be interpreted in Australia.

Für eine einheitliche Markenatmosphäre und Customer Experience bedienen sich alle Stores der gleichen Palette nachhaltiger Materialien aus hellem Ziegelstein, weißen Kacheln und weißem Blockwerk, Terrazzo, schwarzem Zinkstahlgewebe, Holzpaletten, Eiche und Walnuss. In Kombination mit dem Retail Design von Landini Associates schaffen diese Materialien ein einheitliches Bild von der Benennung über die Kundenansprache bis zur Ausschilderung und Navigation: Lebensmittel und Frischwaren, ergänzt durch ein immer größeres Angebot an Ready-to-Eat- und Convenienceprodukten, neben neuen Stationen für „Coffee to go" und einer Hausbäckerei. Ein zentraler Bestandteil des Designkonzepts sind die eigens gefertigten Artworks lokaler Künstler, die jeden Store mit der unmittelbaren Nachbarschaft verknüpfen.

To generate a consistent brand atmosphere and customer experience, each store will feature a sustainable material palette of pale brick, white tiles and blockwork, terrazzo and black and galvanised steel mesh, timber pallets, oak and walnut. These materials combine with the retail graphics solution by Landini Associates that creates a consistent image from naming and messaging to store signage and navigation. Grocery and fresh produce, supplemented by a growing range of ready-to-go meals and convenience products, as well as new take-away coffee and artisanal bakery offerings. A key aspect of the design concept is the commissioning of a local artist to create unique artworks that connect each store with the surrounding neighbourhood.

SPACES   "REINVENTING LOCAL" – ALDI CORNER STORE

Diese Künstler-Kollaborationen „nehmen Rücksicht auf Unterschiede, indem sie betriebliche Vorlieben aufgreifen, und schaffen eine Atmosphäre ganz im Einklang mit der Marke ALDI", sagt Mark Landini, Creative Director bei Landini Associates. Für das Artwork des Erstlings-Stores in der 99 Mount Street in North Sydney zeichnet der ortsansässige Künstler Mulga verantwortlich, der im Auftrag der Agentur sowohl das Ladeninnere als auch die Außenfassade gestaltete.

These artist collaborations "honour differences while embracing operational affinities and create an overall atmosphere that is consistent with the ALDI brand," says Mark Landini, Creative Director of Landini Associates. The debut Store, located at 99 Mount Street in North Sydney, features the work of Sydney artist Mulga, who was commissioned by the agency to interpret both the interior and façade of the site.

GUIJIU BRAND EXPERIENCE STORE NANJING

LOCATION NANJING, CHINA **CLIENT** GUINIANG GROUP LTD., SHANGHAI **CONCEPT / DESIGN** IPPOLITO FLEITZ GROUP – IDENTITY ARCHITECTS, STUTTGART **PHOTOGRAPHS** SUI SICONG, SHANGHAI

Baijiu ist eine chinesische Spirituose, die erst vor kurzer Zeit den internationalen Markt erreicht hat. Seinen Ursprung hat der „Weiße Alkohol" in der Provinz Guizhou, die für die Außenwelt lange als schwer zugänglich galt. Die beeindruckenden Wasserfälle in der bergigen Provinz im Südwesten Chinas wurden zur Inspirationsquelle für den Brand Experience Store.

Baijiu is a Chinese spirit which only reached the international market just recently. The "white alcohol" originated in the Guizhou province which for a long time was virtually cut off from the outside world. The impressive waterfalls in the mountainous province in the south west of China provided the inspiration for the Brand Experience Store.

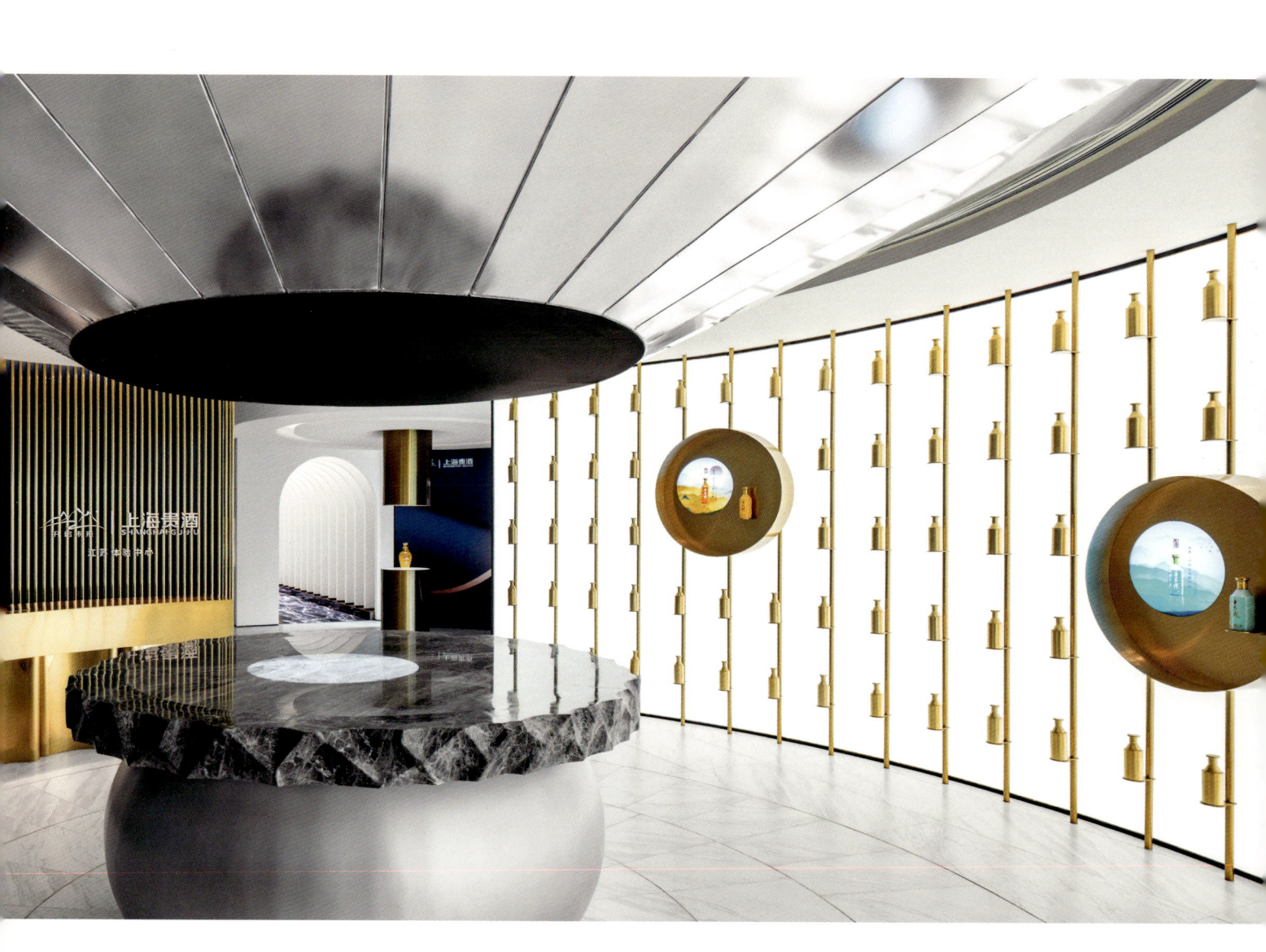

SPACES GUIJIU BRAND EXPERIENCE STORE NANJING

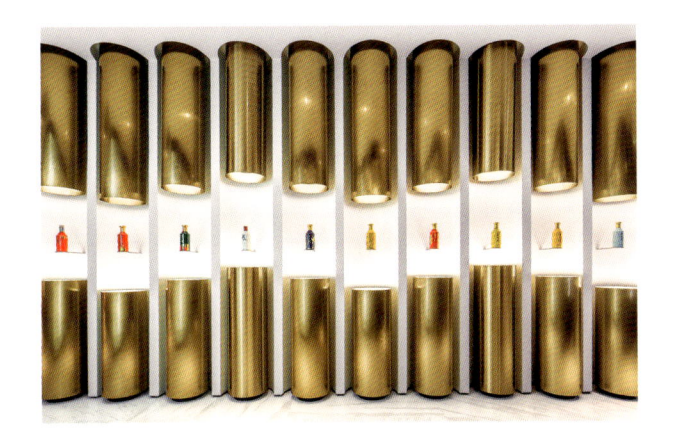

In the Nanjing location, Ippolito Fleitz Group translated the young brand into a themed space which combines tradition with modern lifestyle. The result is an oasis which follows the inspiration of the water to convey the product to the customers. On the fourth floor of a high-rise building, visitors reach the Brand Experience Store by lift. After the doors open, the visitor is guided to a round table made of stone onto which the history of Baijiu is projected. Both the production process of the drink which is distilled from fermented grain as well as the limited production quantities are communicated. At the centre stands the "Hero Product" on a golden pedestal.

In Nanjing hat die Ippolito Fleitz Group die junge Marke in einen Erlebnisraum übersetzt, der Tradition mit modernem Lifestyle verbindet. Es ist eine Oase entstanden, die der Inspiration des Wassers folgt und der Kundschaft das Produkt nahe bringt. In der vierten Etage eines Hochhauses gelegen, lässt sich der Brand Experience Store von den Besucherinnen und Besuchern über einen Aufzug erreichen. Nachdem sich dessen Türen geöffnet haben, wird man zu einem runden Tisch aus Stein geleitet, auf dem die Geschichte von Baijiu mittels einer Projektion erzählt wird. Sowohl der handwerkliche Fertigungsprozess des Getränks, das aus fermentiertem Getreide destilliert wird, als auch die limitierten Produktionsmengen werden kommuniziert. Im Mittelpunkt steht das „Hero Product" auf einem goldenen Podest.

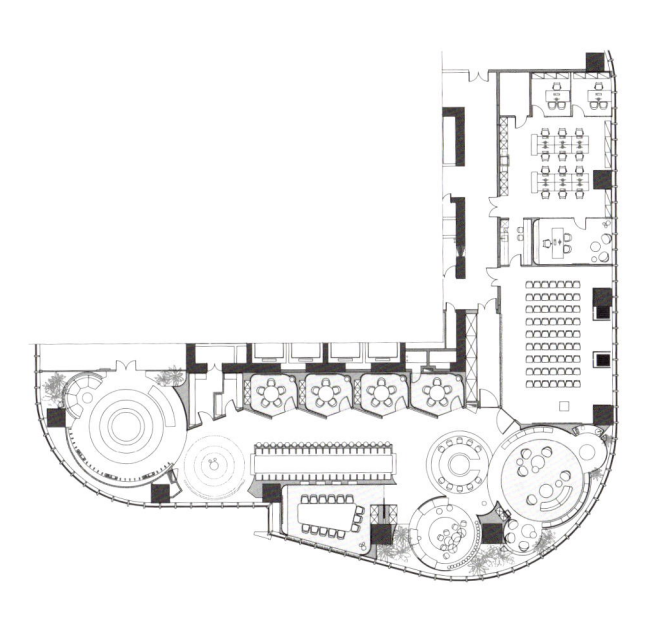

Entlang einer Inszenierung aus Variationen der charakteristischen Flasche an den Wänden gelangt die Kundschaft über einen Catwalk in die Tasting Area. In der Lounge mit kreisförmiger Bar und privaten Nischen werden hier in fünf Schritten alle Sinne angesprochen: Sehen, Riechen, Schmecken, Erfahren und Genießen. Die Farbigkeit und das Licht stellen einen Bezug zur Natur her und lassen die Hektik der Außenwelt für einen Moment vergessen. In der speziellen Customization Area können die Gäste einen Baijiu nach eigenen Vorstellungen kreieren. Die Verkaufsräume bilden abschließend den Weg zurück in den Alltag.

Passing by an installation of variations of the signature bottle presented on the walls, the clientele stride over a catwalk to reach the tasting area. In the lounge with circular bar and private niches, all the senses are addressed in five steps: see, smell, taste, experience and enjoy. The colour scheme and lighting reference nature and let visitors forget the hustle and bustle of the outside world for a moment. In the special customisation area guests can create their own Baijiu. The sales rooms are the final point before re-entering everyday life.

Der Gang durch den Tunnel wird mittels eines digitalen, für jeden Anlass personalisierbaren Bodens zu einem immersiven Erlebnis. Aus dem Spiel mit den Elementen entsteht so ein beliebter Selfie-Spot, der vor allem bei einer exklusiven Anmietung jedes Gästebuch bereichert.

Thanks to the digitally personalised floor, the passage through the tunnel becomes an immersive experience that varies depending on the occasion. The play with the elements makes this a popular selfie spot, which enriches any guest book, particularly when the location has been booked for an exclusive event.

CENTRAL FOOD HALL LAT PHRAO

LOCATION BANGKOK, THAILAND **CLIENT** CENTRAL FOOD RETAIL CO., LTD., NONTHABURI **CONCEPT / DESIGN / GRAPHICS / LIGHTING / REALISATION** INTERSTORE | SCHWEITZER, NATURNS
PHOTOGRAPHS MICHA SCHULTE PHOTOGRAPHY, BANGKOK

Mitten im quirligen Zentrum Bangkoks hat im Dezember 2020 die rund 3.600 Quadratmeter große Central Food Hall Ladprao eröffnet. Der komfortable Feinkosttempel richtet sich sowohl an die vielen Expats in der thailändischen Metropole als auch an die einheimische Kundschaft. Das Projekt gehört zur Central Food Retail Group, die mit 205 Supermärkten die größte Supermarktkette Thailands ist.

In December 2020, Central Food Hall Lat Phrao with a footprint of around 3,600 square metres was opened amidst the hustle and bustle of downtown Bangkok. The convenient delicatessen caters to both the many expats in the Thai metropolis and to the locals. The project belongs to Central Food Retail Group, the largest chain of supermarkets in Thailand with 205 stores across the country.

Die klare Vorgabe für das Design- und Ladenbauunternehmen Interstore | Schweitzer war es, im Zuge der Neugestaltung im Bezirk Ladprao „eine hochwertige Kombination aus inspirierender Food Hall und erstklassigem internationalen Supermarkt" zu schaffen. Das Gesamtkonzept umfasste Architektur, Layout, Design und In-Store-Kommunikation sowie die Entwicklung eigenständiger Marken und des entsprechenden Corporate Designs. Im Fokus standen dabei die Frischeabteilungen, für die individuelle Markenidentitäten, von eigenen Logos über personalisierte Verpackungen bis hin zur Mitarbeiterkleidung, entwickelt wurden. Diese fügen sich nahtlos in das übergeordnete Designkonzept ein und stellen fließende Übergänge her.

The design and shopfitting company Interstore | Schweitzer received a clear brief for the redesign of the store in the Lat Phrao district, namely to create "a high-quality combination of inspiring food hall and first-class international supermarket". The overall concept comprised architecture, layout, design and in-store communication as well as the development of proprietary brands and a corporate design. The focus was firmly on the fresh food departments, for which the individual brand identities were developed, from their own logo and personalised packaging through to the staff uniform. These blend seamlessly into the overarching design concept and create flowing transitions.

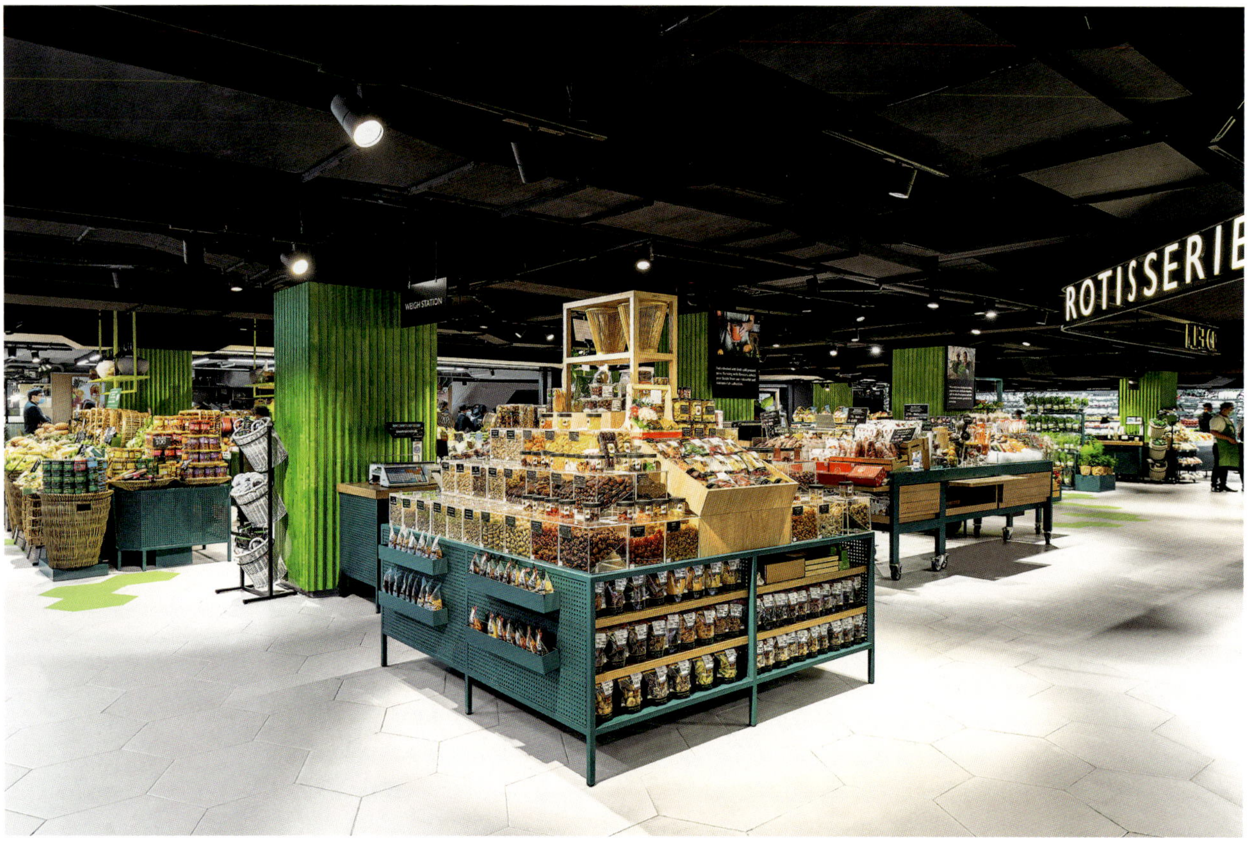
ROTISSERIE
WEIGH STATION

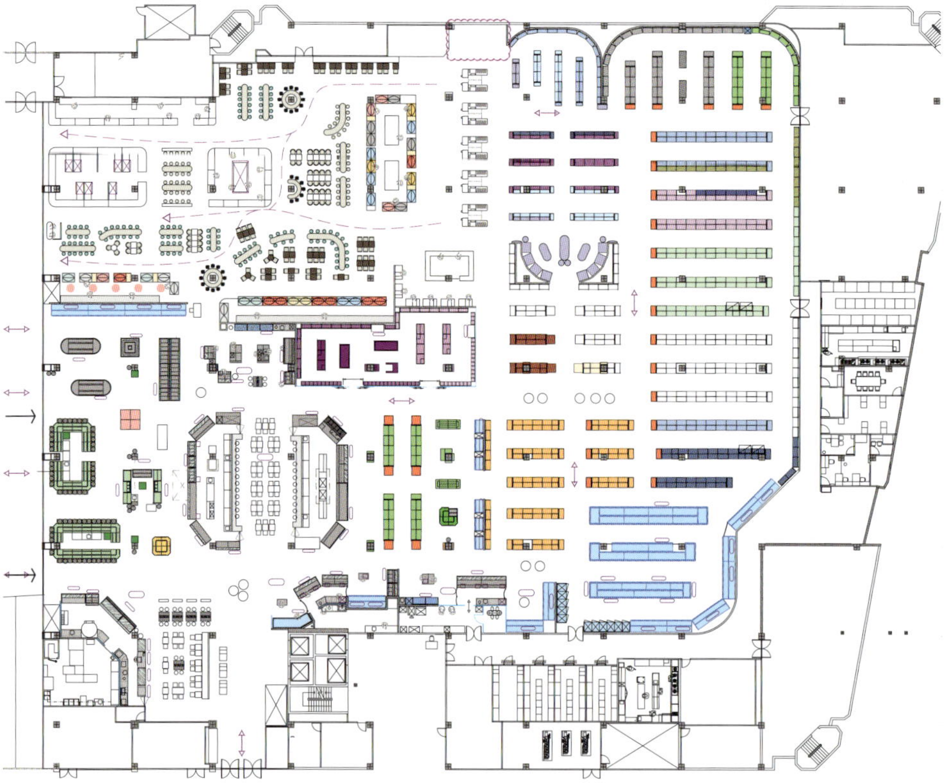

Die einzelnen Abteilungen, vom österreichischen Bäcker über den deutschen Metzger bis hin zum französischen Käse- und Weinexperten, spiegeln die internationale Ausrichtung des Angebots wider. Inmitten der Frischeabteilungen befindet sich das Herzstück der Food Hall, die Central Eatery, mit Showküchen, in denen frische Fusion-Menüs vor Ort zubereitet werden. Die Gerichte können an einem der diversen Sitzareale verspeist oder mitgenommen werden.

The individual departments from the Austrian baker and German butcher through to the French cheese and wine experts reflect the international orientation of the assortment. The Central Eatery, the heart of the food hall, is located in the middle of the fresh food departments. The freshly prepared fusion cuisine from the show kitchens can be either eaten in the various seating areas or taken away.

Neu ist, dass in vielen Abteilungen die fachlich geschulten Verkäuferinnen und Verkäufer der Kundschaft auch neben oder vor den Theken beratend zur Seite stehen und es dadurch weniger Barrieren gibt. Die flexiblen Servicetheken lassen sich mit wenig Aufwand von Bedien- in Selbstbedienungstheken umwandeln. Entsprechend der Unternehmensphilosophie steht der Kunde im Mittelpunkt des innovativen Retail-Konzepts.

What is new is that in many departments the specialist sales staff are available to advise the customers next to or in front of the counters, so that there are fewer barriers. The flexible service counters can be easily converted into service and self-service counters. In line with the corporate philosophy, the innovative retail concept revolves around the customer.

SPACES   CENTRAL FOOD HALL LAT PHRAO

EBIKER BINZEN

LOCATION BINZEN, GERMANY **CLIENT** VISION HOCHRHEIN GMBH & CO. KG, LAUFENBURG **CONCEPT / DESIGN** THEODOR SCHEMBERG EINRICHTUNGEN GMBH, METTINGEN **PHOTOGRAPHS** KOMMUNIKATION & DESIGN GRÖBER GMBH & CO. KG, WALDSHUT-TIENGEN

Es ist ein gutes Zeichen, wenn ausgezeichnete Retail-Konzepte so erfolgreich sind, dass sie schon nach kurzer Zeit einen weiteren Standort eröffnen. So geschehen beim Fachgeschäft „eBiker" in Laufenburg, das nicht nur in der vorigen Ausgabe von Retail Design International vorgestellt, sondern auch zum Store of the Year 2021 gewählt wurde.

It is a good sign when prize-winning retail concepts are so successful that a second store is opened only a short time later as was the case with "eBiker". The specialist store in Laufenburg was not only showcased in the last volume of Retail Design International, it was also named the Store of the Year 2021.

Der Markt für E-Bikes hat während der vergangenen Monate geboomt, nicht zuletzt weil Sport in der freien Natur und an der frischen Luft pandemiebedingt enorm an Zuspruch gewonnen hat. So konnte das Familienunternehmen Theodor Schemberg Einrichtungen GmbH bereits rund ein Jahr nach der Fertigstellung des ersten Stores den zweiten Standort im Gewerbegebiet am Dreispitz in Binzen im Landkreis Lörrach realisieren. Den Spezialisten für Erlebniswelten am Point of Sale ist es ein Anliegen, das Lebensgefühl rund um das beratungsintensive Produkt Fahrrad räumlich umzusetzen. Ein Produkt, zu dem es viele Informationen, Zubehör und Geschichten gibt und das vor allem in jüngster Zeit zu einem wichtigen Bestandteil des täglichen Lebens geworden ist.

The market for e-bikes has been booming in recent months, not least because sport outdoors and in the fresh air has gained hugely in popularity in the wake of the pandemic. Just a year after the completion of the first store, the family-run business Theodor Schemberg Einrichtungen GmbH realised the second location at the Dreispitz industrial estate in Binzen in the Lörrach region. The specialist for themed worlds at the point of sale wanted to find a spatial translation for the lifestyle surrounding the bicycle, a complex product requiring intensive consultation. A product about which there is a great deal of information, loads of accessories and countless stories and which in recent times has become an important part of everyday life.

Im neuen Showroom werden auf 800 Quadratmetern Fläche rund 200 Räder auf Podesten aus Beton und Kiefernholz präsentiert. Die Themenwelten orientieren sich an den unterschiedlichen E-Bike-Typen: von E-Mountainbikes über E-Trekking- und -Rennräder bis hin zu Lastenrädern. In die luftige Gewerbehalle, die früher als Autohaus genutzt wurde, integrieren die Planer:innen einen Indoor-Parcours, der durch eine Outdoor-Teststrecke erweitert wird. Dort können die Fachleute das Fahrverhalten der Kundschaft auf den verschiedenen Terrains genau beobachten und ein individuelles E-Bike darauf abstimmen. In der verglasten Werkstatt sind die Mechatroniker zugange und halten Fahrräder und E-Bikes aller Marken instand.

Die direkte Kundenansprache und die Nähe zur Natur spielten für das Retail Design eine zentrale Rolle. „Wir wollten das Gefühl, mit einem elektrisierten Fahrrad durch die Natur zu fahren, auf den Store übertragen", so der verantwortliche Interior-Designer Benedikt Starke.

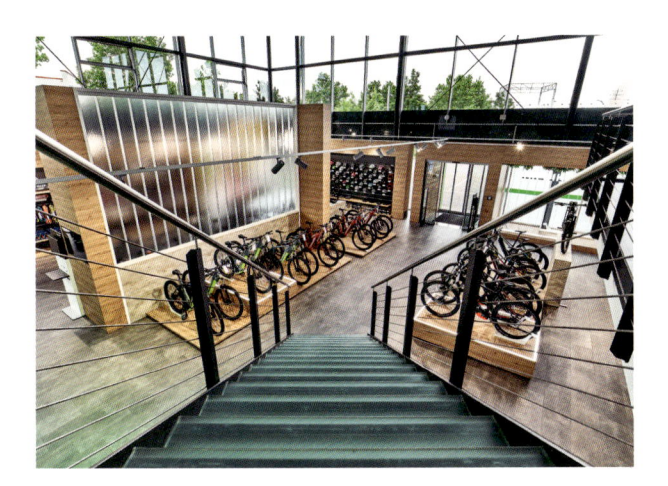

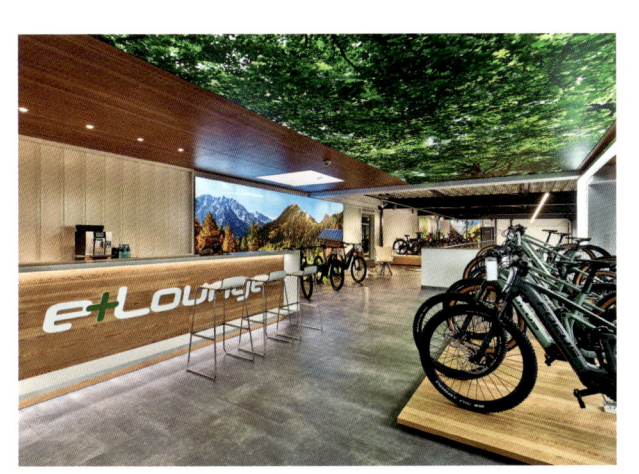

In the new showroom with a footprint of roughly 800 square metres, around 200 bikes are presented on platforms of concrete and pinewood. The themed worlds are built around the various types of e-bike: from e-mountain bikes via e-trekking and racing bikes through to cargo bikes. In the light and airy hall, which used to be a car dealership, the designers integrated an indoor track that is extended by an outdoor test route. Here, the experts can observe the handling of the bikes by the clientele on various types of terrain and, based on this, advise each customer about the right bike for them. In the glazed workshop, the mechatronics are hard at work, repairing and servicing bikes and e-bikes of all brands.

For the retail design, addressing customers directly and the proximity to nature played a central role. "We wanted to transfer the feeling of riding an electric bicycle through the great outdoors to the store", explains Benedikt Starke, the interior designer entrusted with this task.

ASTON MARTIN

استون مارتن

BUILDINGS

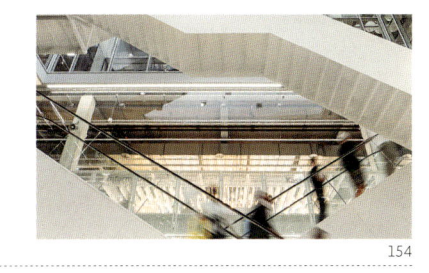

154 174 164

170 180 174

174 164 174

154 160 154

184 154 160

IKEA CITY CENTER

LOCATION VIENNA, AUSTRIA **CLIENT** IKEA EINRICHTUNGEN – HANDELSGESELLSCHAFT MBH, VÖSENDORF
ARCHITECTURE QUERKRAFT ARCHITEKTEN, VIENNA **OTHERS** THOMAS LORENZ ZT GMBH, GRAZ / WERKRAUM INGENIEURE ZT GMBH, VIENNA (STRUCTURAL ENGINEERING, S.E. COMPETITION); IPJ INGENIEURBÜRO P. JUNG GMBH, VIENNA (BUILDING PHYSICS); KRÄFTNER LANDSCHAFTSARCHITEKTUR, VIENNA / GREEN4CITIES GMBH, VIENNA (GREEN SPACE)
PHOTOGRAPHS HERTHA HURNAUS, VIENNA

Noch vor wenigen Jahren galt der Inbusschlüssel als Universalwerkzeug einer Welt, in der nichts unmöglich erschien. Möbel wurden im Katalog ausgesucht, in labyrinthartigen Showrooms probebewohnt und mit dem privaten Auto nach Hause geschafft. Doch alles ist im Wandel, den IKEA-Katalog gibt es nur noch in digitaler Form und in Wien hat das erste autofreie Einrichtungshaus eröffnet.

Just a few years ago, the Allen key was still the all-purpose tool in a world in which nothing seemed impossible. Furniture was selected in the catalogue, tried out in labyrinthine showrooms and transported home in the customer's own car. But everything is changing; the IKEA catalogue is now only available in digital form and in Vienna the first car-free furniture shop has opened for business.

BUILDINGS   IKEA CITY CENTER

Wie ein überdimensionales Billy-Regal öffnet sich der innerstädtische IKEA Wien Westbahnhof zum verkehrsreichen Stadtraum am Gürtel. Er ist bestens an den öffentlichen Nahverkehr angebunden und bietet ein vielfältiges Mixed-use-Konzept. Das Gebäude soll einen wesentlichen Beitrag für die Zukunft einer lebendigen und ökologischen Stadt leisten und ein guter Nachbar werden, beschreiben die Architektinnen und Architekten von querkraft ihre Vision. Das fast ausschließlich weiblich besetzte Team unter Carmen Hottinger als Projektleiterin konnte sich in einem dreistufigen Architekturwettbewerb mit mehreren Workshops durchsetzen. Bereits im Briefing formulierte das schwedische Unternehmen den Leitsatz: „We want to be a good neighbour."

Like an oversized Billy shelf unit, the downtown IKEA Wien Westbahnhof (Vienna West Station) opens onto the busy Gürtel street. Easily accessible by public transport, it offers a diverse mixed-use concept. The architects from querkraft formulate their vision for the building as making an important contribution to the future of a lively and ecological city and becoming a good neighbour in the process. The almost all-female team under Carmen Hottinger as project manager was selected in a three-step architecture competition with several workshops. Already in the briefing the Swedish company described its guiding principle: "We want to be a good neighbour."

Die Lösung für diesen Anspruch zeigt sich in einem Gebäude, das auch für die Umgebung einen Mehrwert darstellt. Die 4,3 Meter tiefe Außenzone legt sich wie ein Schatten spendendes Regal um das Volumen und bietet Platz für Terrassen, Begrünung und dienende Elemente wie Lifte, Fluchttreppen und Haustechnik. Die vorgefertigten Stahlbetonstützen folgen einem Raster von zirka 10 mal 10 Metern, was eine vielseitige Nutzung und Gestaltung der Räume ermöglicht. In den unteren Geschossen findet man den IKEA-Retail, in den oberen zwei Stockwerken ist das Jo&Joe-Hostel mit 345 Betten untergebracht.

The solution for this claim is manifested in a building which adds value to its surroundings. The 4.3-metre-deep outer zone is wrapped like a shady shelf round the structure and offers space for terraces, greenery and service elements like lifts, fire escapes and utilities. The prefabricated reinforced concrete supports follow a grid of around 10 × 10 metres which allows the varied usage and design of the spaces. While the lower floors house IKEA retail, the two upper floors are occupied by the Jo&Joe Hostel with 345 beds.

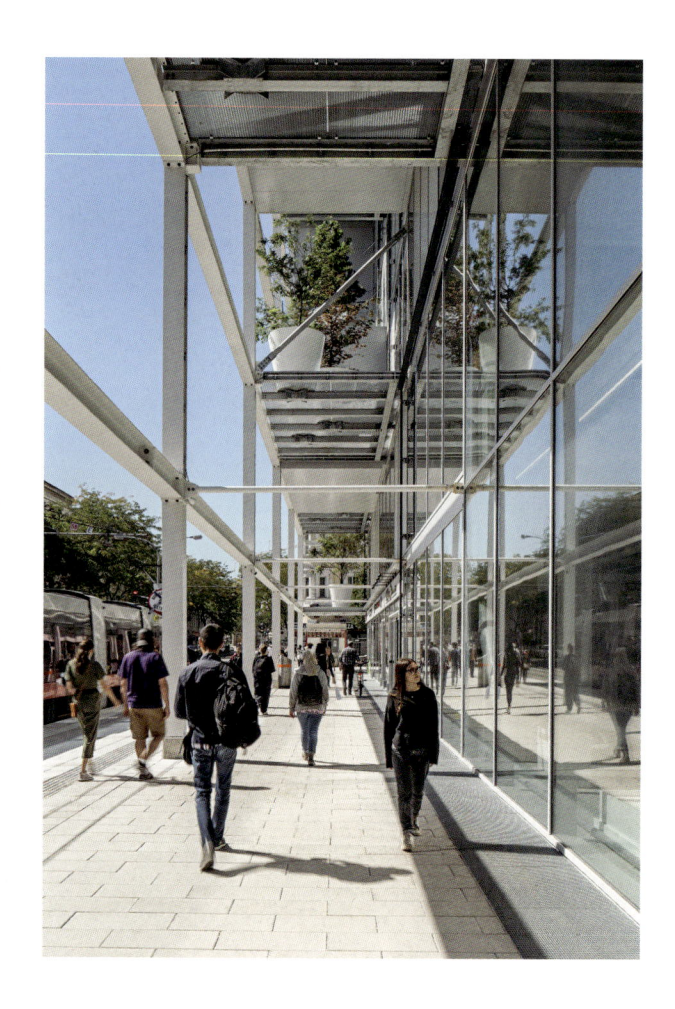

BUILDINGS   IKEA CITY CENTER

rooftop terrace
hostel
hostel
retail & restaurant
retail
retail
retail
external retail

BUILDINGS   IKEA CITY CENTER

Die der Öffentlichkeit zugängliche Dachterrasse mit der Möglichkeit, einen Kaffee zu trinken, zu entspannen und die Aussicht auf die Stadt zu genießen, trägt zur guten Nachbarschaft bei. Durch den Mix wurde ein urbanes Haus geschaffen, das 24 Stunden lang 7 Tage die Woche bespielt wird.

The roof terrace that is open to the public offers the opportunity to drink a coffee, relax and enjoy the view of the city and is indeed a great addition to the neighbourhood. The mixed usage has created an urban house which is filled with life 24/7.

ASTON MARTIN SHOWROOM

LOCATION DOHA, UAE **CLIENT** ASTON MARTIN INHOUSE, GAYDON **CONCEPT / DESIGN** VIZONA GMBH, WEIL AM RHEIN **PHOTOGRAPHS** ASTON MARTIN INHOUSE, GAYDON

Im 25. Bond-Film „Keine Zeit zu sterben" kehrt nicht nur der Schauspieler Daniel Craig als Agent in den Dienst seiner Majestät zurück, sondern es gibt auch ein Wiedersehen mit den Automobilklassikern der britischen Marke Aston Martin. Das von Lionel Martin und Robert Bamford 1913 in einer kleinen Werkstatt in London gegründete Unternehmen ist zu einer international agierenden Luxusmarke geworden und regelmäßig in den Kultfilmen vertreten.

In the 25th Bond film "No Time to Die" not only actor Daniel Craig returns to the service of her Majesty. The Aston Martin, the classic British car marque, also puts in an appearance again. The firm founded in a small workshop by Lionel Martin and Robert Bamford in 1913 has become an internationally renowned luxury brand and is regularly to be seen in iconic films.

BUILDINGS   ASTON MARTIN SHOWROOM

Nicht nur in Regionen, deren Vergangenheit durch den britischen Lebensstil geprägt wurde, steht die Marke bis heute für Tradition und Technik „made in Great Britain". Dieses Selbstverständnis spiegelt sich in der Gestaltung und Materialwahl der weltweiten Filialen wider. Der größte Showroom im Mittleren Osten wurde von Vizona in den Alfardan Towers in der boomenden Wüstenstadt Katar realisiert. Das Ladenbauunternehmen aus Weil am Rhein hat den Automobilhersteller bereits erfolgreich in der Ausstattung von mehr als 100 Filialen unterstützt.

To this day, the car brand stands for tradition and technology made in Great Britain, and not only in regions whose past has been shaped by British lifestyle. This self-image is reflected in the design and choice of materials of the showrooms around the world. The biggest showroom in the Middle East was realised by Vizona in the Alfardan Towers in the booming desert city of Qatar. The shopfitters from Weil am Rhein have successfully helped the car manufacturer fit out more than 100 locations.

Technologisch auf dem allerneuesten Stand, soll der Showroom Bestands- und mögliche Neukunden in eine immersive Brand Experience versetzen. Er bietet Platz für bis zu zwölf Fahrzeuge und beherbergt neue oder neu belegte zeitlose Ausstellungsflächen, einen extra Übergaberaum, eine Welcome-Lounge mit Kaffeebar sowie einen Konfigurationsbereich, wo die Kunden ihre maßgefertigten Autos mit allen erdenklichen Ausstattungsoptionen selbst entwerfen können. Das neue Design ist großräumig, gediegen und besitzt für die Sportwagen sogar eigene Parkettflächen inmitten hochwertiger Baumaterialien, die von Vizona modern integriert wurden: Details aus amerikanischer Walnuss und Leder, champagnerfarbenes Aluminium und Edelstahl. Exzellenter Service und elegantes Interieur – ein perfektes Zuhause für die britische Autokultur der Luxusklasse.

Featuring state-of-the-art technologies, the showroom is designed to present existing and prospective customers with an immersive brand experience. Accommodating up to 12 vehicles, it comprises new and timeless pre-owned car display areas, a dedicated handover space, a welcoming lounge and coffee bar, and a configuration zone where customers can create their own bespoke vehicles with the ultimate in specification options. The new design is spacious and comfortable, and even has the sports cars parked on parquet flooring among high-quality materials which Vizona incorporates with a modern twist: American walnut and leather details, champagne-coloured aluminium and stainless steel. Excellent service and an elegant interior – the perfect home for luxurious British car culture.

BUILDINGS   ASTON MARTIN SHOWROOM

Um zahlungskräftigen Kunden und ihren Besuchern dieses Lebensgefühl auch im privaten Umfeld zu demonstrieren, bietet Aston Martin seit Kurzem einen individuellen Designservice an, der es den Fahrzeughaltern erlaubt, Garagen, Wohnraum und schurkenhafte „Geheimverstecke" zu entwerfen, die ihre Lieblinge gut zur Geltung bringen.

In order to also transport this feeling to the private ambiance of affluent customers and their guests, Aston Martin recently introduced a bespoke design service that allows drivers to create garages, homes and villain-esque "lairs" that showcase their favourite cars.

FEUCHT / SPORTLER INNSBRUCK

LOCATION INNSBRUCK, AUSTRIA **CLIENT** MODE VON FEUCHT GMBH / SPORTLER AG, INNSBRUCK **CONCEPT / DESIGN** BLOCHER PARTNERS, STUTTGART **LIGHTING** HAILIGHT LICHTPLANUNG, INNSBRUCK (FEUCHT); ARCLITE GMBH, BARGTEHEIDE (SPORTLER) **OTHERS** SCHLEGEL GMBH, BIETIGHEIM-BISSINGEN (SHOPFITTING FEUCHT); KRAISS GMBH, BAD URACH (SHOPFITTING SPORTLER) **PHOTOGRAPHS** JOACHIM GROTHUS FOTOGRAFIE, HERFORD

In die markant grüne Hülle eines teilweise leer stehenden Möbelhauses im Osten von Innsbruck ist neues Leben eingezogen. Wo einst Möbel verkauft wurden, ergänzen sich nach einer umfangreichen Sanierung zwei traditionsreiche Handelshäuser unter einem gemeinsamen Dach. Zusammen mit dem Südtiroler Sportartikelhändler Sportler eröffneten die drei Brüder und Geschäftsführer von Mode von Feucht, Wolfgang, Leopold und Christoph Feucht, das größte Mode- und Lifestylehaus Westösterreichs.

New life has been breathed into the striking green shell of the partly vacant furniture store in the eastern part of Innsbruck. Where furniture was once sold, two heritage retail firms now complement each other after an extensive refurbishment under a shared roof. Together with the South Tyrolean sports equipment retailer Sportler, the three brothers and general managers of Mode von Feucht, Wolfgang, Leopold and Christoph Feucht, have created the biggest fashion and lifestyle store in western Austria.

Die Tiroler Modehändler haben sich ein Store Design gewünscht, das höchsten Ansprüchen an Nachhaltigkeit gerecht wird und einen Erlebnisraum für die Besuchenden schafft. Das transdisziplinär arbeitende Team von blocher partners hat in einer Umbauzeit von vier Monaten ein Konzept umgesetzt, das beiden Marken Raum zur Entfaltung und ein geschossübergreifendes Erlebnis bietet. Verbindende Elemente sind der Bezug zur Region sowie eine nachhaltige Ausführung. Mitten in den Alpen gelegen, ist die Hauptstadt Tirols eine beliebte Wintersportregion, deren Nähe zu alpinen Aktivitäten durch den Umbau hervorgehoben wurde. Wo früher eine Rampe durch die Möbelausstellung führte, tut sich nun ein eindrucksvoller Luftraum auf, der wie in der Bergwelt Ausblicke gewährt und verschiedene Höhenniveaus verbindet.

The Tyrolean fashion retailers wanted a store design which met their high standards of sustainability and have created a genuine shopping experience for visitors. In a rebuild time of four months, the transdisciplinary team from blocher partners realised a concept which offers both brands space to evolve and a cross-storey experience. The connecting elements of this are regional references and the sustainable execution. Situated in the middle of the Alps, the capital of Tyrol is a popular winter sport region, whose proximity to Alpine activities has been emphasised by the refurbishment. Where a ramp used to guide customers through the furniture exhibition, an impressive air space has now emerged which – like in the mountains – offers views and links various height levels.

Auch die Farb- und Materialpalette des Feucht-Stores ist von der Landschaft inspiriert: Flächen in Betonoptik kombiniert mit Fichtenholz bilden die Hülle und beziehen sich auf die unmittelbare Natur. Die Mittelmöbel sind aus recyceltem Kunststoff gefertigt, die Polsterstoffe größtenteils nach dem Cradle-to-cradle-Prinzip hergestellt.

The palette of colours and materials used in the Feucht store was also inspired by the landscape: Areas in concrete optic combined with spruce wood form the setting and make reference to the nature in the immediate vicinity. The centre furniture elements are made of recycled plastics, the upholstery materials largely produced according to the cradle-to-cradle principle.

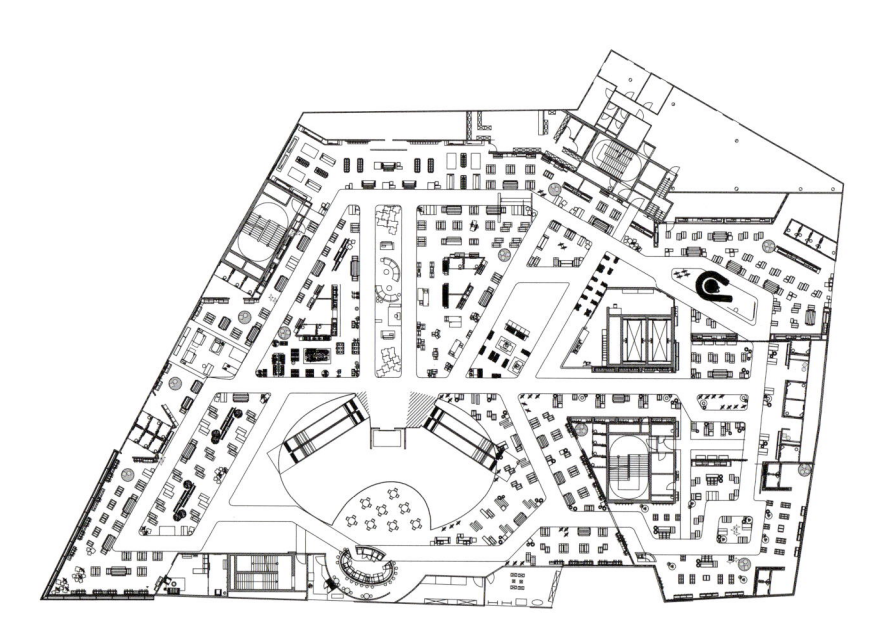

BUILDINGS   FEUCHT / SPORTLER INNSBRUCK

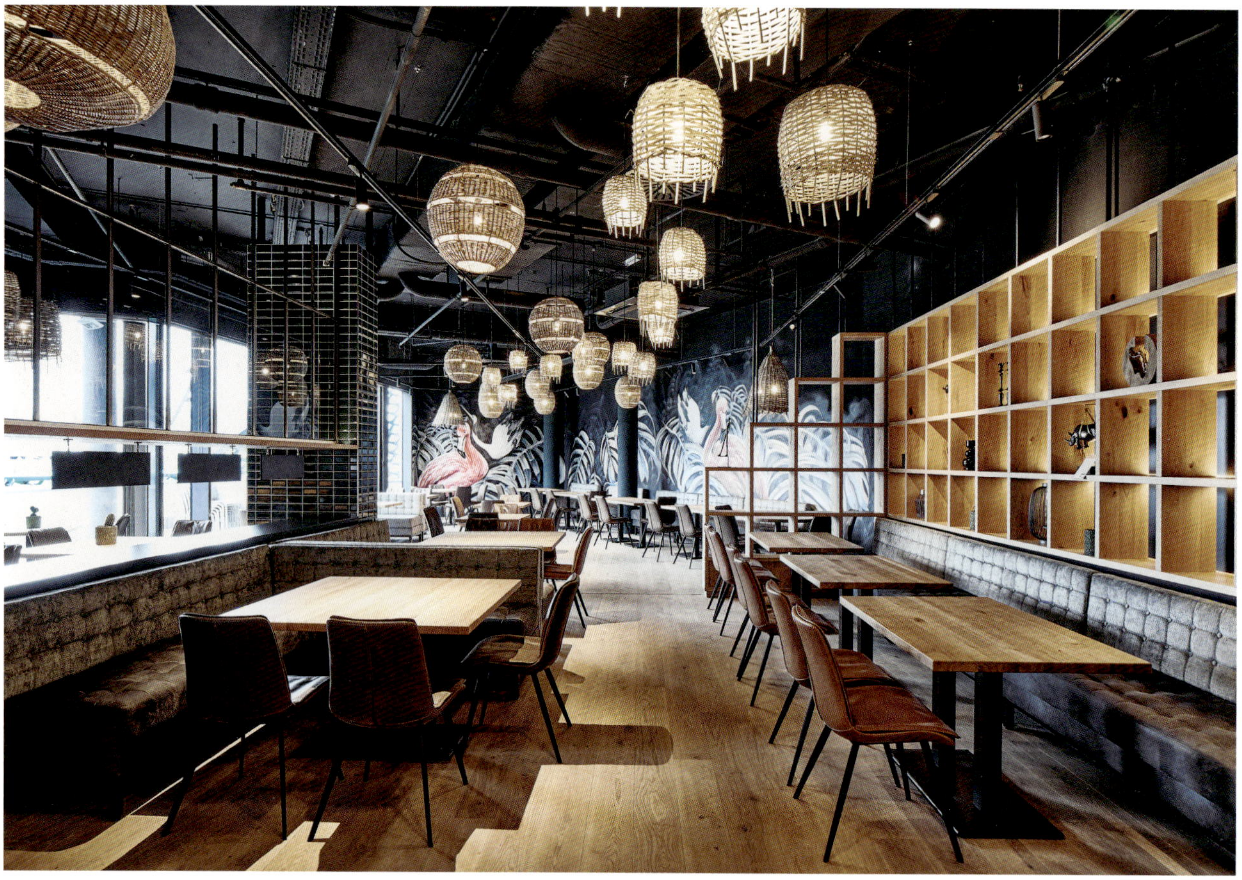

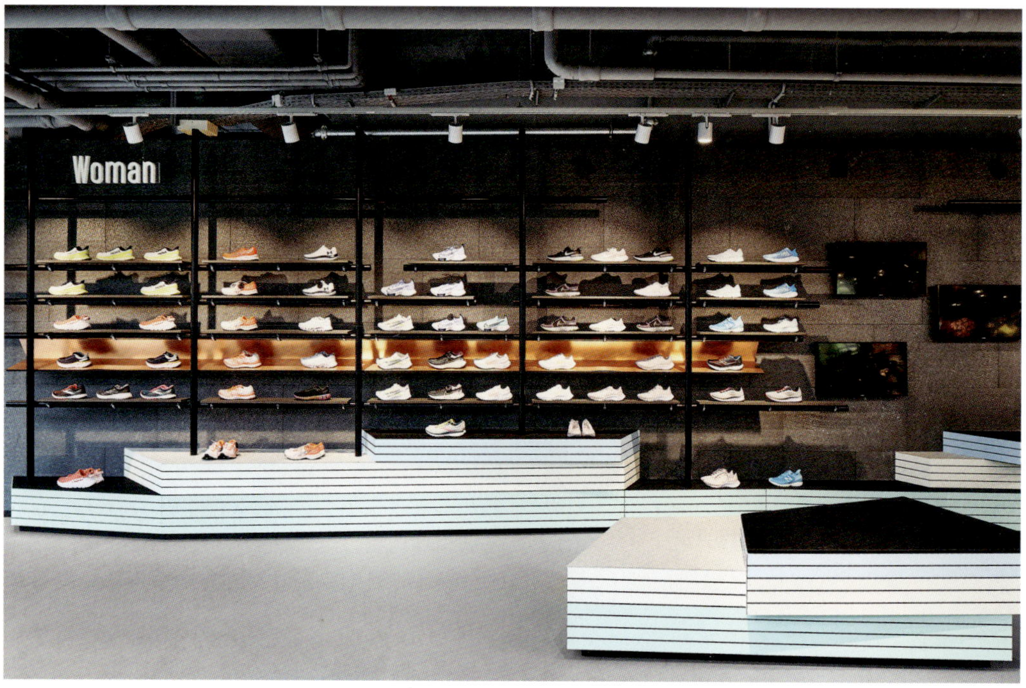
Woman

BUILDINGS   FEUCHT / SPORTLER INNSBRUCK

Neben maximaler Wandelbarkeit liegt auch in den oberen Etagen bei Sportler der Fokus auf natürlichen, regionalen und unverbundenen Materialien. Den Store zeichnet außerdem ein hoher Experience-Charakter aus, denn alle Produkte können getestet werden: die Bikes auf einer Halfpipe, die Running-Schuhe auf einer Laufstrecke, die Kletterschuhe an einer Kletterwand – sogar ein spezieller Rucksacktest ist möglich.

On the upper floors at Sportler, the focus – besides maximum versatility – is on natural, regional and pure materials. The store is also big on experience and all products can be tested: the bikes in a halfpipe, the running shoes on a running track, the climbing shoes on a climbing wall – even a special rucksack test is possible.

CUPRA FLAGSHIP STORE

LOCATION HAMBURG, GERMANY   **CLIENT** DICOM, BARCELONA   **CONCEPT / DESIGN** VIZONA GMBH, WEIL AM RHEIN
PHOTOGRAPHS ROMAN THOMAS FOTOGRAFIE, CELLE

Viele innovative Erfindungen, technische Neuentwicklungen oder auch Start-ups haben ihren Ursprung in einfachen Garagen. Die Garage scheint ein Ort zu sein, an dem sich der kreative Unternehmer- und Gründergeist besonders gut entfalten kann. Nach einem dynamischen Rollout mit rund 200 eigenen Präsentationsbereichen für Seat-Händler weltweit hat Vizona in Hamburg die erste CUPRA-Garage Europas realisiert.

Many innovative inventions, new technical developments and even start-ups originated in simple garages. The garage seems to be a place in which the entrepreneurial spirit thrives particularly well. After a dynamic rollout with around 200 presentation areas for Seat dealers around the world, Vizona realised Europe's first CUPRA Garage.

BUILDINGS   CUPRA FLAGSHIP STORE

Die zum Volkswagen-Konzern gehörende Marke Seat hat ihre sportlichen Fahrzeuge unter dem Namen CUPRA ausgegliedert und alle Motorsportaktivitäten auf die neue Marke übertragen. Die Bezeichnung geht auf die Kurzform von Cup Racing zurück und soll die Leistungsfähigkeit und die Rennsport-Gene der Performance-Marke unterstreichen. Schon der Eingang der anthrazit gestrichenen Halle weckt mit seinem breiten Eichenholzrahmen Assoziationen zu einem offen stehenden Garagentor und sorgt für Aufmerksamkeit auf der Händlermeile im Nedderfeld.

Seat, a Volkswagen brand, has spun off its sporty vehicle under the name CUPRA and transferred all its motor sport activities to the new marque. The name comes from the short form of Cup Racing and is intended to underline the power and the racing sport gene of the performance brand. With its wide oak wood frame, the entrance to the hall that has been painted in anthracite already arouses associations with an open garage door and catches the attention of visitors to the Nedderfeld car dealership strip.

Im Inneren dominiert die markentypische Materialwahl mit roher Betonoptik, petrolverputzten Wandpaneelen, setzkastenartigen Boxen aus Holz und kupferfarbenen Streckgittern. Auf der Ausstellungsfläche mit Wohnzimmeratmosphäre finden bis zu fünf Fahrzeuge Platz. Unter der Decke laufen Kabel und Schienen eines alten Industriekrans. Die rennsportlich inspirierte Erlebniswelt wird mit einer Experience Zone, einer Racing Area sowie einem Test-Drive-Bereich hervorgehoben. Im VR-Raum haben Kund:innen die Möglichkeit, die Fahrzeuge dank digitaler Unterstützung „on the road" zu erleben. Möblierung und Ausstattungselemente bilden ein authentisches Setup für Veranstaltungen wie Fahrzeugpräsentationen und Launches von neuen Modellen.

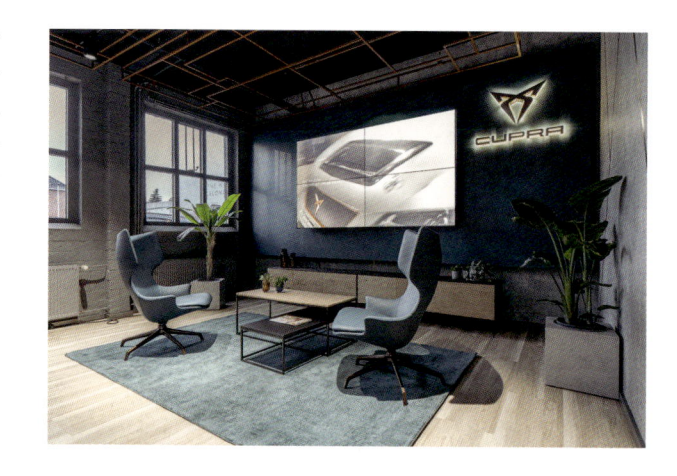

The inside is dominated by the choice of materials typical for the brand including raw concrete optic, petrol-coloured plasterwork wall panels, wooden boxes arranged like letter cases and copper-coloured expanded metal. The exhibition space has the atmosphere of a living room and can accommodate up to five vehicles. Cables and tracks of an old industrial crane run along the ceiling. Inspired by motor racing, the themed world has an Experience Zone, a Racing Area and a Test-Drive area. In the VR room, customers have the opportunity – with digital support – to experience vehicles "on the road". Furnishing and decoration elements create an authentic set-up for events and vehicle presentations and launches of new models.

BUILDINGS CUPRA FLAGSHIP STORE

Die Hamburger CUPRA-Garage ist nach Mexiko-Stadt der zweite Standort des neuen Retail-Konzepts. Das Garagenmotiv fügt sich schlüssig in den denkmalgeschützten Industriebau aus den 1950er-Jahren ein, in dem früher unter anderem Uhren für den öffentlichen Raum, Kraftmessgeräte für Jahrmärkte und Lostrommeln gefertigt wurden.

After Mexico City, the Hamburg CUPRA-Garage is the second location with the new retail concept. The garage motif has been seamlessly integrated into the listed industrial building from the 1950s where once clocks for public spaces, strength testers for fun fairs and lottery drums were produced.

KASTNER & ÖHLER KAUFHAUS TYROL

LOCATION INNSBRUCK, AUSTRIA **CLIENT** KASTNER & ÖHLER MODE GMBH, GRAZ **CONCEPT / DESIGN** DIOMA AG, BERNE
LIGHTING VEDDER.LICHTMANAGEMENT, MUNICH **PHOTOGRAPHS** JENS PFISTERER, STUTTGART

Trotz Lockdown im Frühling wurde Mitte September 2020 die neue Filiale von Kastner & Öhler im Innsbrucker Kaufhaus Tyrol eröffnet. Der Department Store ist nach dem Stammhaus in Graz der größte Standort des 1873 gegründeten Familienunternehmens und soll zum neuen Treffpunkt für Modeinteressierte in der Tiroler Landeshauptstadt werden.

Über zehn Jahre nach der Neueröffnung von K & Ö in Graz wurde Marco Dionisio, Geschäftsführer der dioma ag, erneut beauftragt, die Art-Direction für den Standort Innsbruck zu übernehmen. Anhand einer genau definierten Vision wurde unter dem Arbeitstitel „Urban – Alpin" das gesamte Design der Ladengestaltung neu aufgestellt. „Urban" steht für ein offenes und modernes Innsbruck in Tirol, während „Alpin" die bergige und natürliche Landschaft der Umgebung mit großem Wohlfühlcharakter spezifiziert. Den urbanen Mittelpunkt bildet dabei der offene Rolltreppen-Lichthof über mehrere Etagen.

Despite the lockdown in the spring, the new branch of Kastner & Öhler was opened in Innsbruck's Kaufhaus Tyrol in mid-September 2020. After the main store in Graz, the department store is the second largest location of the family business founded back in 1873 and its owners want it to become the new meeting point for fashionistas in the capital city of Tyrol.

More than ten years after the opening of K & Ö in Graz, Marco Dionisio, general manager of dioma ag, was once again tasked with the art direction for the Innsbruck store. Based on a precisely defined vision, the whole design of the store was revamped under the working title "Urban – Alpine". "Urban" stands for an open and modern Innsbruck in Tyrol, while "Alpine" refers to the surrounding mountainous and natural landscape with a cosy, feel-good character. At the heart of the store, the open escalator in the inner courtyard that extends over several storeys.

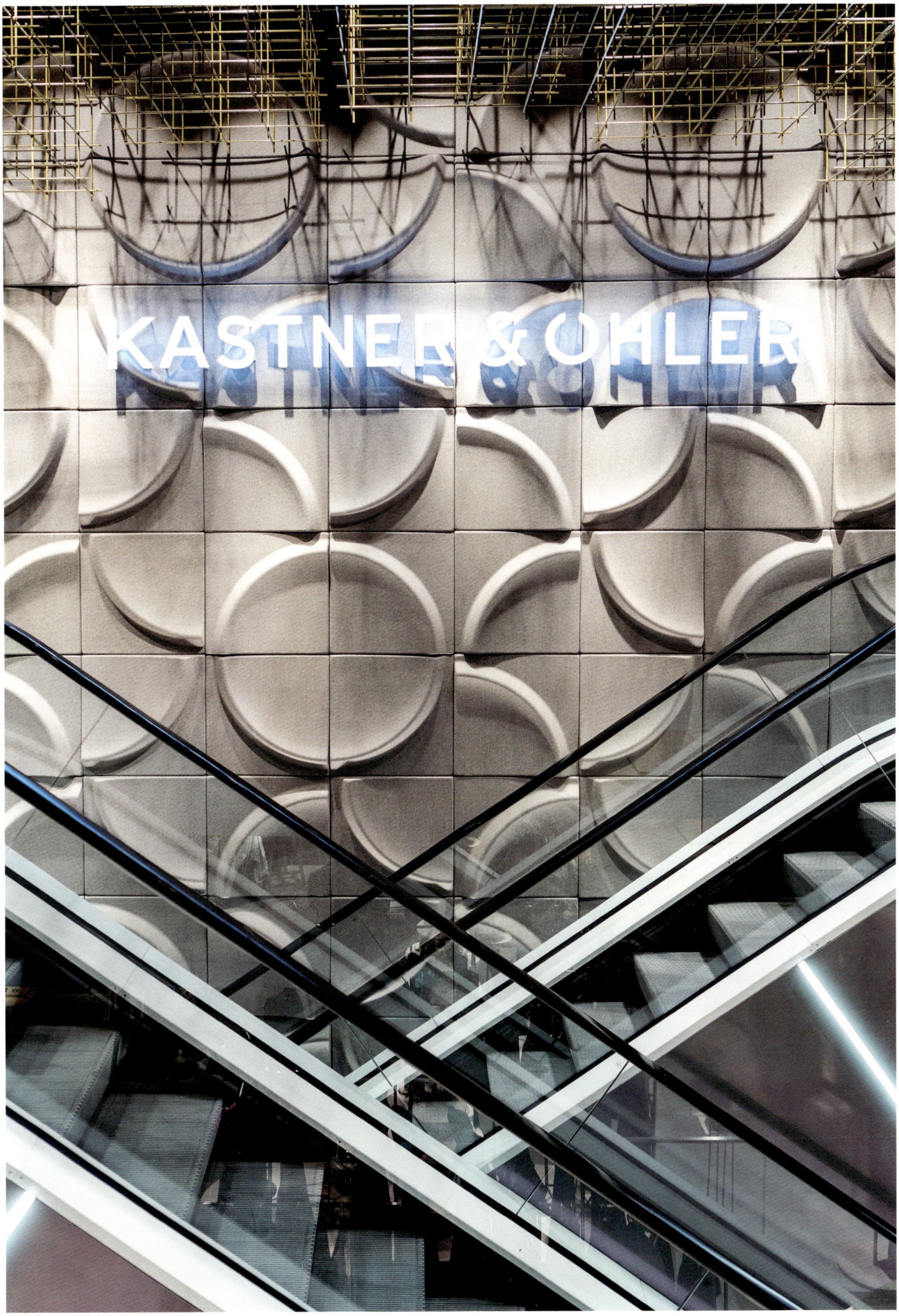
KASTNER & ÖHLER

Die Kernelemente des neuen Erscheinungsbilds nehmen regionale Bezüge auf: Eichenholz in diversen Farbnuancen mit Sandeiche in der Damenabteilung und Steineiche bei den Herren. Ein Karomuster kommt als dezent alpines Motiv sowohl am Boden als auch an Wänden und den überdimensionalen Vorhängen zum Einsatz. Dank der imposanten Raumhöhe von 4,5 Metern konnte im Erdgeschoss eine großzügige Lösung mit einem Baldachin aus abgerundetem Gipskarton realisiert werden. In der ersten Etage für Damenmode mit der Champagnerbar setzt zartes Rosé in Kombination mit brüniertem Messing Akzente. In der zweiten Etage für Herrenmode kommt alpines Grün mit rostfarbenen Akzenten zum Einsatz. Frisches Gelb und tiefes Schwarz bestimmen neben wellblechartigen Elementen die Gesamtstimmung im Bereich der Young Fashion.

The core elements of the new appearance have regional associations: oak wood in various shades, for instance common oak in the ladies' department and holly oak in menswear. A check pattern has been used as a subtle alpine motif both on the floor and on the walls and the oversized curtains. Thanks to the imposing ceiling height of 4.5 metres, it was possible to realise a generously dimensioned solution with a canopy of curved plasterboard. On the first floor for ladies' fashion with a champagne bar, features have been emphasised with dashes of pale pink in combination with blued brass. On the second floor for menswear, alpine green has been used with rust-coloured accented features. The overall mood in the young fashion area has been created by combining elements in corrugated iron style with a colour scheme of fresh yellow and pitch black.

Marco Dionisio konzipierte für K & Ö eine eigene Visual-Merchandising-Toolbox. Sämtliche Mannequins und Büsten für Mode und Accessoires wurden in Spanien nachhaltig produziert. Bemerkenswert ist, dass die Parfümerie-Mannequins in Zusammenarbeit mit der Künstlerin Rebecca Moses entstanden sind.

Marco Dionisio developed a visual merchandising toolkit specially for K & Ö. All the mannequins and dummies for fashion and accessories were produced in Spain under sustainable conditions. The mannequins for the perfume department were designed in collaboration with the artist Rebecca Moses.

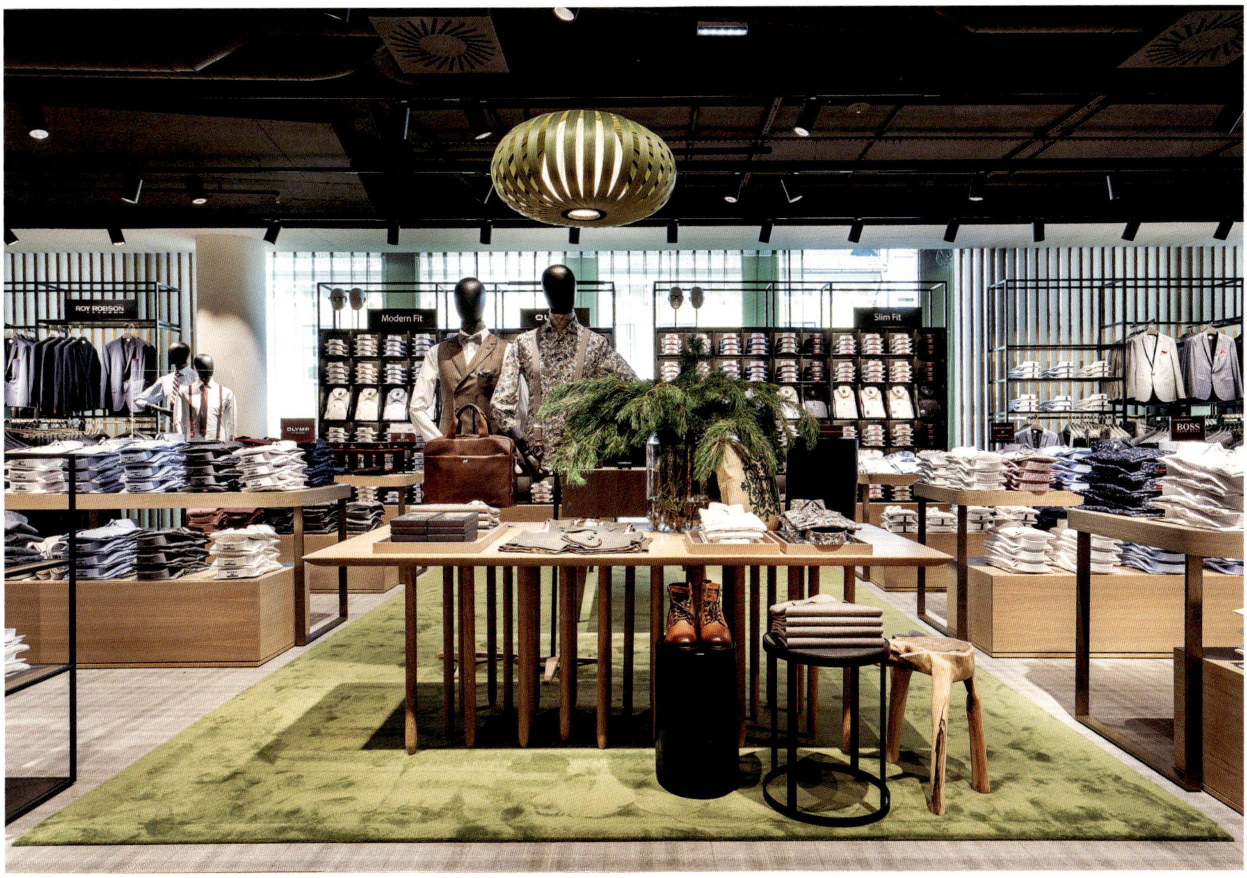
ROY ROBSON
Modern Fit
Slim Fit
BOSS

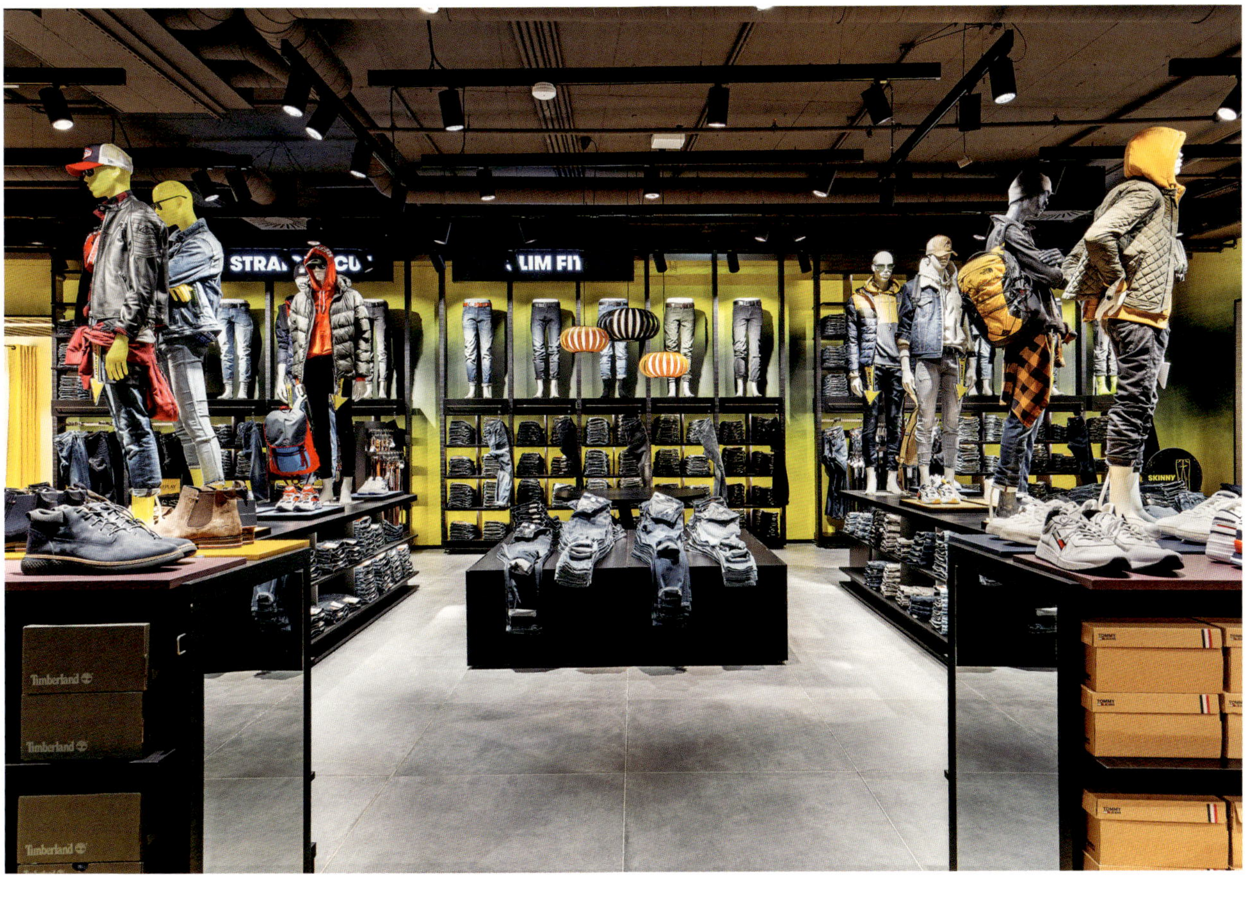
SKINNY
Timberland

K11 MUSEA SHOPPING MALL, B2 LEVEL

LOCATION HONG KONG, CHINA **CLIENT** NEW WORLD DEVELOPMENT, HONG KONG
CONCEPT / DESIGN STEFANO TORDIGLIONE DESIGN LTD, HONG KONG **PHOTOGRAPHS** NICOLA LONGOBARDI, HONG KONG

An Hongkongs Küstenmeile hat eine neue Mixed-use-Retail-Destination eröffnet, die den in Tsim Sha Tsui gelegenen Hafen von Victoria überragt. Der „Victoria Dockside" genannte Komplex wurde 1910, als die industrielle Revolution Honkong erreicht hatte, als Holt's Wharf gegründet. In den 1970ern nutzte man ihn für Einzelhandel, Freizeit und Kommerz, heute ist der Distrikt als Kunst- und Kulturviertel in Gebrauch, mit dem K11 MUSEA als einem seiner neuen Wahrzeichen.

A new mixed-use cultural-retail destination has opened on Hong Kong's waterfront, overlooking Victoria Harbour in Tsim Sha Tsui. Victoria Dockside was originally founded as Holt's Wharf in 1910 as the industrial revolution reached Hong Kong. In the 1970s, the site was transformed into a retail-leisure-commercial complex. Today, it has evolved into an art and cultural district with the new landmark K11 MUSEA.

BUILDINGS   K11 MUSEA SHOPPING MALL, B2 LEVEL

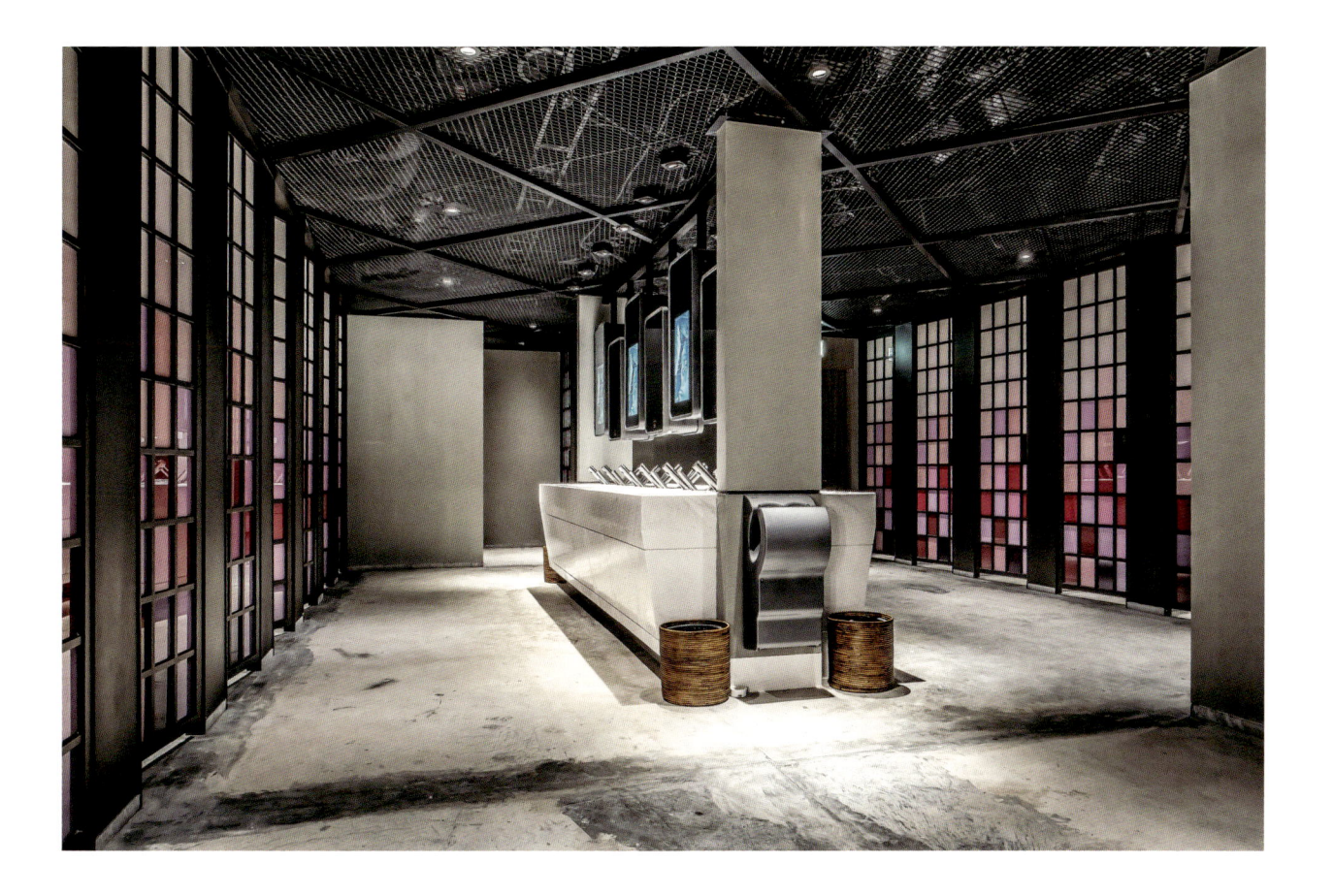

ST Design inszeniert das Art-meets-Retail-Center, die B2-Ebene des K11 MUSEA, und bereichert Hongkongs Retail-Szene damit um einen Neuzugang. Im Herzen der Victoria Dockside gelegen, vereint die Experience-Location immersive Erlebnisse in Retail, Kunst, Kultur, Unterhaltung und Gastronomie unter einem Dach. Stefano Tordiglione, Kreativ-Direktor von ST Design, hat hier weniger eine herkömmliche Einkaufsumgebung als vielmehr eine künstlerisch-theatralische Raumerfahrung geschaffen, in der Millennials aus aller Welt zusammenkommen und Inspirationen sammeln können.

For the art-meets-retail center, ST Design staged the K11 MUSEA's B2 Level as a new addition to Hong Kong's retail scene. Located in the heart of the Victoria Dockside area, this experiential space combines immersive experiences in retail, art, culture, entertainment and gastronomy under one roof. Stefano Tordiglione, Creative Director of ST Design, created an artistic, theatrical spatial experience rather than a conventional shopping environment, where global millennials can come together to discover their muse.

Das hohe schwarze Metalldach überspannt drei unterschiedliche Bodenbefliesungen, darunter sechseckige Cementine-Fliesen, die den Charme des italienischen Designs aus dem 19. Jahrhundert aufgreifen und verschiedene Zonen markieren. Der Gebrauch schwarzer Gitter-Schiebetüren in allen Läden sorgt durchgängig für ein einheitliches und zeitloses Ambiente. Es bietet den Shops zudem eine Plattform für die werbewirksame Präsentation der Persönlichkeit ihrer Marken, wobei die Anmutung einer Shopping Mall stets erhalten bleibt. Die Materialien sind glatt, elegant und in Schwarz gehalten, sodass keine Konkurrenz zum Merchandise entsteht. Ein großer Bereich dient der Ausstellung zeitgenössischer Kunstwerke, und viele Stellen eignen sich gut als Insta-Spots, was sie für das modebewusste Publikum attraktiv macht.

Under the high black metallic ceiling, three different types of floor tiles, including the hexagonal Cementine tiles that embody the charm of 19th century Italian design, have been used to demarcate different zones. The use of sliding doors in a black frame for all shops gives the whole environment a homogeneous and timeless atmosphere. It also provides a standard platform for the shops to present their brand personality in an effective way while maintaining the overall look of a shopping mall. The materials are slick and sleek, and in black so as to not compete with the merchandise. A large amount of space is dedicated to exhibiting contemporary art pieces. Many areas are designed to be grammable and attractive to the fashion-conscious shoppers.

BUILDINGS   K11 MUSEA SHOPPING MALL, B2 LEVEL   183

„Beim Retail geht es nicht mehr nur ums Einkaufen, es geht um das Schaffen einer einzigartigen Customer Experience, besonders für die, die sich ein ‚phygitales', also physisches und digitales Erlebnis zugleich versprechen", sagt Tordiglione, dessen Art-Direction intuitiv östliche und westliche Einflüsse vereint – als Tribut sowohl an seine italienischen Wurzeln als auch an die örtlichen Kulturen Asiens.

"Retail is not about shopping any more, it's about creating a one-of-a-kind experience for consumers, especially for those who crave a 'phygital', both physical and digital shopping experience", says Tordiglione, whose art direction is an intuitive blend of East and West, respecting both his Italian roots and the local cultures of Asia.

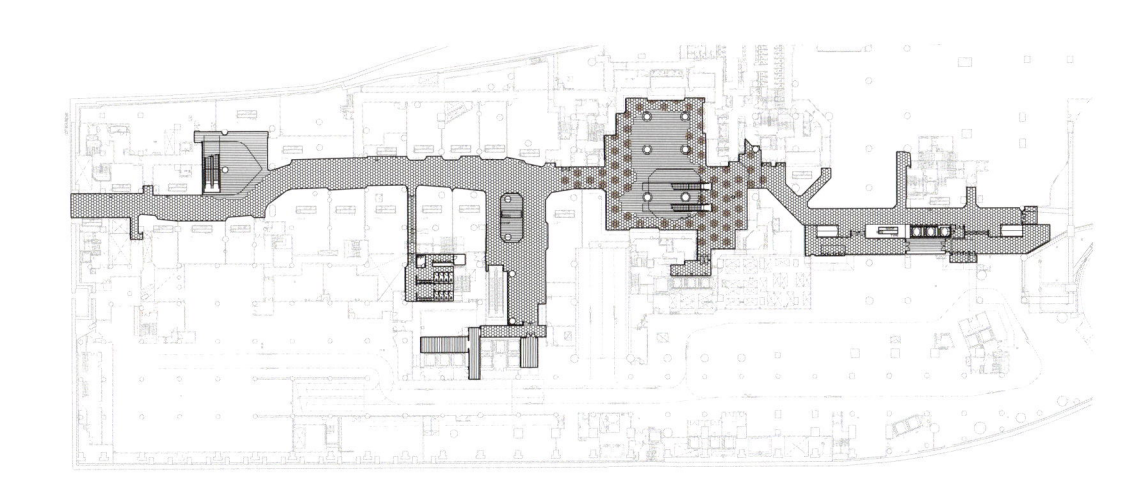

SEAT CUPRA DUSSELDORF AUTOMEILE

LOCATION DUSSELDORF, GERMANY   **CLIENT** GOTTFRIED SCHULTZ AUTOMOBIL HANDELS SE, RATINGEN   **CONCEPT / DESIGN** STUDIO K, MÜLHEIM A. D. RUHR   **LIGHTING** ANSORG GMBH, MÜLHEIM A. D. RUHR   **OTHERS** VIZONA GMBH, WEIL AM RHEIN (SHOPFITTING)   **PHOTOGRAPHS** BORIS GOLZ, ARNSBERG

Im Jahr 2001 hatte ein Konsortium von Autohändlern und Investoren die Idee, in Düsseldorf eine „Automeile" nach amerikanischem Vorbild zu errichten. Die Konsorten konnten ein rund 100.000 Quadratmeter großes Grundstück der ehemaligen Betriebshöfe der Düsseldorfer Stadtwerke erwerben und mit benachbarten Arealen arrondieren. Auf dem parzellierten Grundstück entstanden Retail- und Markenwelten der Automobilindustrie rund um das Thema Mobilität.

Als neueste Markenpräsentation wurde auf der bis heute erfolgreichen Automeile das gemeinschaftliche Autohaus von Seat und CUPRA eröffnet. Erstmals werden in dem transparenten Neubau aus Stahl, Glas und Holz beide Konzernmarken unter einem Dach zusammengefasst.

Back in 2001, a consortium of car dealers and investors had the idea of setting up an American-style "car mile" in Dusseldorf. The consortium members were able to purchase a roughly 100,000 square-metre plot of the former depots of the Dusseldorf municipal utilities and combine it with adjacent areas. On the parcelled-out land, there have emerged retail and brand worlds of the automotive industry on all topics relating to mobility.

The most recent brand addition to the successful car mile was the joint car showroom of Seat and CUPRA. In the new transparent building of steel, glass and wood, the two group brands have been combined under a single roof for the first time.

BUILDINGS   SEAT CUPRA DUSSELDORF AUTOMEILE

Die einheitliche Dachkonstruktion und Deckenbeleuchtung sorgen für ein ganzheitliches Erscheinungsbild. Gleichzeitig werden die beiden Automarken über die differenzierten markenbildenden Designelemente des Interieurs sowie der Farb- und Bildwelt abgrenzend in Szene gesetzt. Die Corporate-Design-Maßgaben beider Marken wurden von STUDIO K unter Leitung von Besnik Kalo architektonisch umgesetzt. Hierzu gehört auch das vom Beleuchtungsexperten Ansorg für den internationalen Rollout entwickelte und umgesetzte Corporate-Lighting-Konzept.

A holistic appearance is provided by the consistent design of the roof structure and the ceiling lighting. And yet, the two car marques have nonetheless been presented separately by means of differentiated brand-building design elements in the interior and also through the colour palettes and imagery used. The Corporate Design requirements of the two brands were translated into an architectural dimension by STUDIO K under the creative lead of Besnik Kalo. This includes the corporate lighting concept, which was developed and realised by lighting expert Ansorg for the international rollout.

Ein besonderer Wunsch der Bauherren war es, auf der kühlen Präsentationsfläche auch ruhige Wohlfühlinseln für die Kundinnen und Kunden zu schaffen. Hierzu wurden punktuelle Rückzugsbereiche sowie Stehtische und Beratungseinheiten in die Fläche integriert und mit warmem Licht ausgeleuchtet. Im Zentrum des Showrooms befindet sich die Lounge „Central Island", eine mit Highboards, Vitrinen und Sofas ausgestattete Sitzecke, um Gespräche zu führen, innezuhalten oder Kaffee zu trinken. Durch ein abgehängtes Deckengitter mit einer transluzenten Lichtabdeckung, kombiniert mit pointierten Pendelleuchten, entsteht ein gemütlicher Bereich, der zum Verweilen einlädt.

In einer ersten Phase werden in Deutschland, Italien, Schweden und Spanien weitere 35 Niederlassungen mit dem neuen Corporate Lighting aus dem Hause Ansorg ausgestattet.

BUILDINGS   SEAT CUPRA DUSSELDORF AUTOMEILE

For the clients, it was particularly important to create peaceful feel-good islands for customers within the cool presentation zones. With this wish in mind, a number of retreats were created, and high tables and consultation units were integrated into the space and bathed in warm light. At the centre of the showroom, the "Central Island" lounge furnished with highboards, showcases and sofas offers seating areas for consultations, for a brief pause or for a cup of coffee. Thanks to the suspended ceiling grid with a translucent light cover, combined with deliberately placed pendant lights, the cosy area invites visitors to take a break for a while.

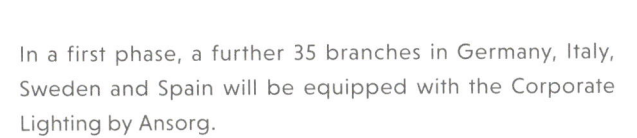

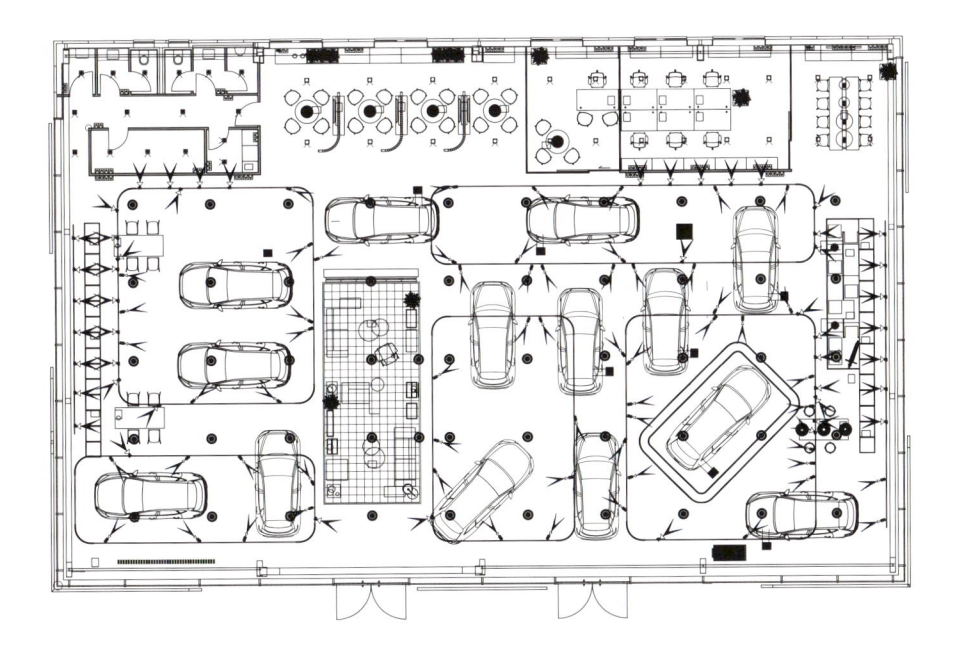

In a first phase, a further 35 branches in Germany, Italy, Sweden and Spain will be equipped with the Corporate Lighting by Ansorg.

THE AUTHORS

RETAIL DESIGN INTERNATIONAL VOL. 7

Dr. Jons Messedat

lehrt seit 2016 das Modul Bau und Raum an der HAWK Hochschule für angewandte Wissenschaft und Kunst Hildesheim. Er studierte Architektur an der RWTH Aachen, der Universität Stuttgart und als Stipendiat an der London South Bank University. Parallel dazu machte er sein Diplom als Industriedesigner bei Richard Sapper. Es folgte eine Hochschulassistenz an der Bauhaus-Universität Weimar, die er 2004 mit der Promotion zum Thema Corporate Architecture abschloss. Im Büro von Sir Norman Foster plante er das heutige Red Dot Design Museum in Essen und das Interior Design im Reichstagsgebäude in Berlin. Als zertifizierter Preisrichter wirkt er in internationalen Architektur- und Designwettbewerben mit. Er war Jurymitglied im Wettbewerb für das bauliche Corporate Design im Berliner Humboldt Forum und wurde 2018 von der Architektenkammer Niedersachsen in die Jury zum Staatspreis für Architektur berufen. Für den Kulturkreis der deutschen Wirtschaft im BDI e. V. engagiert er sich im Bronnbacher Stipendium – Kulturelle Kompetenz für künftige Führungskräfte.
www.messedat.com

Prof. Christoph M. Achammer

Der Architekt und Univ.-Prof. beschäftigt sich als Inhaber des Lehrstuhls für Integrale Bauplanung und Industriebau an der TU Wien mit der Forschung zu Integraler Planung, Green Deal, Lebenszyklus, BIM und Digitalisierung. Als Vorstandsvorsitzender von ATP architekten ingenieure, dem führenden Büro für Integrale Planung in Europa mit 900+ Mitarbeitenden, erarbeitet er im Rahmen der Initiative „New Life" in strategischer Partnerschaft mit Immobilienconsultants, Placemakern und Nachhaltigkeitsexpert:innen innovative Multi-use-Konzepte für die Wiederbelebung leer stehender Einzelhandelsimmobilien in europäischen Innenstädten.
www.atp.ag

Dr. Jons Messedat

has been teaching the building and space module at the HAWK University of applied sciences and art in Hildesheim since 2016. He studied architecture at the RWTH Aachen University, the University of Stuttgart and had a scholarship to the London South Bank University. In parallel, he qualified as industrial designer under Richard Sapper. This was followed by a university assistantship at the Bauhaus University Weimar, which he completed in 2004 with a doctorate in the field of Corporate Architecture. In the office of Sir Norman Foster he worked on the design of today's Red Dot Design Museum in Essen and was responsible for the interior design of the Reichstag building in Berlin. As certified competition judge, he is involved in a number of international architecture and design competitions. He was on the panel for built Corporate Design in the Berlin Humboldt Forum and in 2018, he was appointed onto the jury of the state prize for architecture by the chamber of architects for the federal state of Lower Saxony. For the Kulturkreis der deutschen Wirtschaft im BDI e. V. (Association of Arts and Culture of the German Economy at the Federation of German Industries e. V.) he is involved in the Bronnbacher Scholarship that supports the cultural education of prospective leaders.
www.messedat.com

Prof. Christoph M. Achammer

In his capacity as chair of Industrial Building and Interdisciplinary Planning at the Vienna University of Technology, the research of architect and university professor focuses on integrated design, the green deal, life cycle, BIM and digitalisation. As Chairman of the Executive Board of ATP architekten ingenieure, Europe's leading integrated design company with more than 900 employees, he develops innovative multi-use concepts as part of the "New Life" initiative in strategic partnerships with property consultants, placemakers and sustainability experts with a view to revitalising large vacant retail properties in European city centres.
www.atp.ag

Stefan Herbert

absolvierte 2001 an der PBSA Düsseldorf und wurde in die Baukunstklasse der Kunstakademie Düsseldorf aufgenommen. Nach seinem Abschluss im Jahr 2004 trat er in die METRO ein. Als leitender Architekt verantwortet er eine Vielzahl von Projekten im In- und Ausland. Seit 2013 leitet er das Corporate Project Development Studio, ein Team aus Architekt:innen und Designer:innen, das an Konzepten mit Fokus auf die neuesten Trends im Immobiliensektor arbeitet. Der Schwerpunkt der Arbeit liegt auf der Masterplanung und Entwicklung prototypischer Lösungen im Bereich der zeitgenössischen Architektur und des Städtebaus.
www.metro-properties.de

Annika Gründel

ist Absolventin der Hochschule Düsseldorf im Fachbereich Betriebswirtschaftslehre. Sie ist seit 2016 für die METRO PROPERTIES Unternehmenskommunikation tätig und betreut nationale sowie internationale Immobilienprojekte des METRO Konzerns. Seit ihrem Abschluss als Master of Business Administration (MBA) im Jahr 2020 verantwortet sie die Kommunikations- und Marketingbegleitung für die METRO Campus Projektentwicklung in Düsseldorf.
www.metro-properties.de

Stefan Herbert

has a degree from the PBSA Düsseldorf and was admitted to the architecture course at the Düsseldorf Academy of Arts. After concluding in 2004, he joined the METRO. As lead architect, he is responsible for a large number of projects in Germany and abroad. Since 2013, he has led the Corporate Project Development Studio, a team of architects and designers that work on concepts focusing on the latest trends in the real estate sector. The focal point of their work is the master planning and development of prototypical solutions in the fields of contemporary architecture and city planning.
www.metro-properties.de

Annika Gründel

has a degree in business administration from the University of Applied Sciences Dusseldorf. She joined the corporate communications department of METRO PROPERTIES in 2016 and in this capacity accompanies the national and international real estate projects of the METRO group. Since acquiring her Master of Business Administration (MBA) in 2020, she has been responsible for communication and marketing support for the METRO Campus project development in Dusseldorf..
www.metro-properties.de

Prof. i. Vtr. Sabine Krieg

begann im März 2021 eine Vertretungsprofessur für Retail Design am Fachbereich Design der Hochschule Düsseldorf. Seither hat sie dort einen Lehrauftrag inne und unterstützt nun die Professorenschaft mit ihrem umfassenden Retail-Wissen. Von 1996 bis 2003 studierte sie BWL und Jura und schloss mit deutsch-französischem Doppeldiplom an der Carl von Ossietzky Universität Oldenburg, Université Jean Monnet de St. Etienne der Academie de Lyon sowie Université du Havre ab. Danach folgten Tätigkeiten für verschiedene Fashion-Marken wie Louis Vuitton, adidas, BOSS und Falke sowie für den Möbelhersteller Vitra. Ihre interdisziplinäre Auseinandersetzung mit Kunst, Medien und Kommunikation hat Sabine Krieg jahrelang geprägt. In ihrem Podcast, den sie gemeinsam mit der Alumna Aurelie Jahns umsetzt und der von den Retail-Digitalexperten invidis veröffentlicht wird, geht es um die Transformation der Fläche durch die Veränderung des Konsumenten- und Sozialverhaltens. Ihre großen Schwerpunkte neben Marke und Markenführung sind die durch Digitalisierung und die Änderung der Innenstädte beeinflusste Transformation der Fläche sowie Konsum- und Sozialverhalten. Außerdem ist sie Teil der FRAME-Designjury 2022.
pbsa.hs-duesseldorf.de/20210519_sabine_krieg

Prof. i. Vtr. Sabine Krieg

joined Dusseldorf University in March 2021 as deputy professor for retail design in the Design Faculty. This is a teaching assignment but also includes supporting the other professors with her in-depth retail knowledge. From 1996 to 2003, she studied business administration and law and completed her studies with a German/French double diploma from Carl von Ossietzky University Oldenburg, Université Jean Monnet de St. Etienne der Academie de Lyon and Université du Havre. After her studies, there followed various jobs for a number of fashion labels like Louis Vuitton, adidas, BOSS and Falke and the furniture manufacturer Vitra. Her interdisciplinary interaction with art, media and communication has had a major impact on Sabine Krieg for many years. In her podcast, which she co-hosts with former student Aurelie Jahns and which is published by the retail digital experts invidis, she explores the transformation of space by changing consumer and social behaviour. Her focal points beside brand and brand management are the transformation of space caused by the digitalisation and changing inner cities as well as consumer and social behaviour. She is also on the 2022 FRAME design jury.
pbsa.hs-duesseldorf.de/20210519_sabine_krieg

IMPRINT

EDITOR / AUTHOR
Jons Messedat

EDITING / TYPESETTING
Mario Ableitner

TRANSLATION
Beverley Locke, Mario Ableitner

LAYOUT
Tina Agard Grafik & Buchdesign, Stuttgart

LITHOGRAPHY
corinna rieber prepress, Marbach / Neckar

PRINTING
Schleunungdruck, Marktheidenfeld

BINDING
Hubert & Co. GmbH & Co. KG BuchPartner, Göttingen

FONTS
Niveau Grotesk

PAPER
Condat Matt Périgord Vol. 1,1, 150 g/m²

COVER PHOTO
Christina Häusler, Vienna
IKEA Einrichtungen – Handelsgesellschaft mbH, Vösendorf
querkraft architekten, Vienna

PHOTO CREDITS
Mint Architecture (p. 9–10, 12–13); METRO PROPERTIES / ACME (p. 15–25); Hans Höhenrieder (p. 29 top left, 30 top left); Franziska Stasch (p. 29 bottom left, 30 bottom); Janna Jakobs, Svenja Krach, Niklas Riechmann (p. 29 right, 31); Oliver Tjaden, Dusseldorf (p. 32/33); Philip Kottlorz Fotografie, Stuttgart (p. 54/55); Aston Martin Inhouse, Gaydon (p. 152/153)

IMAGE RECOGNITION
www.ayscan.de

avedition GmbH
Publishers for Architecture and Design
Senefelderstraße 109
70176 Stuttgart
Germany

Tel.: +49 (0)711 / 220 22 79-0
Fax: +49 (0)711 / 220 22 79-15

retaildesign@avedition.de
www.avedition.com

© Copyright 2022 **av**edition GmbH, Stuttgart

© Copyright of photos with individual companies, agencies and photographers

This work is subject to copyright. All rights are reserved, whether the whole or part of the material is concerned, and specifically but not exclusively the right of translation, reprinting, reuse of illustrations, recitation, broadcasting, reproduction on microfilms or in other ways, and storage in databases or any other media. For use of any kind, the written permission of the copyright owner must be obtained.

ISBN 978-3-89986-366-6